MEDFORD
THROUGH TIME

PATRICIA SAUNDERS
AND BARBARA KERR

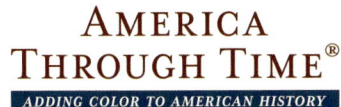

America Through Time is an imprint of Fonthill Media LLC

First published 2016

Copyright © Patricia Saunders and Barbara Kerr

ISBN 978-1-63500-039-9

All rights reserved. No part of this publication may be reproduced, stored in a retrieval system or transmitted in any form or by any means, electronic, mechanical, photocopying, recording or otherwise, without prior permission in writing from Fonthill Media LLC

Typeset in Mrs Eaves XL Serif Narrow

Published by Arcadia Publishing by arrangement with Fonthill Media LLC
For all general information, please contact Arcadia Publishing:
Telephone: 843-853-2070
Fax: 843-853-0044
E-mail: sales@arcadiapublishing.com
For customer service and orders:
Toll-Free 1-888-313-2665

Visit us on the internet at www.arcadiapublishing.com

Introduction

Medford, Massachusetts, has been a part of history since the 1630s, when Governor John Winthrop named a rock in the Middlesex Fells after the cheese in his lunch. Since that time a lot has happened. Many of the sites and structures from Medford's early centuries remain, while others have vanished, and are remembered only in stories and vintage images. In the pages of this book, you will see a mix of Medford's centuries as you journey through the past and present of this ever changing city.

Like many early Massachusetts towns, Medford was settled near water. Medford Square was originally the site of a ford in the river. The Square also became a crossroads in the early days with roads extending out to all point of the compass. Medford's growth over the centuries had a lot to do with changes in transportation. Until the train, trolley, and automobile changed the landscape, Medford's businesses and life were local. Up until the Civil War, Medford was a country town of farms, estates, houses, and business areas centered on town squares. In the 1870s however, trains and streetcars created easier access to Boston. Desirable farm and estate land was divided up into house lots and Medford started to grow. In 1860 there were 4,800 residents and in 2015 there are over 57,000.

Growing population brought growing changes. The town became a city in 1894. Business areas added national chains and houses replaced open land. As new parts of the city were developed, city services expanded to meet new demands. Schools, churches, entertainment venues and businesses gave each new neighborhood a special personality all its own. To keep busy and entertained Medford's citizens founded clubs and sports teams, performed, took photographs, went to the movies, rode bicycles, fought for social causes, and never ever ever said no to a good celebration!

Medford is uniquely blessed with natural spaces. The Mystic River served as a source of industry and transportation in the eighteenth and nineteenth centuries when brick, ship, and rum industries thrived. As these industries faded, Medford's enthusiasm for the water did not, and generation after generation swam, boated, and fished in the river, lakes, and ponds. The Middlesex Fells provided an inspiration to early residents who banded together to preserve this natural resource. Today, Medford's green spaces answer the city's recreational and spiritual needs and Medford's waters and woods are tended by those who live here.

From John Winthrop's lunch to the present day, Medford has grown and changed and reinvented itself over and over. It has always been a unique place and it has never been boring. As you read this book we hope you will laugh and remember and learn, but most of all we hope you enjoy your journey through the history, culture, nature, and fun that has created this one and only place.

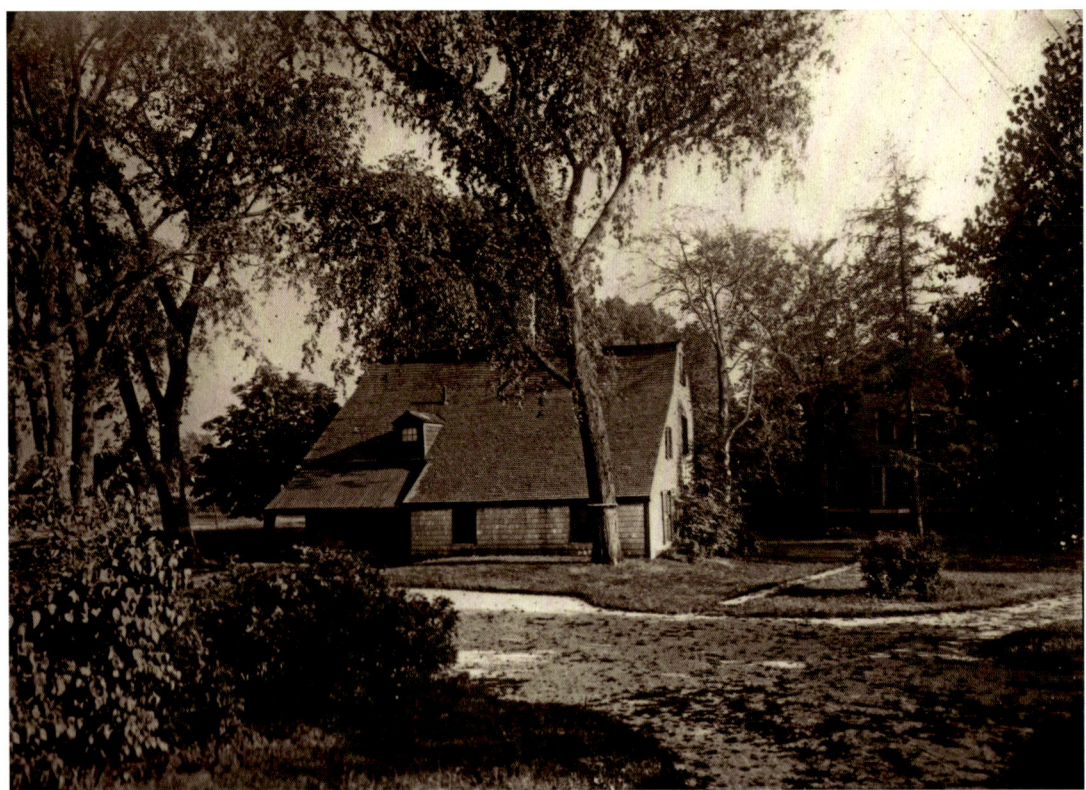

BLANCHARD HOUSE: One of the earliest houses built in the town was the George Blanchard House, also known as the old Wellington farmhouse. The house was constructed in the 1650s in the Salt Box style. Salt Box houses like this one have a long, pitched roof that slopes down to the back, with one story in the back and two stories in the front. The house was demolished in the twentieth century.

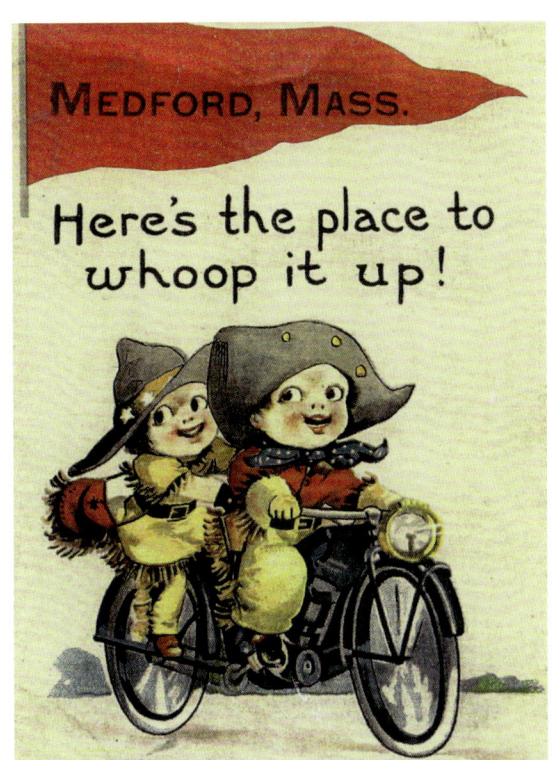

WHOOPING IT UP: Medford Square has always been a crossroads with visitors passing through and sometimes stopping to enjoy themselves. Things were hopping here in 1911 when this postcard and its happy motorcyclist was mailed. The motorcycle tradition continued in 2002, when these fun loving motorcyclists rode through Medford on their way to a New Hampshire charity event.

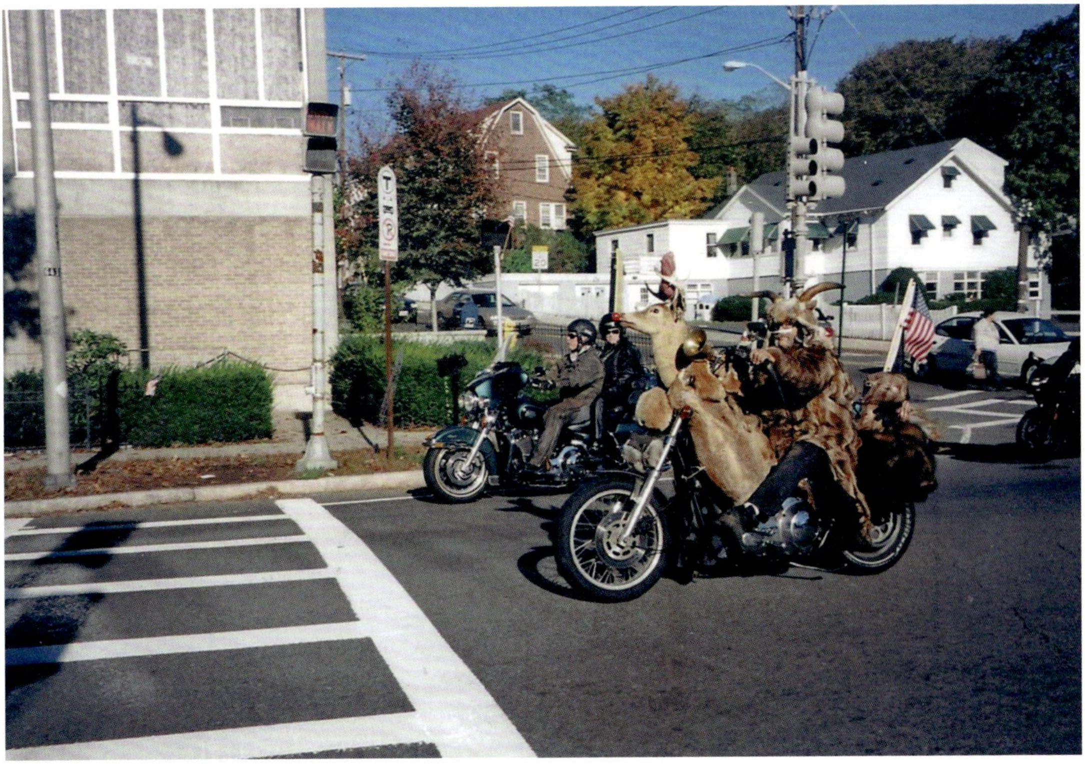

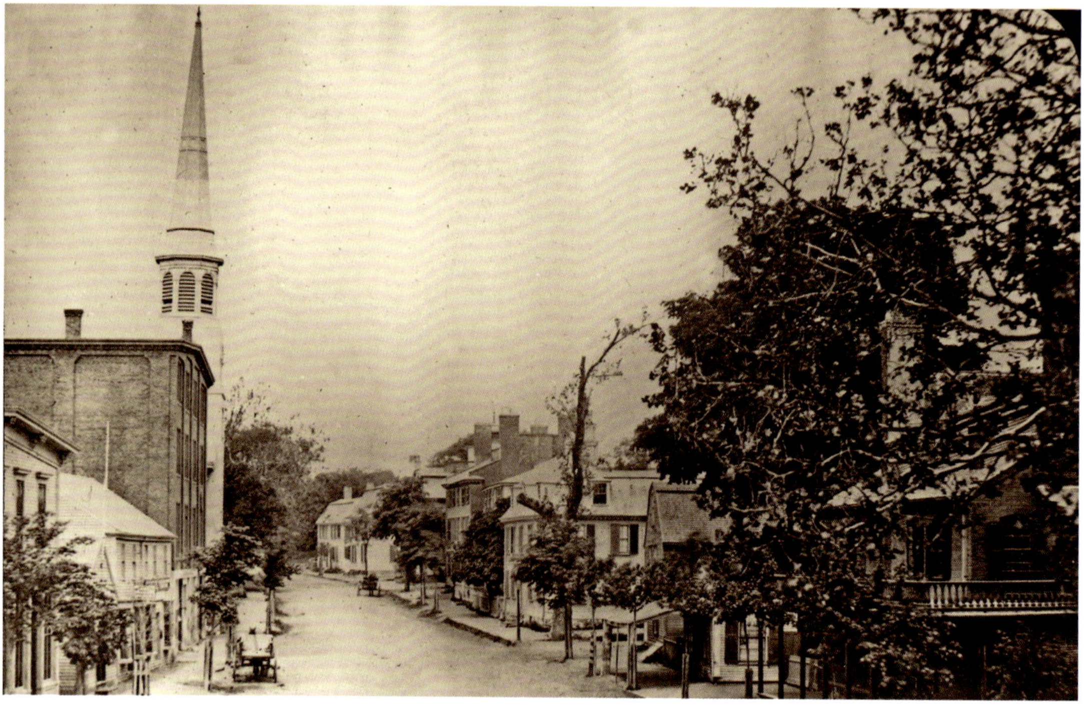

MEDFORD SQUARE: Originally the site of a ford in the river, Medford Square was also at the center of Medford's first public roads: Main, Salem and High Streets. The Square has changed a great deal over the years. In this early 1860s photo you see quiet country town with a population of about 5,000. Medford boomed after the Civil War, however, and by the time of this 1890s postcard there were 18,000 residents in the growing town.

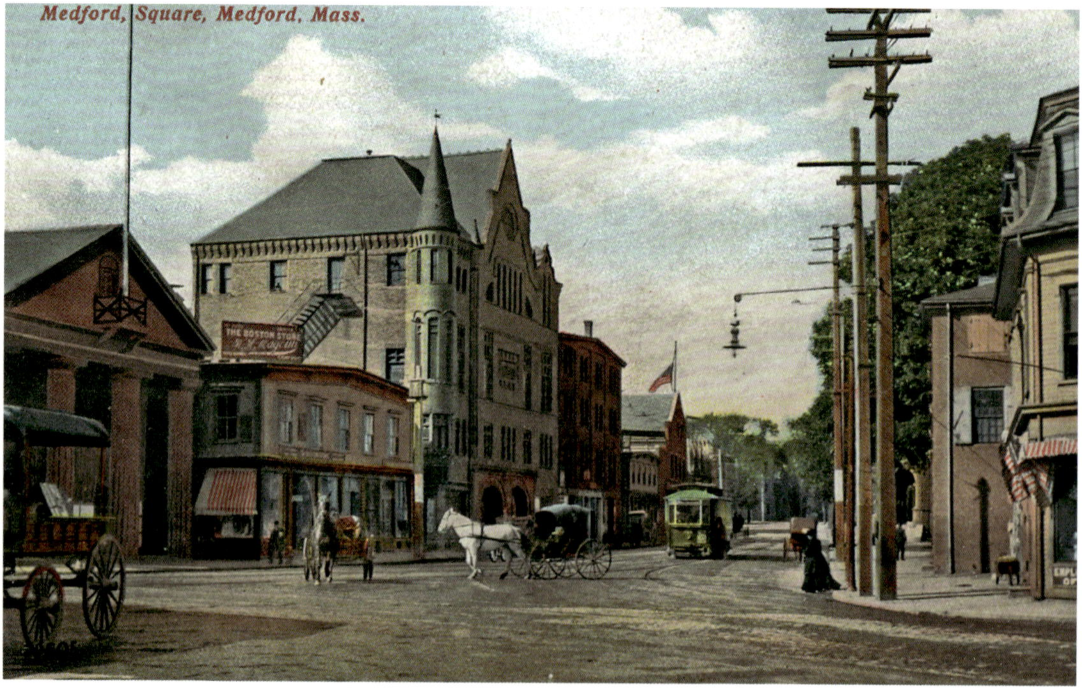

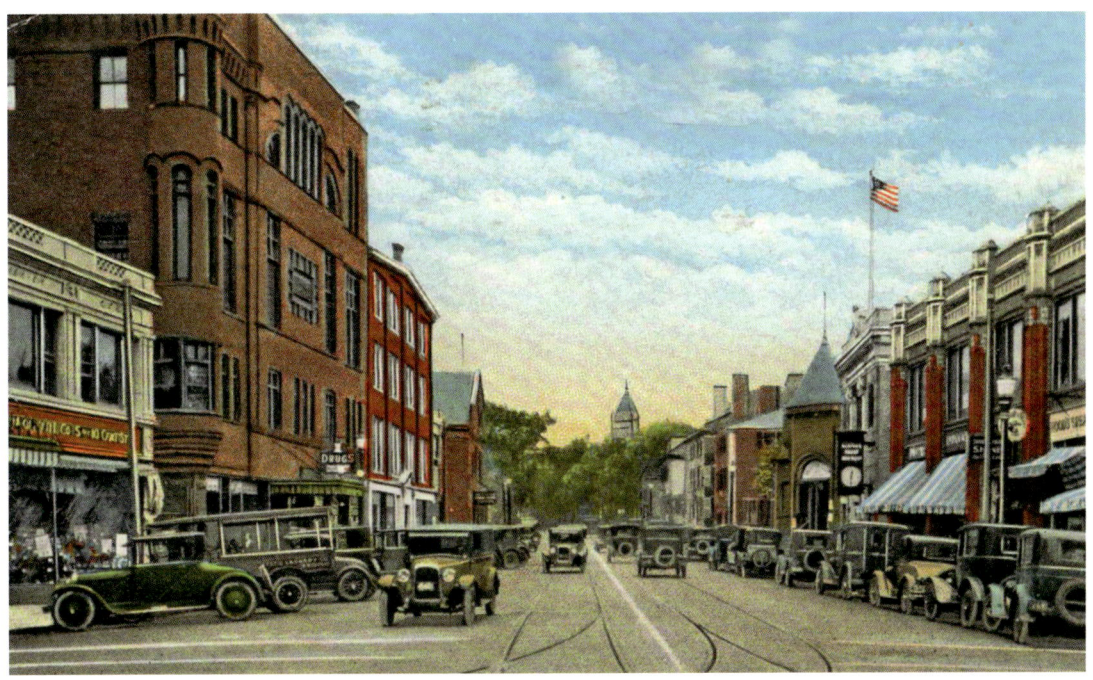

TWENTIETH CENTURY SQUARE: By the middle of the twentieth century, Medford Square was a typical suburban city center with a mix of small businesses and larger chains like the Woolworth's seen on the left. Today the Square still offers that busy business mix.

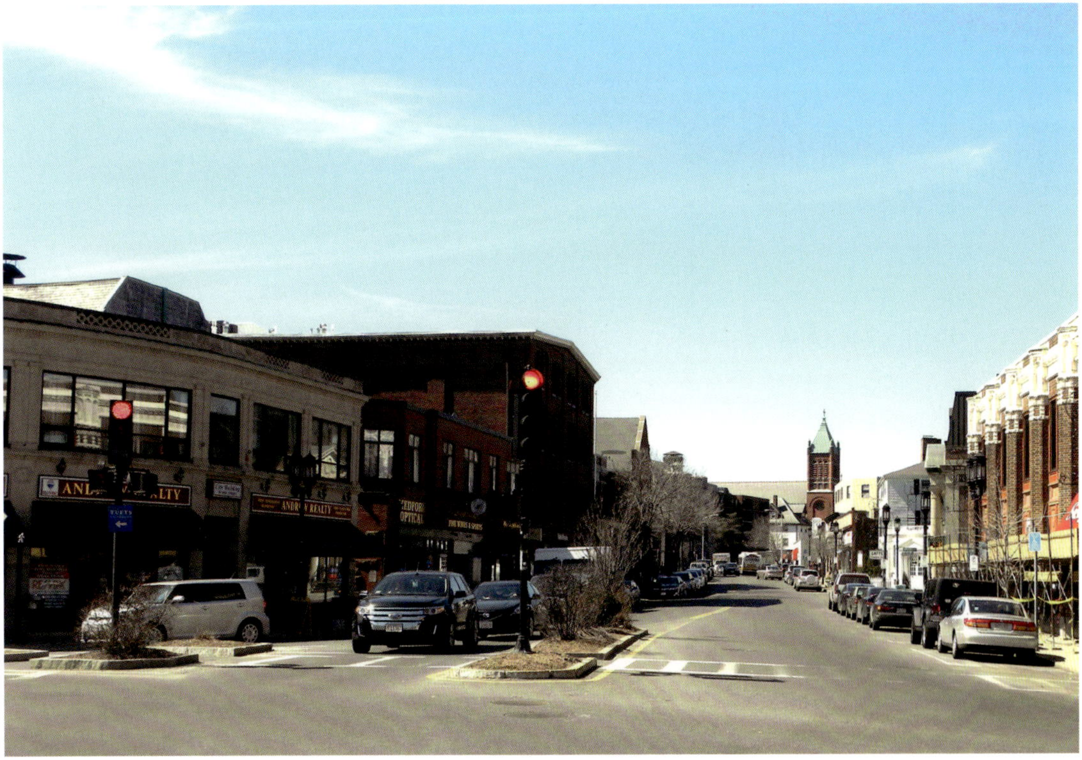

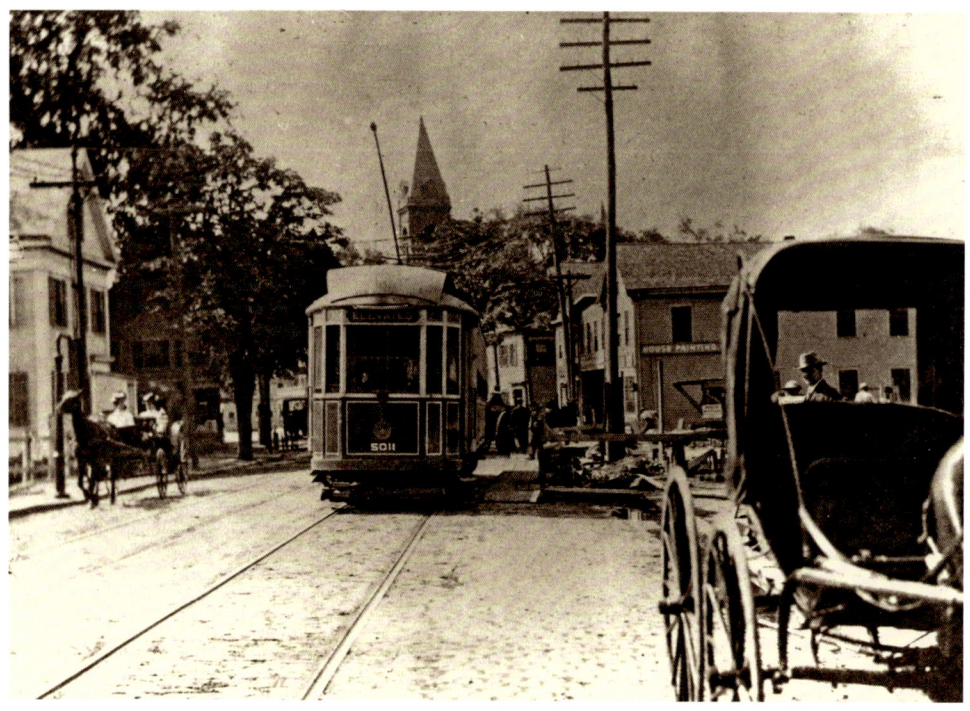

MAIN STREET: This first public road in Medford was the primary road to Boston until superseded by highways in the twentieth century. The number of different kinds of vehicles in this late nineteenth century photo gives an idea of what a busy street it was. Those who live here know that it is just as busy today even without the horses and trolley cars!

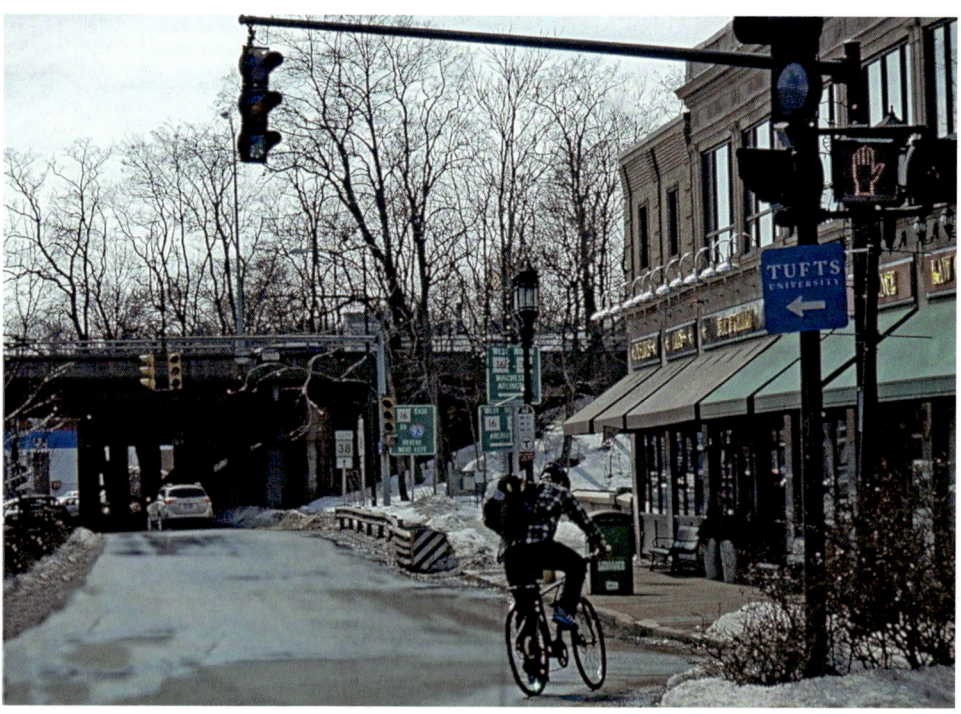

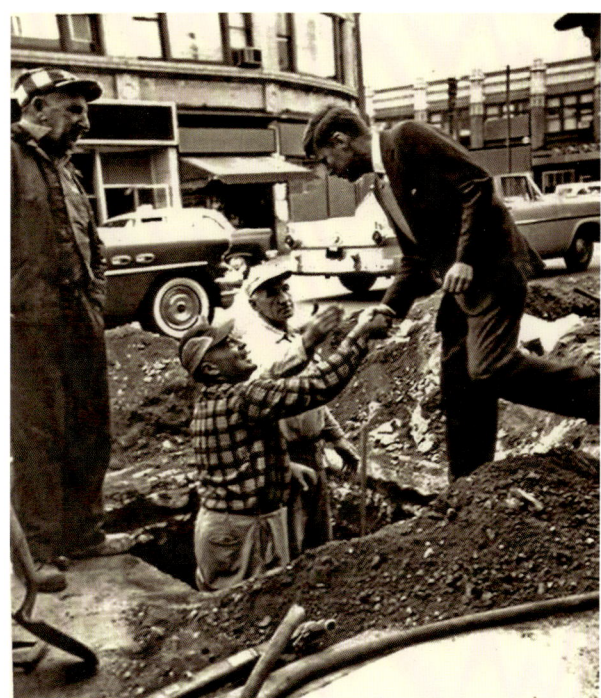

TRAFFIC STOPPERS: During his second senatorial campaign in June 1958, Senator John F. Kennedy braved the Main Street traffic to shake hands with DPW workers. That traffic island still remains in the center of this always busy street.

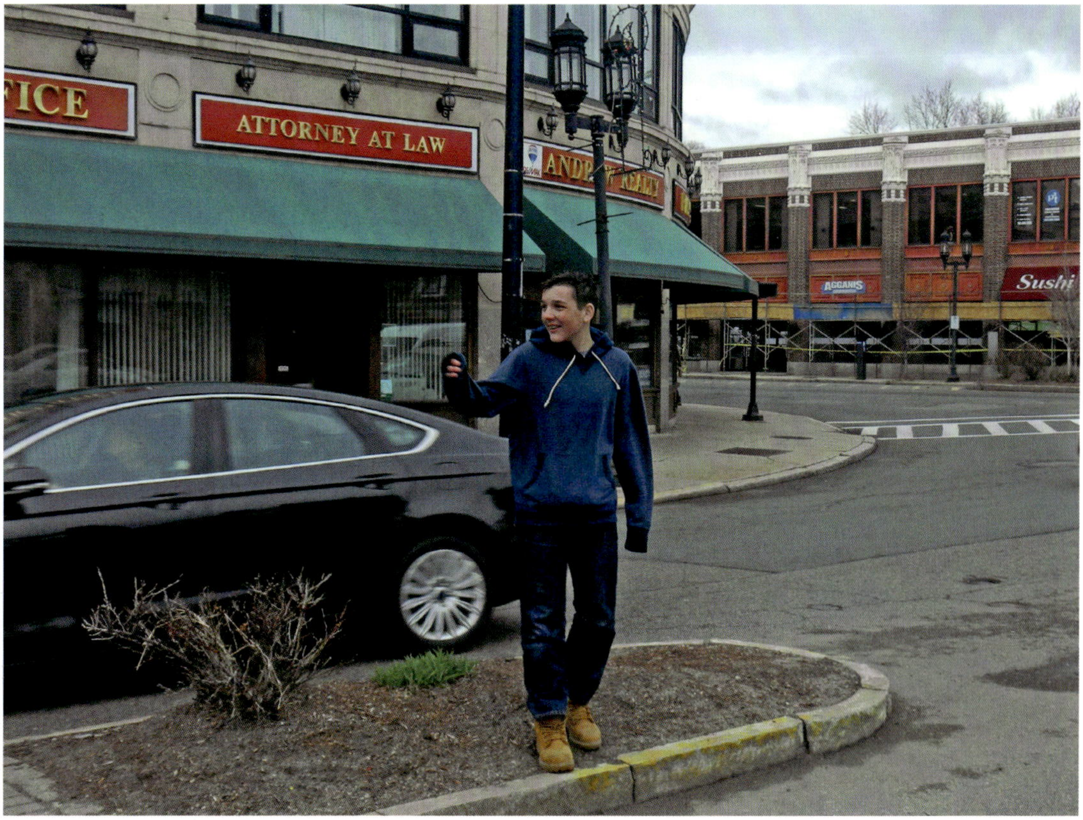

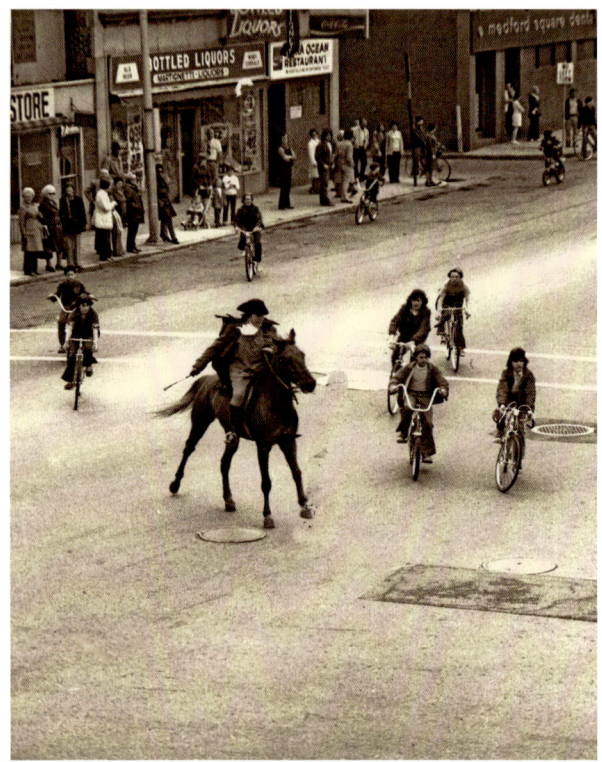

Paul Revere: On April 19, 1775, Paul Revere travelled along Main Street on his famous ride. Revere stopped at the house of Medford militia captain Isaac Hall, now Gaffey's funeral home. Since 1914 the rides of Revere and William Dawes are re-enacted every year on Patriot's Day. Revere occasionally shares the road with companions, like these 1970s boys on bikes, and in 2015 a member of the National Lancers who participates in the ride every year.

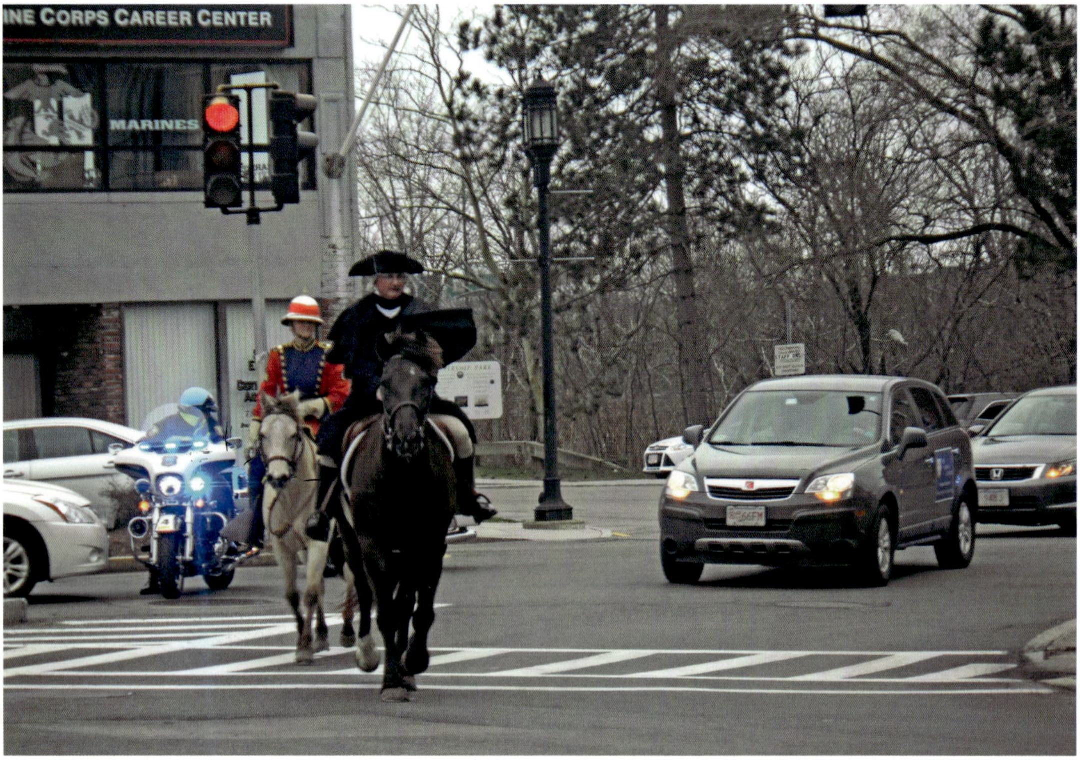

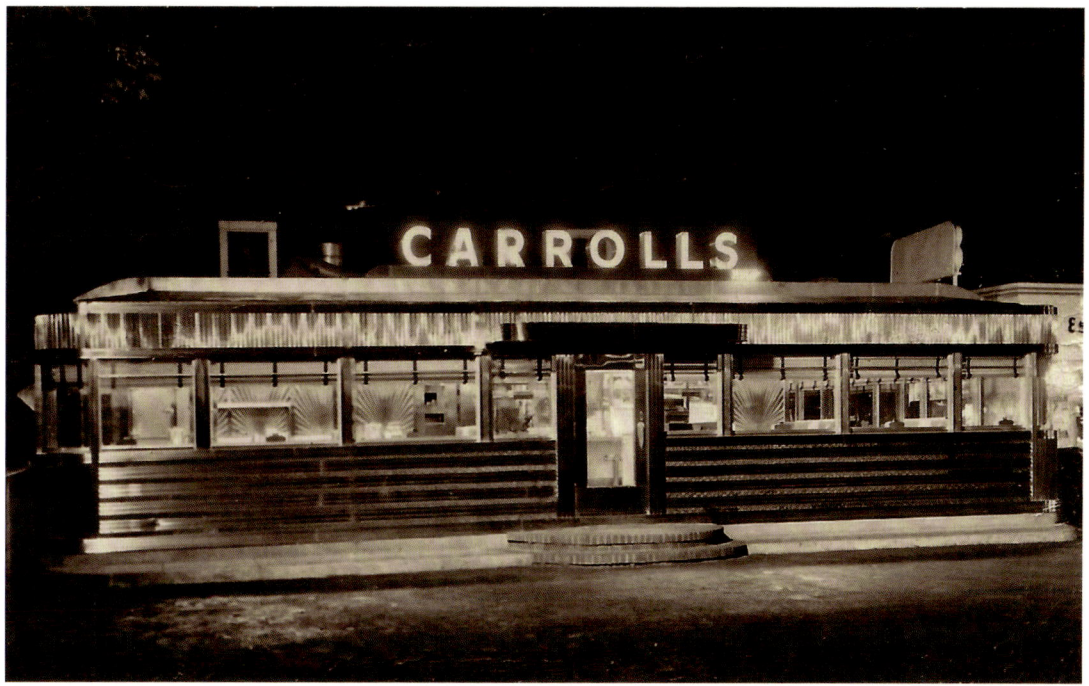

CARROLL'S: Everyone in Medford went to Carroll's Diner. The original Carroll's opened in 1930 when Maurice W. Carroll moved a used steel diner to Main Street next to the Medford Battery Company which he also owned. A new diner car was added to an expanded Carroll's in 1948 and again 1961. The diner closed in 1986, but the Carroll family brought tradition back to Medford Square in 2012 when they opened the new Carroll's restaurant at 21 Main Street.

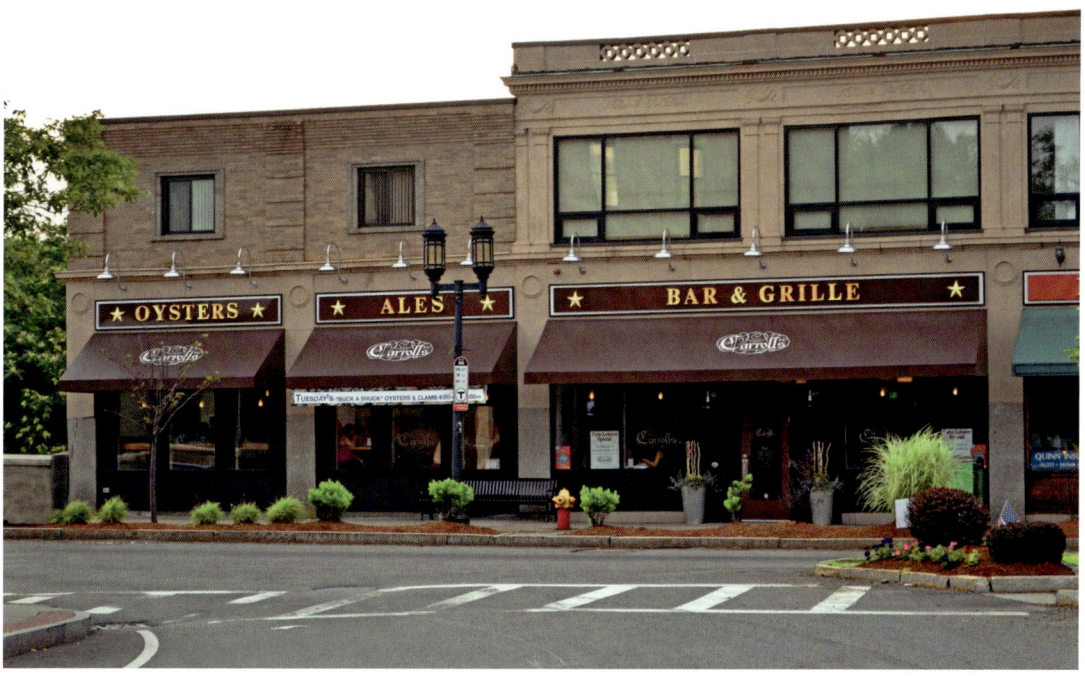

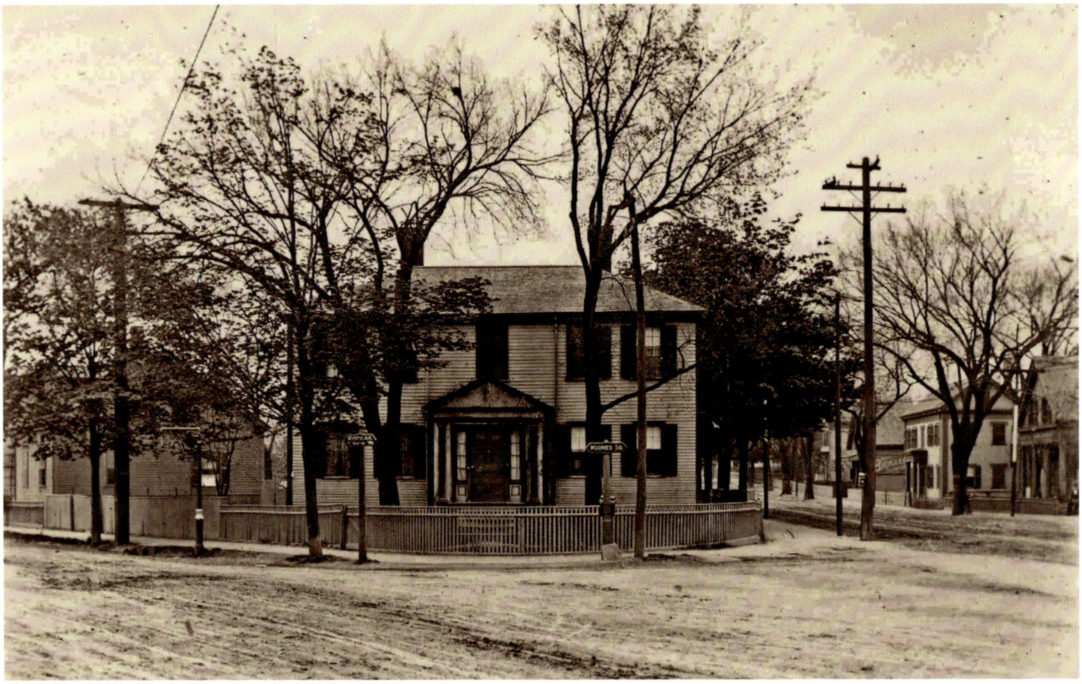

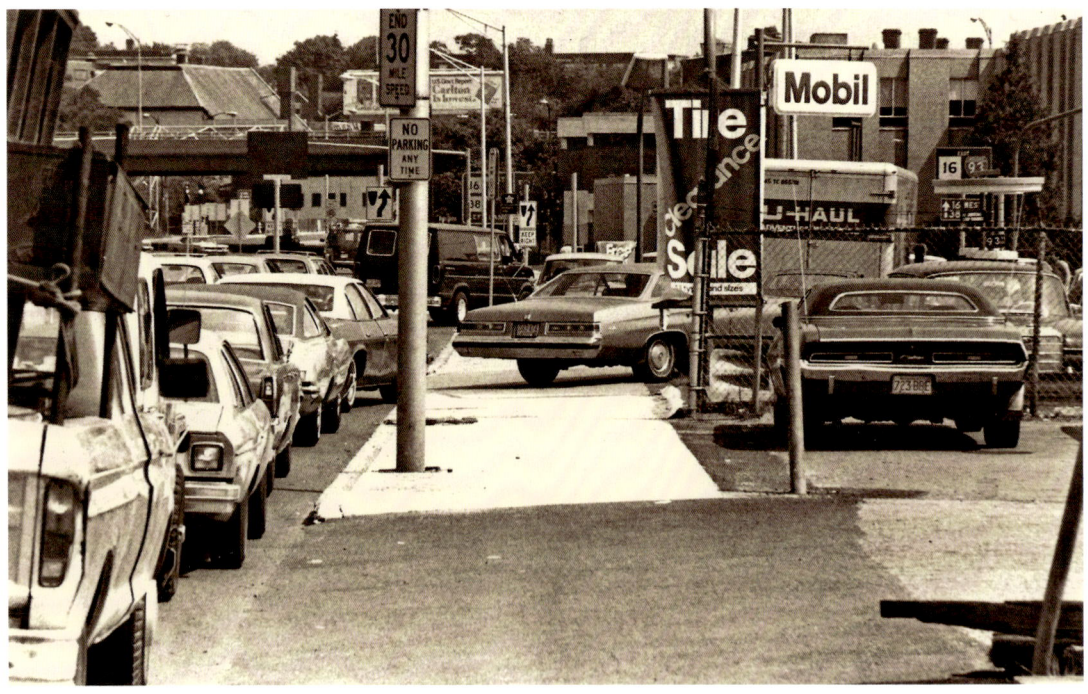

MOORE HOUSE: Local legend once had it that blacksmith Henry Moore was the model for Henry Wadsworth Longfellow's "Village Blacksmith." This has been since disproven – Moore was only twelve years old the year Longfellow published the poem! Main Street's transportation history endures in this spot where the grown up Moore shoed many a Medford horse. During the oil crisis in 1979, horseless carriages (or cars as we know them) lined up at Main Street gas stations near the site.

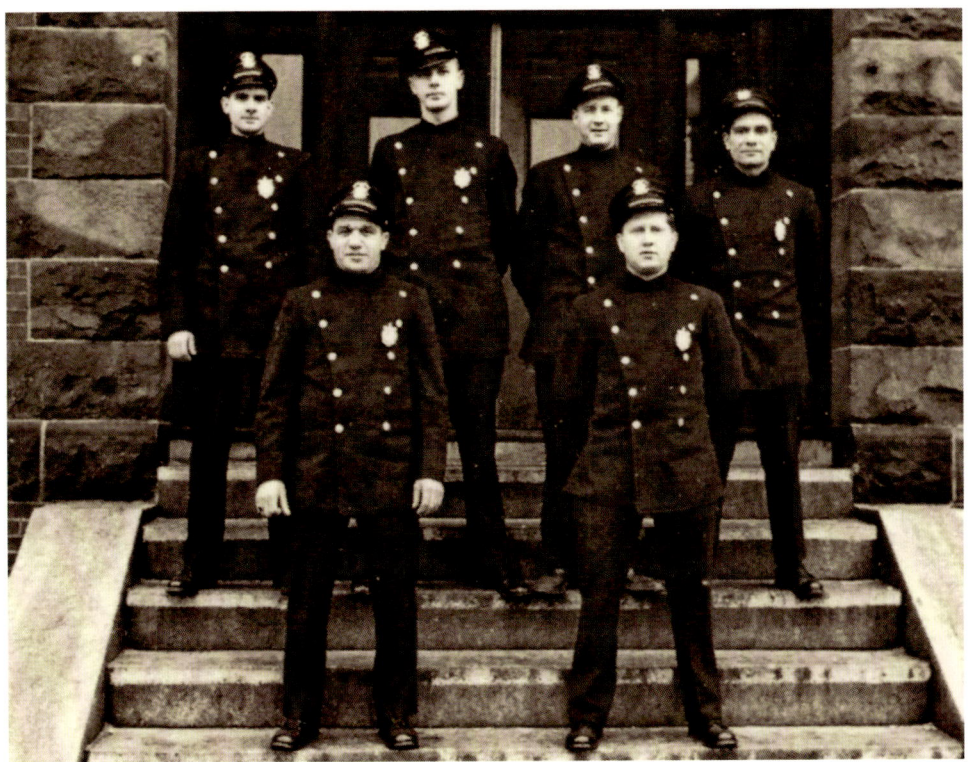

POLICE DEPARTMENT: Main Street has always been home to Medford's police. The first police station was built in 1895 at Main and Swan Streets, very close to its current location. The department itself was founded in 1870 when the city selectmen decided to establish a full time police department with a force of eight policemen. Since then the force has grown considerably and adapted to meet the needs of the modern city. The current building was built in 1963.

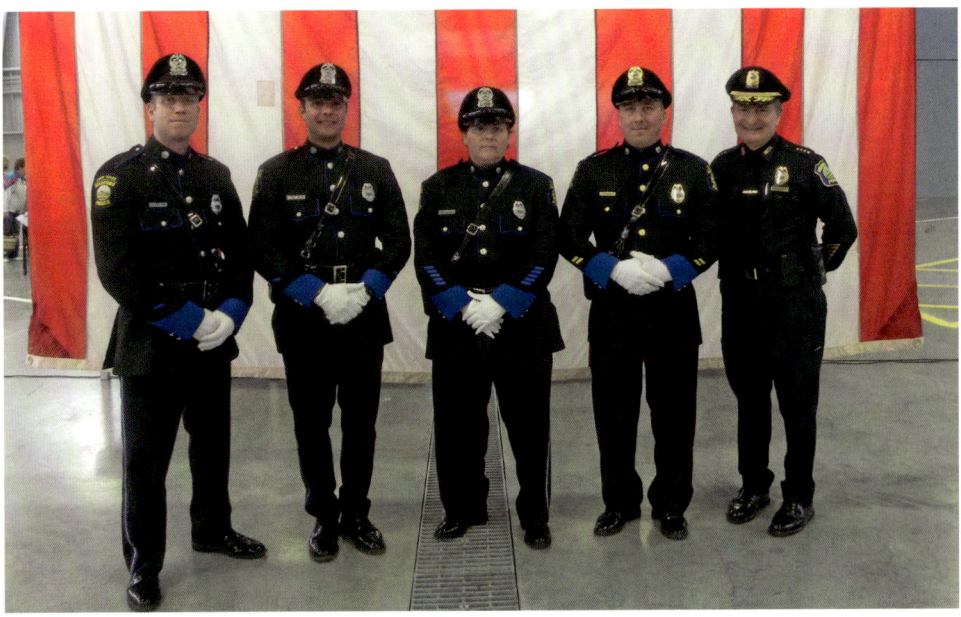

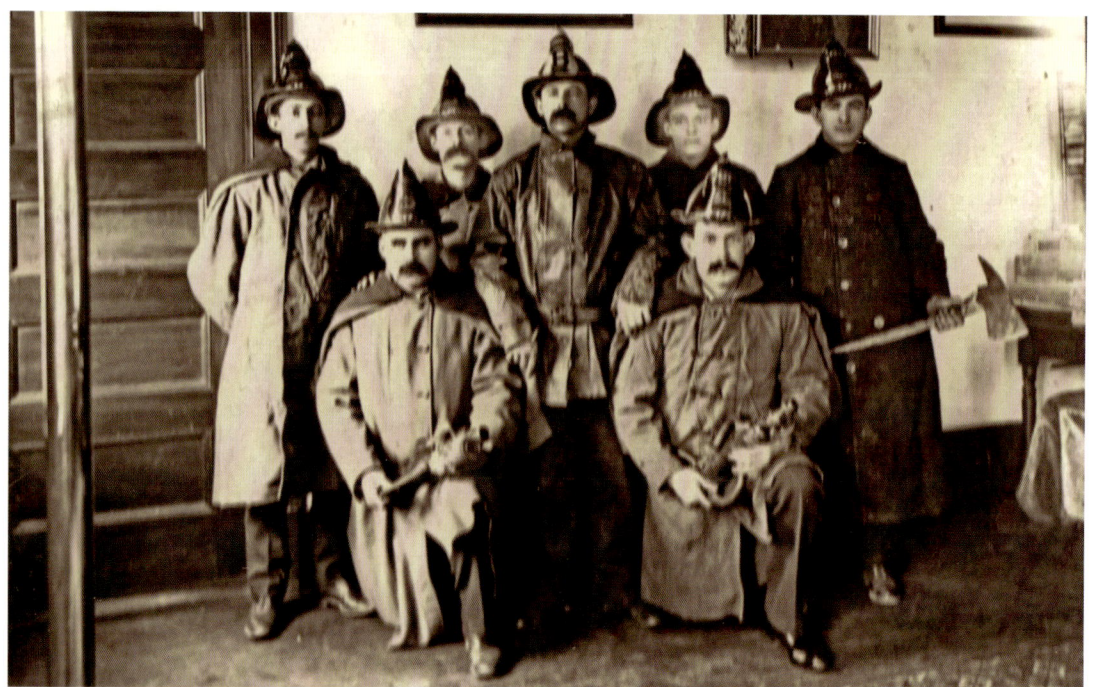

FIRE DEPARTMENT: Medford has had an organized fire department since 1760. In 1900 when the crew of the Medford Street Station posed for a photo the city used horse-drawn equipment. The first motorized engine was purchased in 1912. In 2015, when the crew of the Main Street station posed, the Medford Fire Department has left horses long behind. The modern department has 130 firefighters, six stations and a training building.

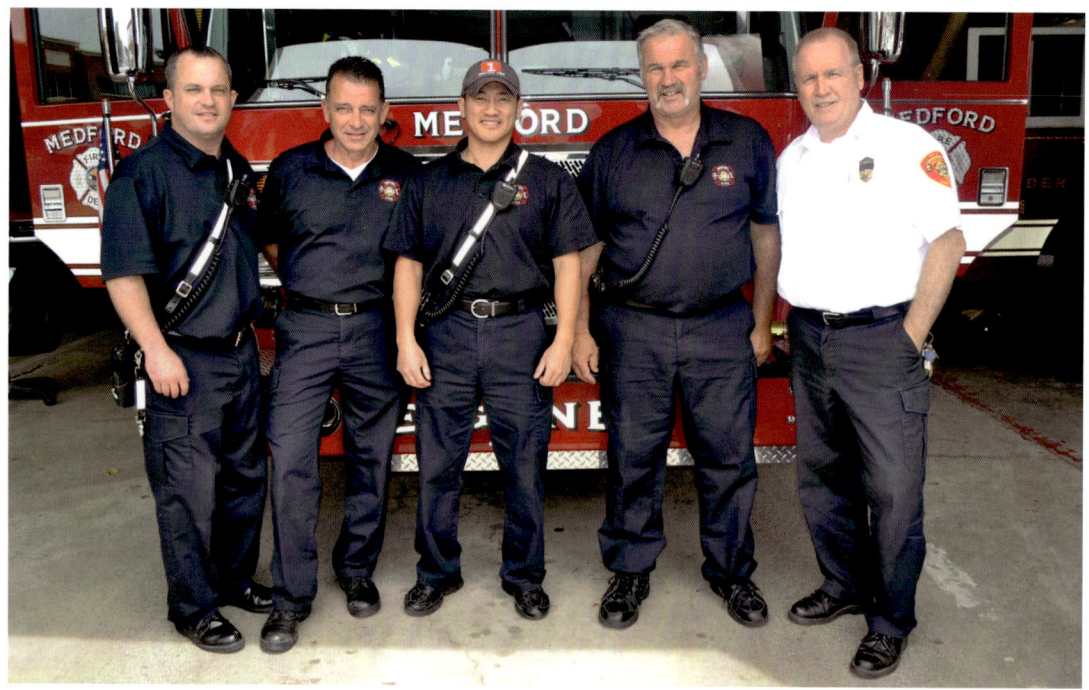

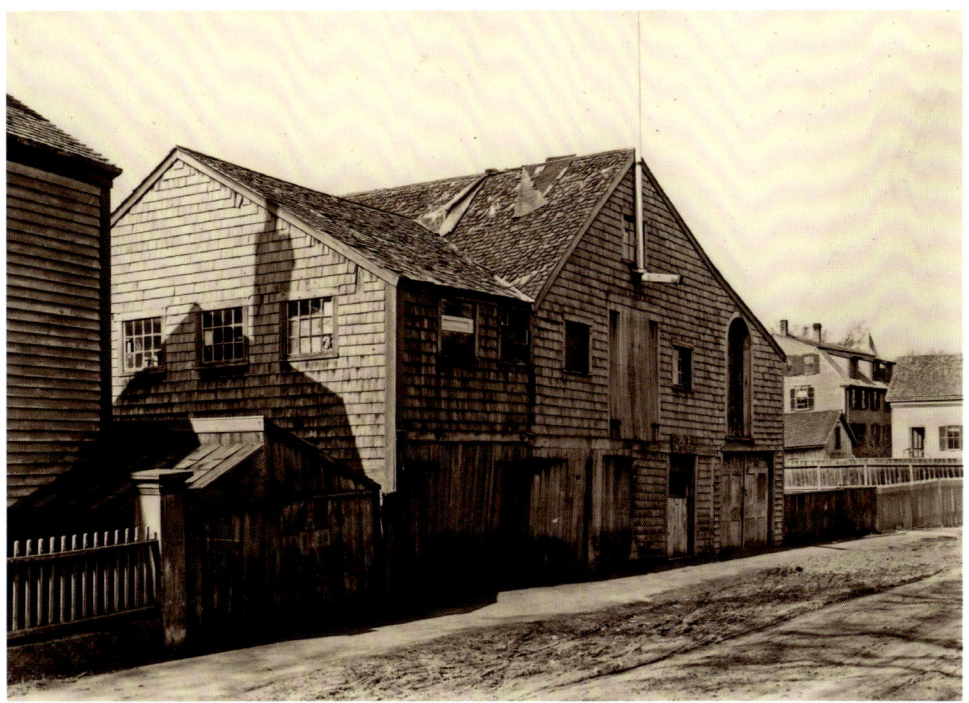

THOMAS STREET: Many older Medford houses were moved to new locations. In the background of this image is the Bigelow House which was moved before 1880 from the corner of Forest and Salem to make room for the Bigelow Building. The structure in front was the Thomas Barn. When it was torn down the Bigelow House was moved off Main Street and onto the barn site.

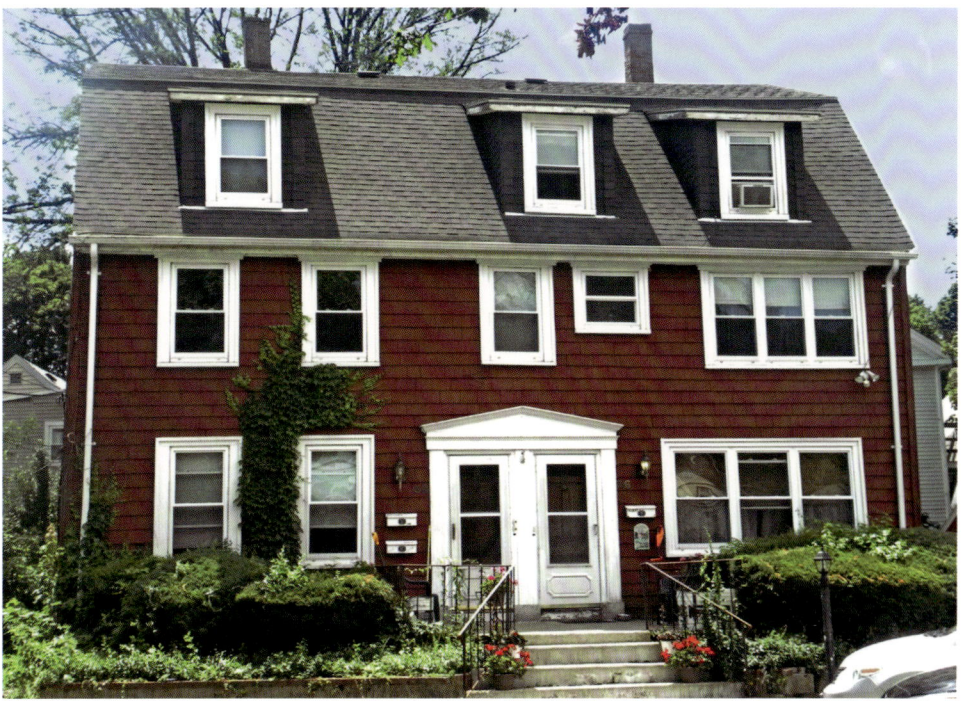

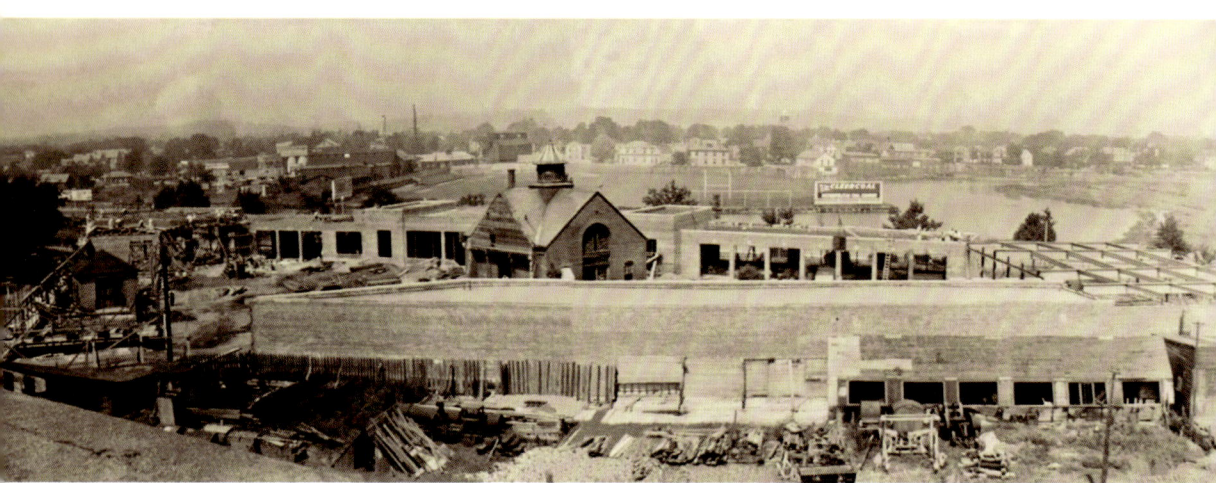

DPW: Medford's first consolidated Department of Public Works was built on James Street in 1937 as a WPA project. In 2015 a new public works facility was built on the same land. The original Medford Municipal Garage lettering, the DPW weather vane, and the original city seal were reconditioned and installed in the new building which was named after former Mayor Alfred Pompeo.

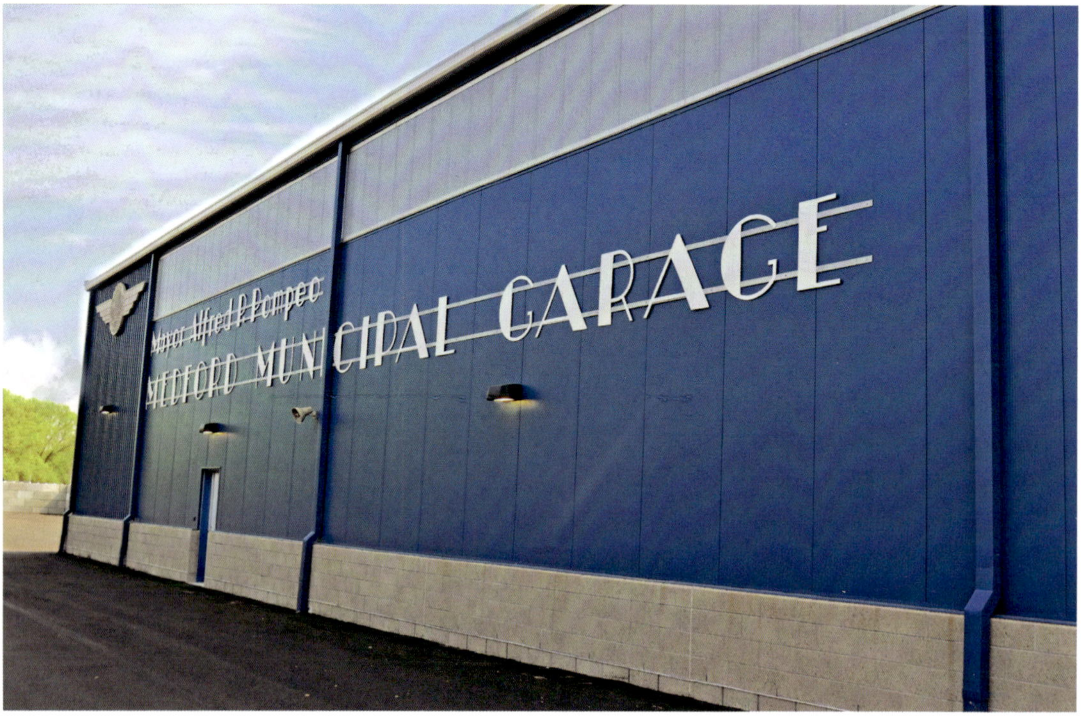

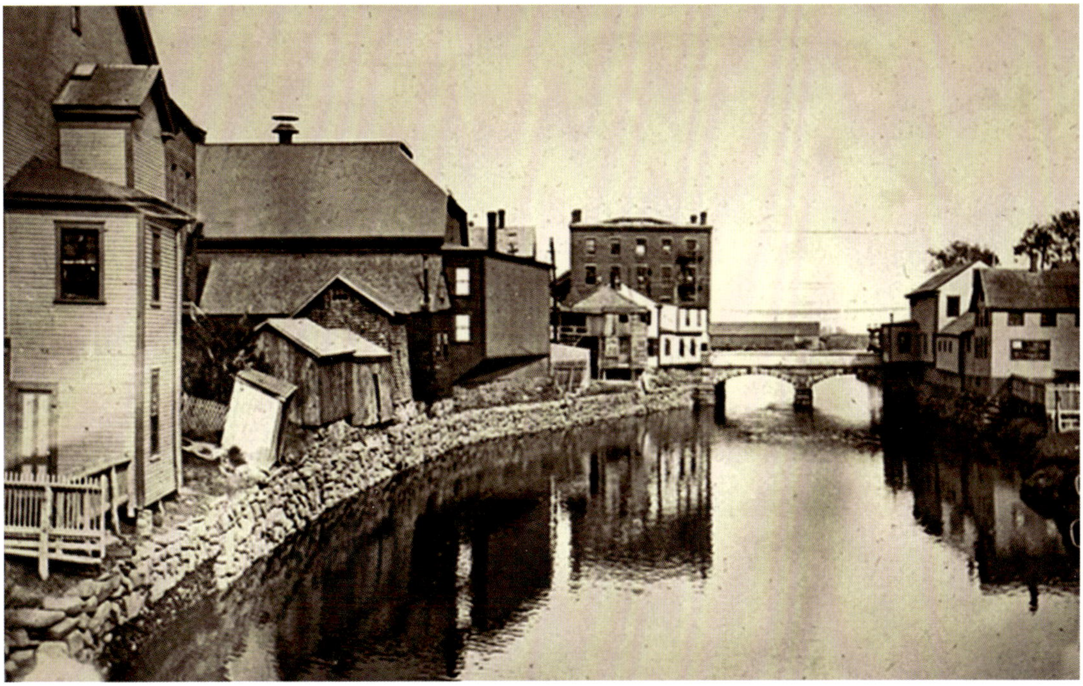

MYSTIC RIVER: In the eighteenth and nineteenth centuries, much of Medford's industry and town life focused on the Mystic River. Until 1879 the Main Street Bridge in the foreground of this photo was a wooden drawbridge which accommodated the frequent large boat and barge traffic up and down the river. In 1880 the bridge was rebuilt in stone, a sign that age of large ships was over. From that time until this, however, pleasure craft of all shapes and sizes have sailed the river and it is one of Medford's great natural treasures.

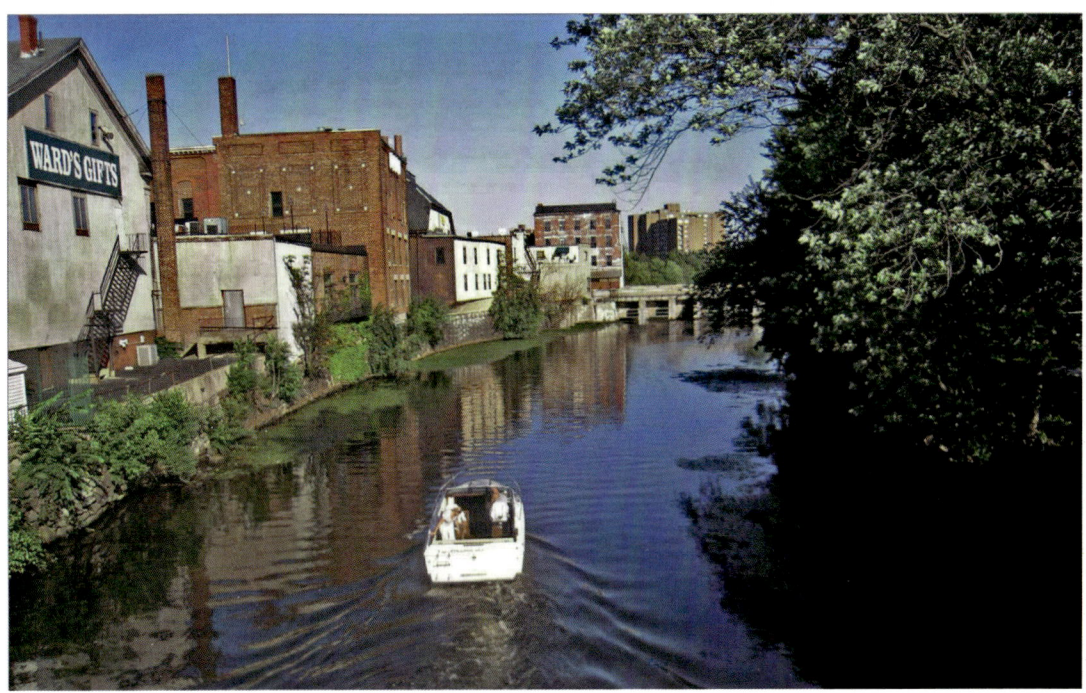

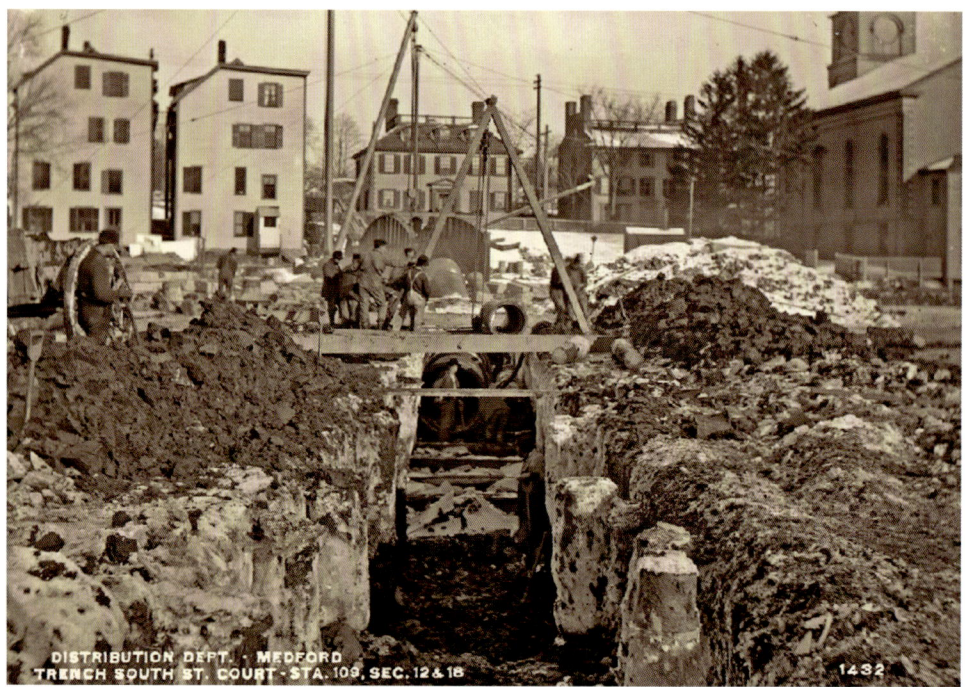

SOUTH STREET VIEW: In the 1880s and 1890s, plumbing came to Medford, and for years the streets were dug up to accommodate pipes, first for water and then for sewage. This 1897 view from South Street into the Square, shows water pipes being installed on the other side of the river. Two of the four eighteenth century Hall Houses can be seen in the foreground. Today the foot bridge from South Street to Shipyard Way spans the river in the same location.

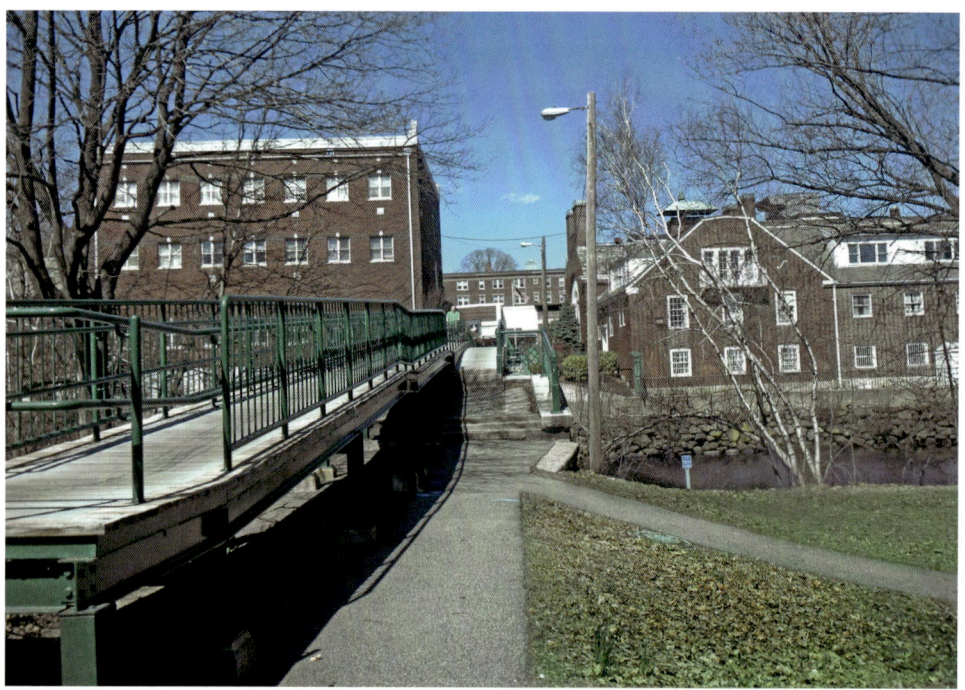

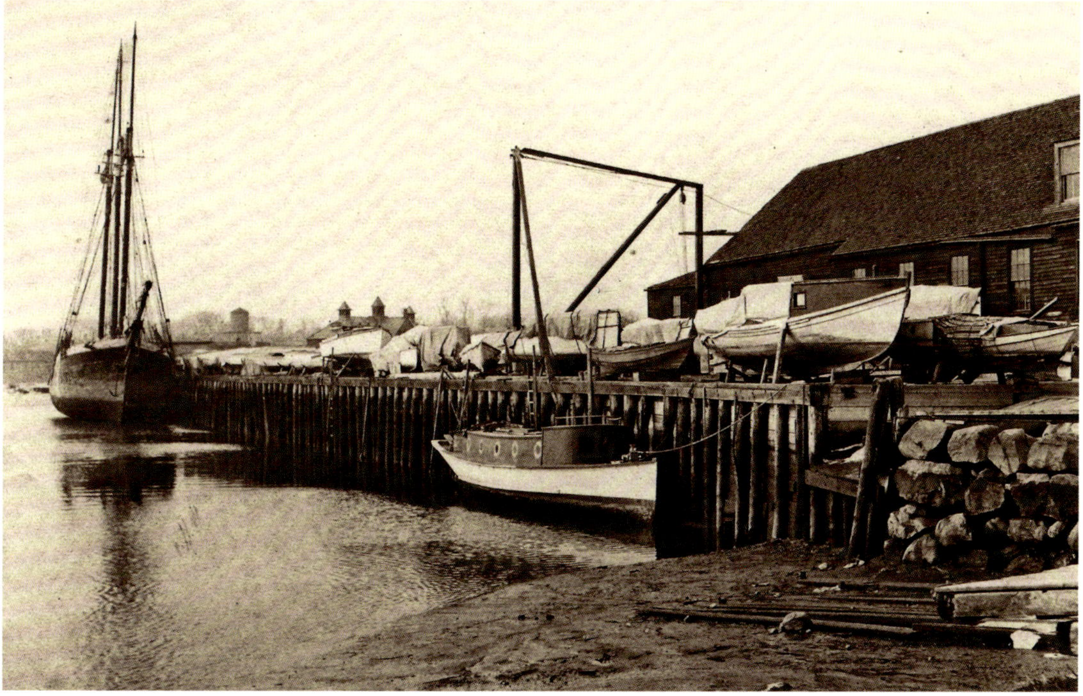

MYSTIC BOAT COMPANY: In the nineteenth century, Medford was a major shipbuilding town. Although the last merchant ship was launched in 1875, smaller boatyards flourished on the river into the twentieth century. The Mystic Boat Company, seen here *c.* 1916, built both motor and sailboats. Viewing the peaceful river from the former site of the yard, it is hard to imagine the busy maritime industry of earlier times.

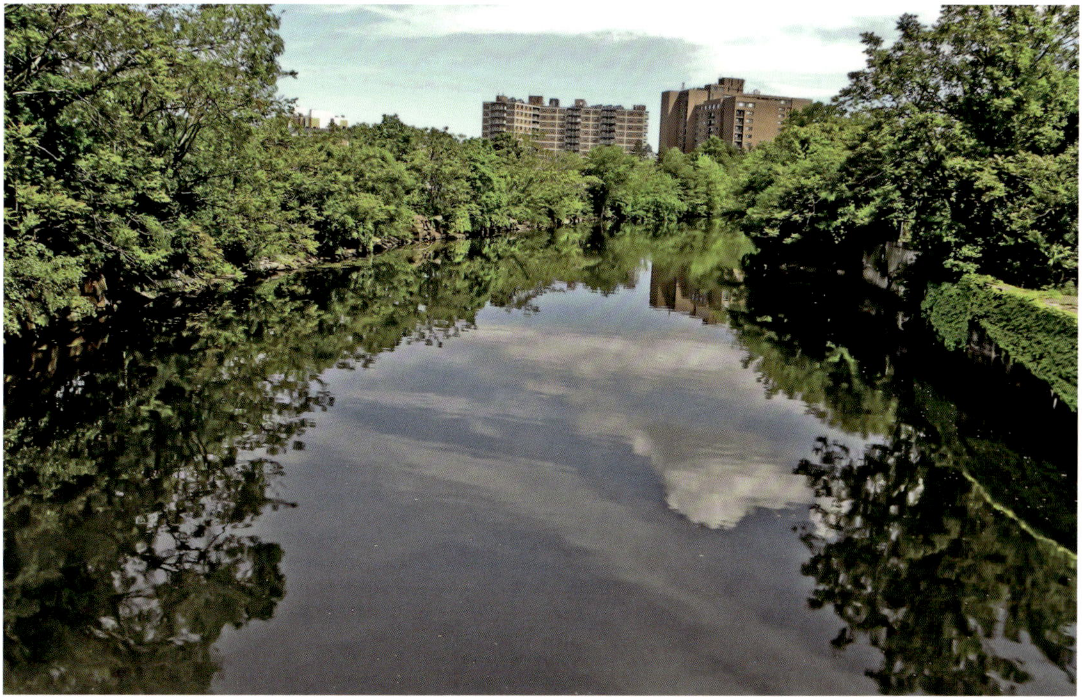

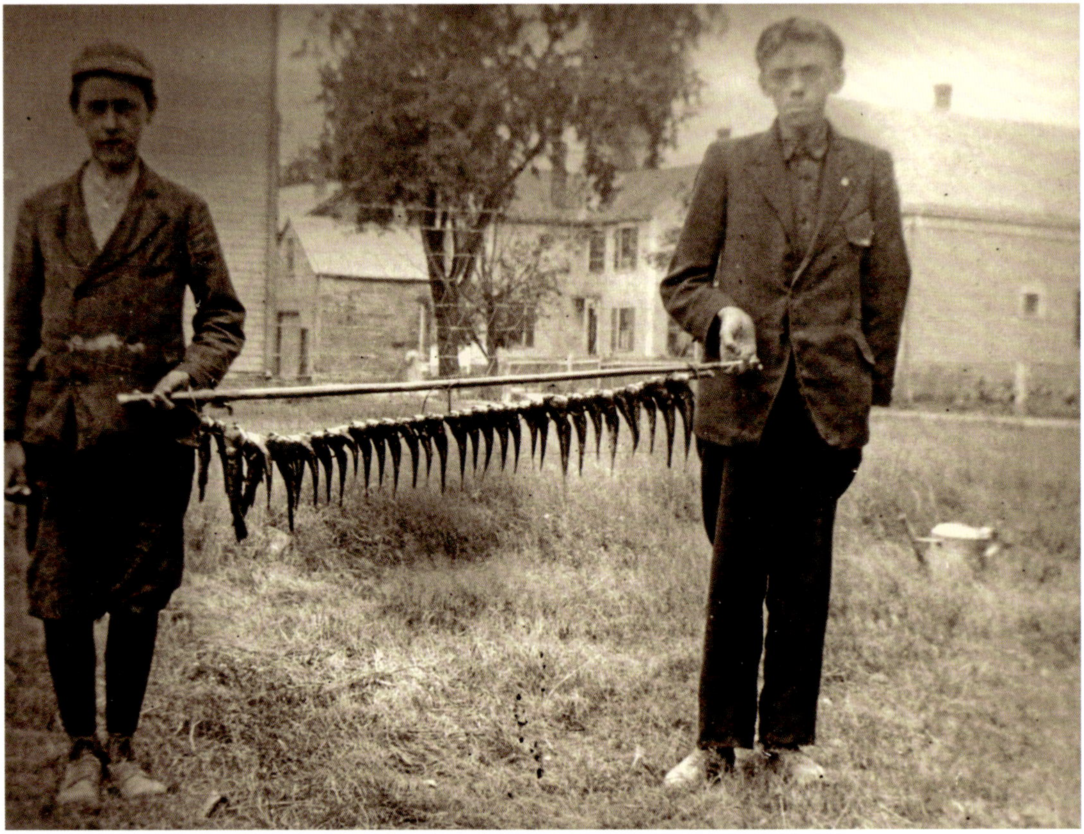

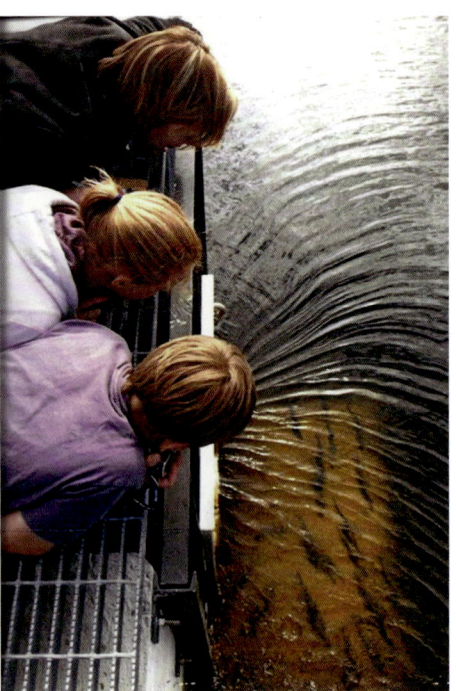

ALEWIVES: The alewife, a type of herring, was first mentioned in 1639 in a document granting John Winthrop permission to catch fish. Alewives were very abundant in Medford's first three centuries. There was still a sizeable population in the river at the time the George brothers showed off their catch in this 1910 photo. In recent years, however, the alewife population has declined and volunteers like these pictured help conservation by taking part in an annual monitoring program.

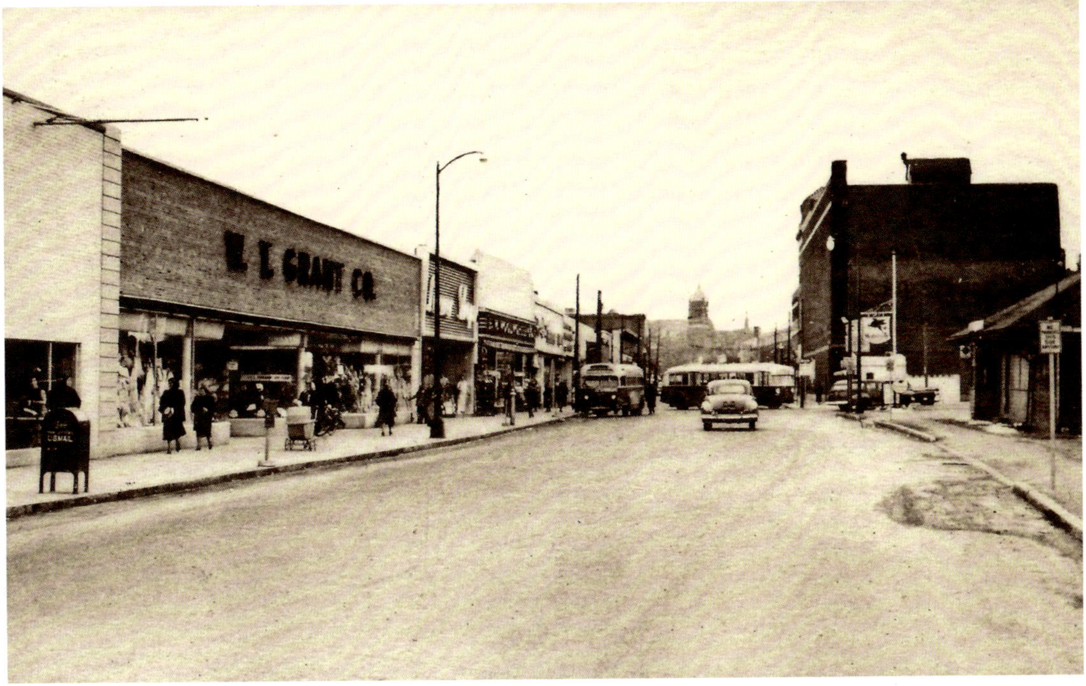

RIVERSIDE AVE: Before shopping malls, suburban city centers were home to national department stores like W. T. Grant seen in this 1950s postcard. The first Grant's opened in 1906 and the chain went out of business in 1975. The Medford store opened in 1928. Grant's store-branded electronics and other goods were named Bradford after Bradford County, Pennsylvania, where the chain's founder was born. The in-store restaurants were named Bradford House, and their mascot was a pilgrim named Bucky Bradford.

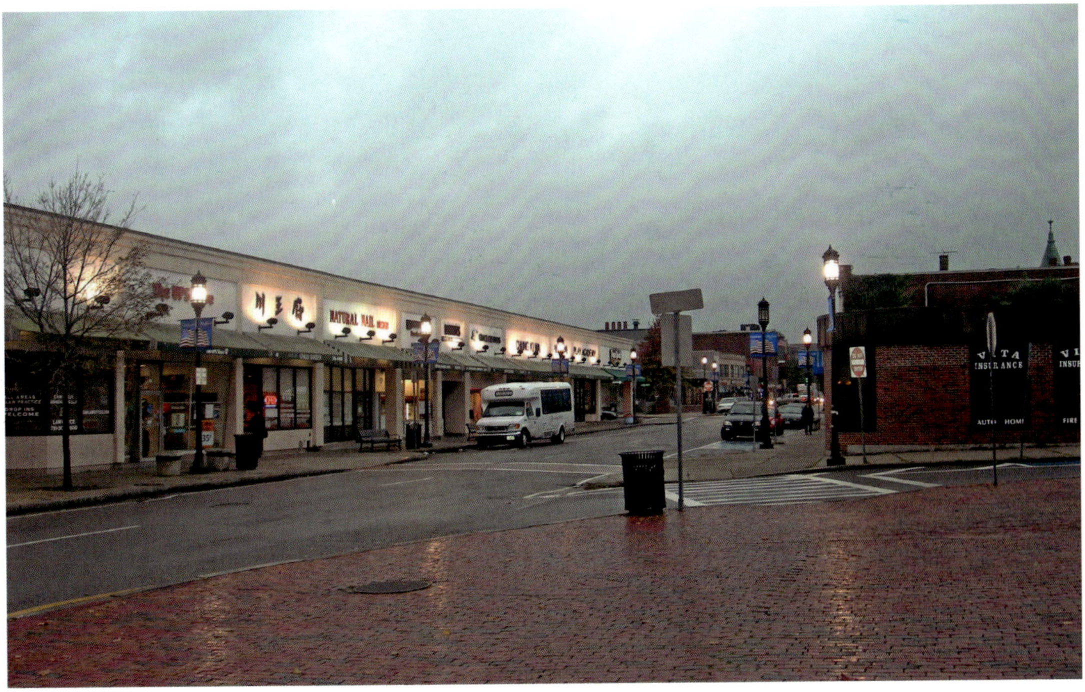

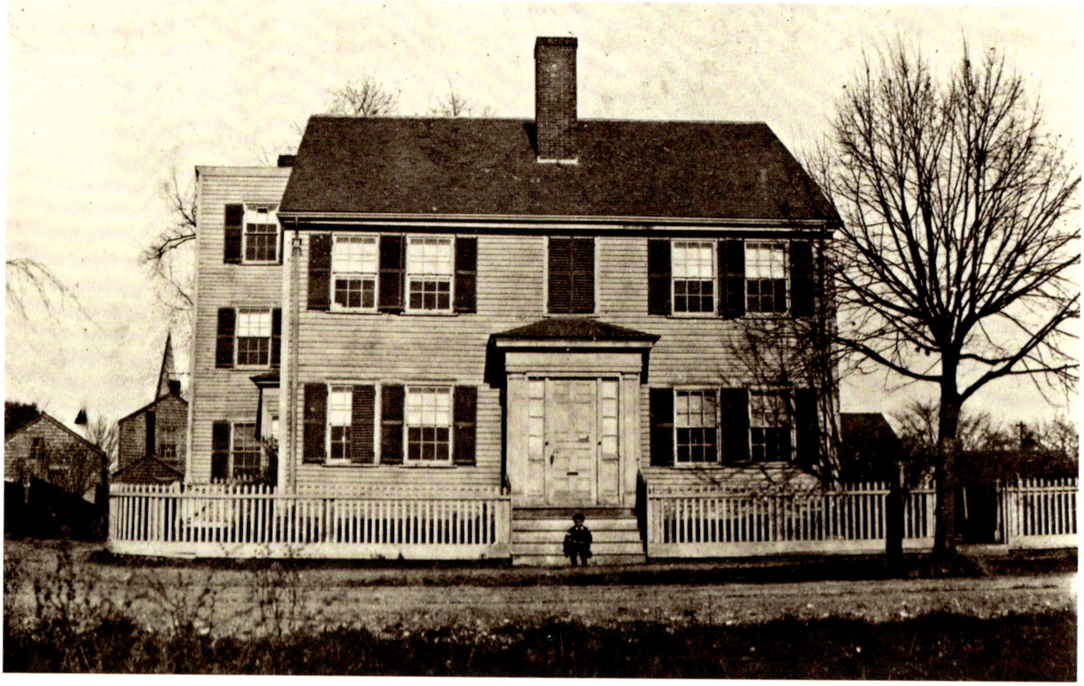

SABLES COURT: Medford's landscape was forever altered by the construction of Route 93 in the 1960s. Entire neighborhoods full of residences and small businesses were replaced by the highway and its many embankments and ramps. The house in this late nineteenth century photo was on Sables Court, where the Hyatt Regency now stands. Much of the Sables Court neighborhood was razed for the highway construction, including the Cross Street cemetery which was moved to Oak Grove in West Medford.

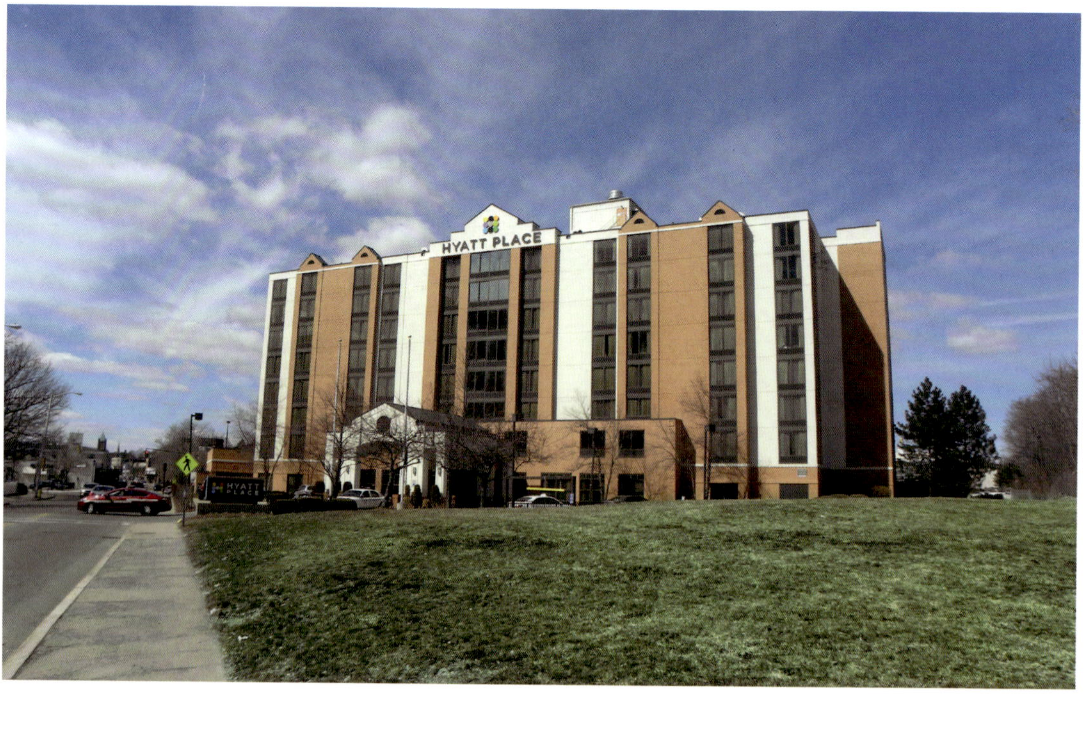

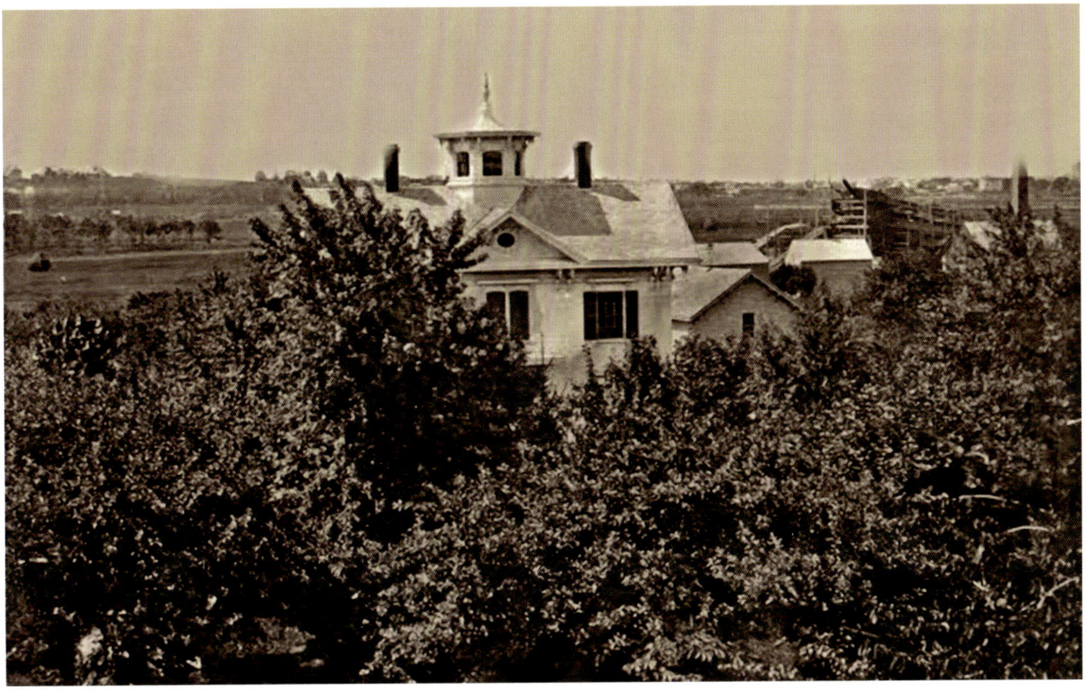

FOSTER HOUSE: This 1870s photo of the house of shipbuilder Joshua Foster is one of the few photographic images of a Medford ship. In the upper right corner you can see the last Medford ship, *The Pilgrim*, under construction in Foster's shipyard. During the shipbuilding era, Riverside Avenue was called Ship Street because of all the yards. As a tribute to the old shipbuilding area these modern condo buildings on the site of Foster's yard are on Ship Avenue.

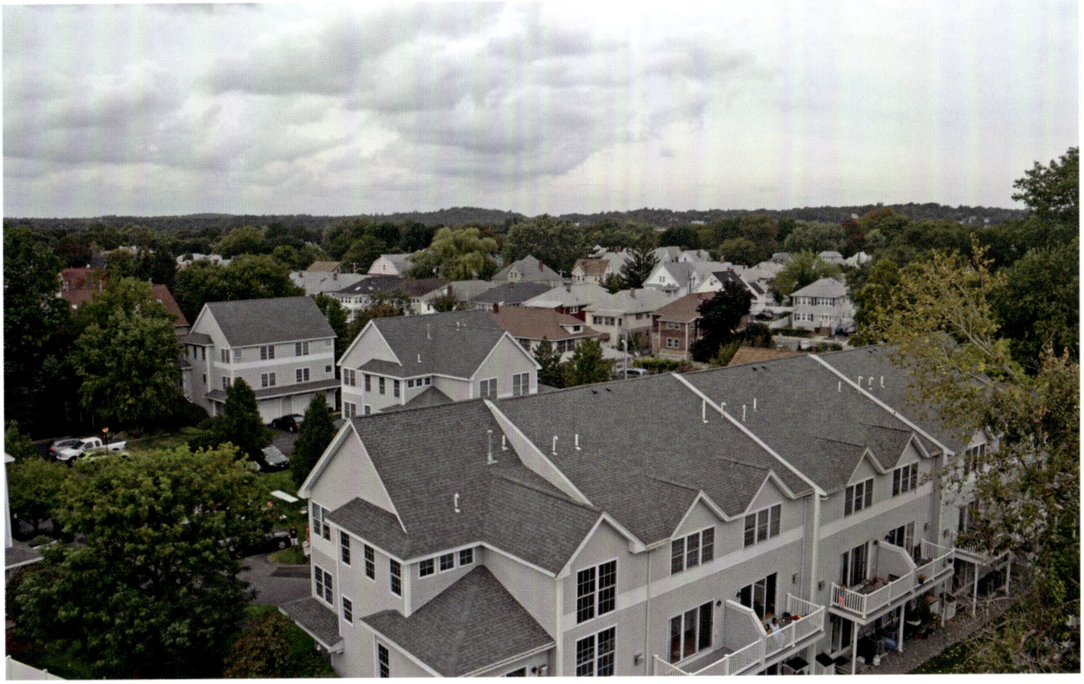

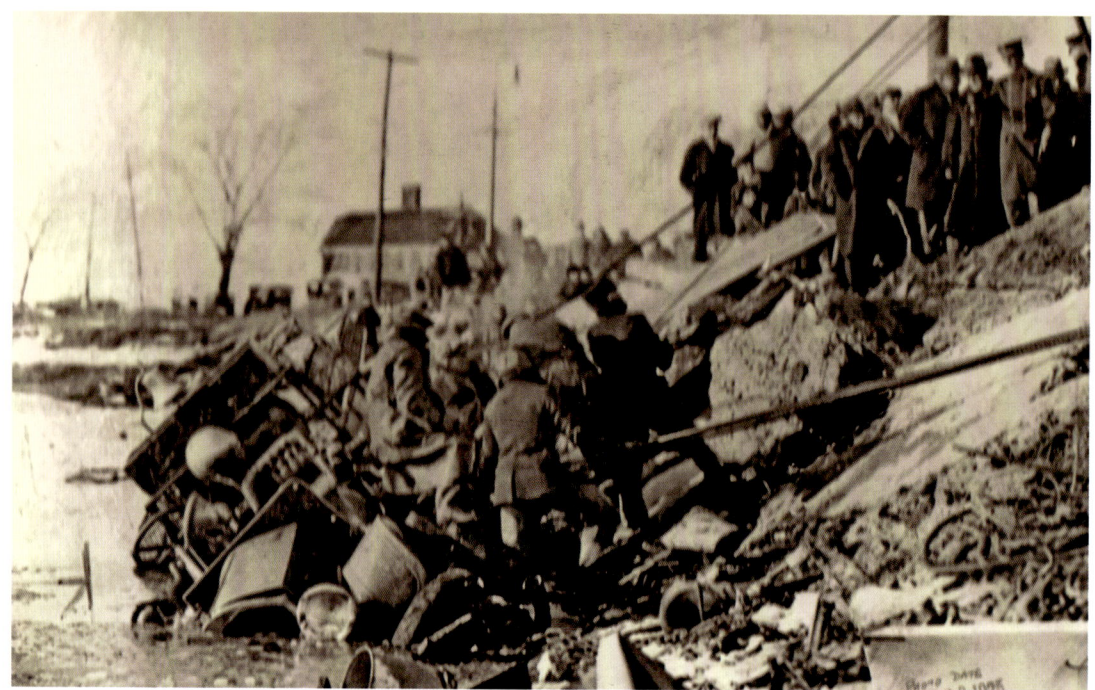

Clay Pits: In 1925 one of Medford's fire vehicles slid off Riverside Avenue into clay pit once used by the Bay State Brick Company. Brickmaking was one of Medford's major eighteenth and nineteenth century industries. In 1900 the original company was purchased by the New England Brick Company which closed its doors in the late 1920s. Today Riverside Avenue shows little trace of this once major industry.

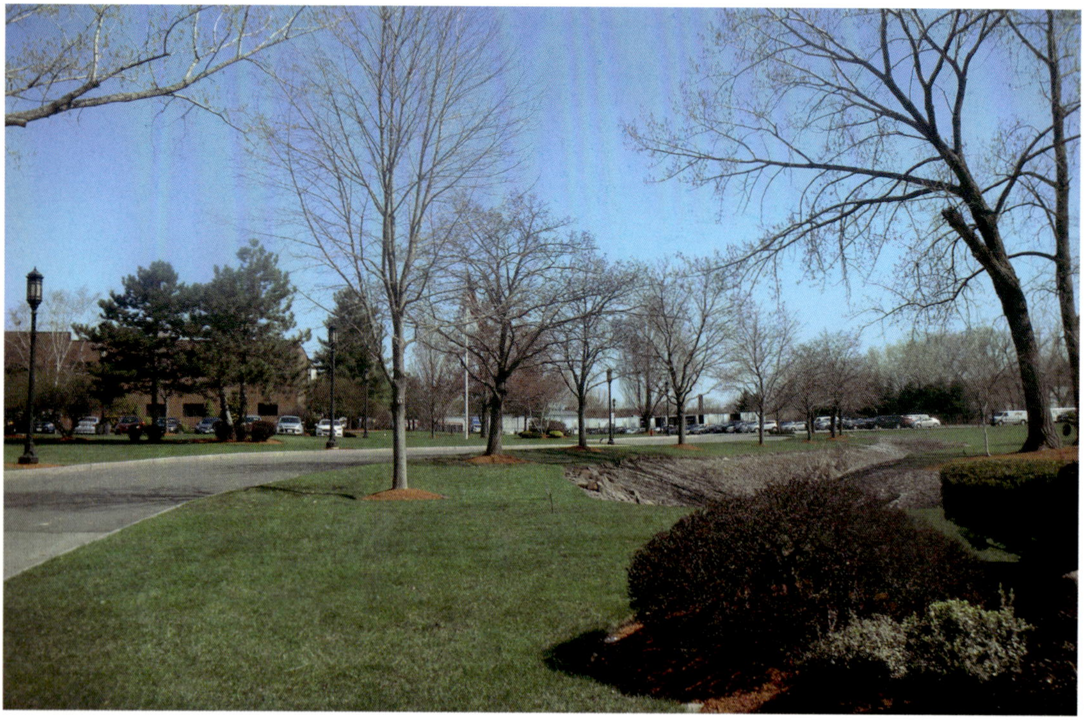

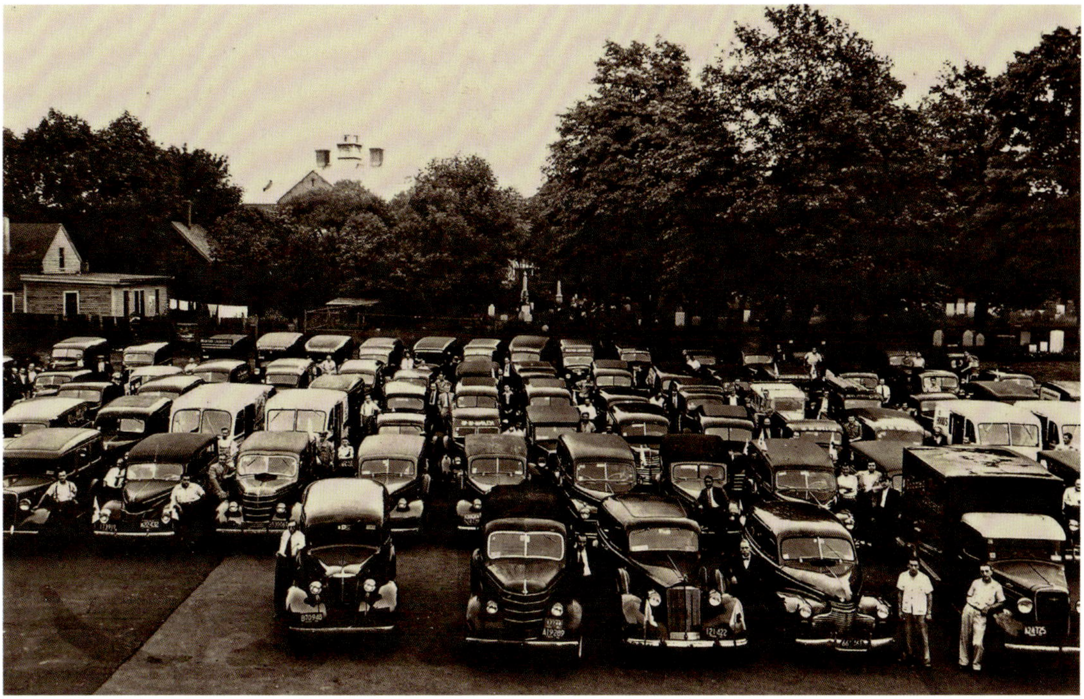

CITY HALL: The first Medford town hall was built on the corner of Main and High Street in the 1830s. The current city hall was dedicated on September 11, 1937. The new Colonial revival style building was built on the site of the old town common and the Everett school. In 2013 the building was decked with a large flag in memory of Krystle Campbell who was killed in the Boston Marathon bombing.

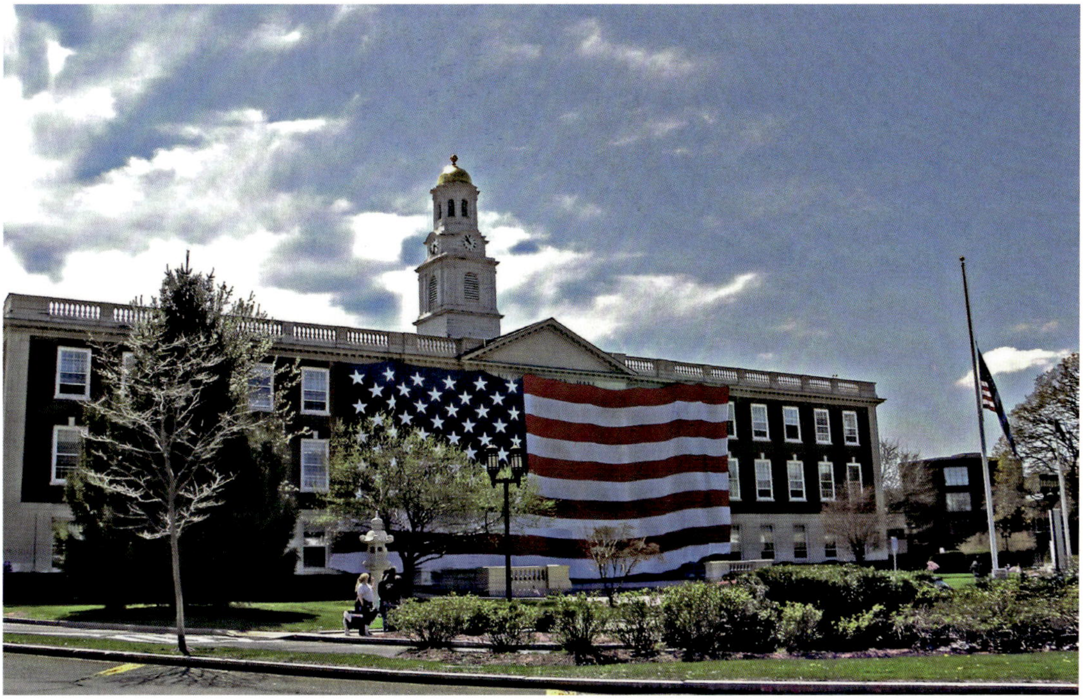

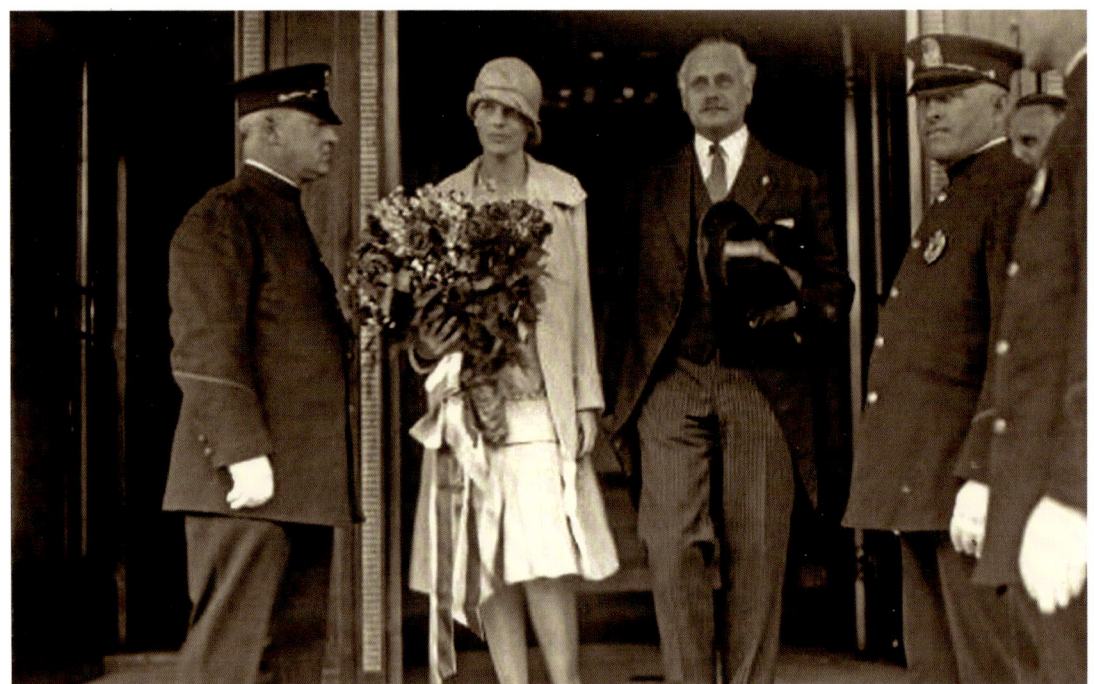

FAMOUS VISITORS: In July 1928, after she became the first woman to fly across the Atlantic, Amelia Earhart was met with a huge celebration in Medford. Earhart had lived in Medford a few years earlier while working as a social worker in Boston. Earhart is seen here with then Medford Mayor Edward Larkin on her arrival. In 2012, the Dalai Lama posed with then Mayor Michael McGlynn during the visit to the Center for Tibetan Buddhist Studies on Magoun Avenue.

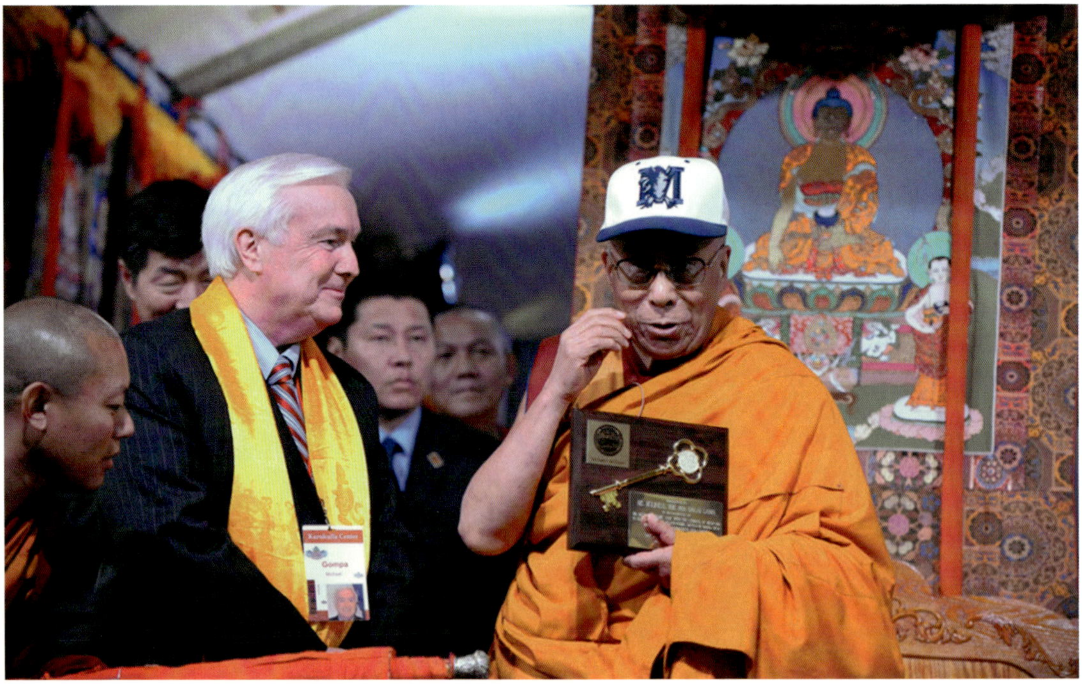

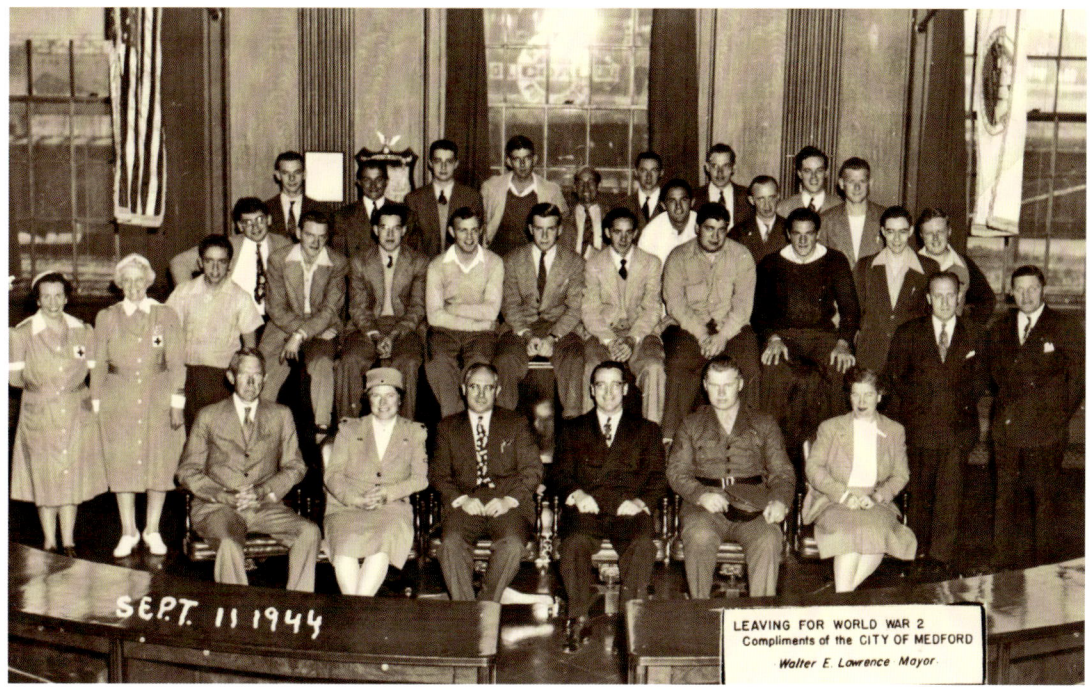

WORLD WAR II: Medford men and women have served in every conflict since the American Revolution. In September of 1944 one of many groups of recruits was photographed in the council chambers at Medford City Hall. By the time the war ended, more than 8,600 Medford men and 287 women had served. Some sixty years later, surviving World War II veterans gathered at the unveiling of the city's World War II monument on Winthrop Street.

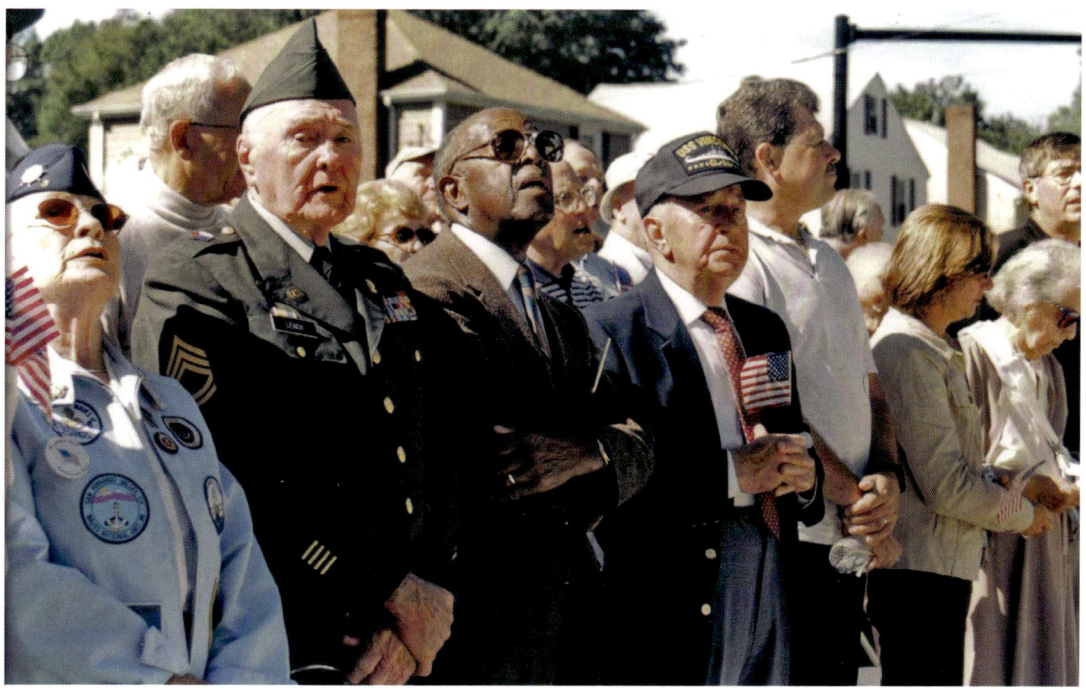

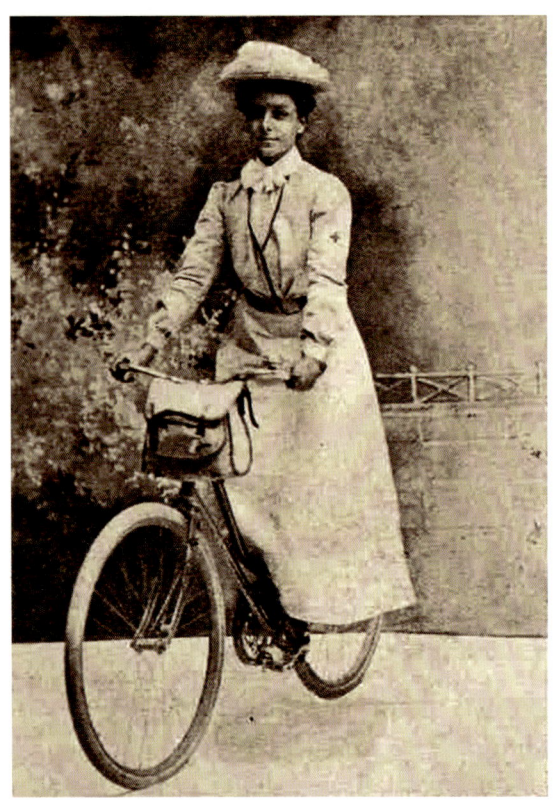

NURSES: Medford women have always served the community in war and peace. The first visiting nurse, Miss Row, was hired in June 1900, at fifty dollars per month and served three years. Miriam Larkin O'Hearn (1897-1954) was the daughter of Medford mayor Edward Larkin. Like many Medford women, she volunteered with the Red Cross during World War I. After the war, O'Hearn, a talented pianist, played in local theaters accompanying silent movies. She married John O'Hearn and had six children.

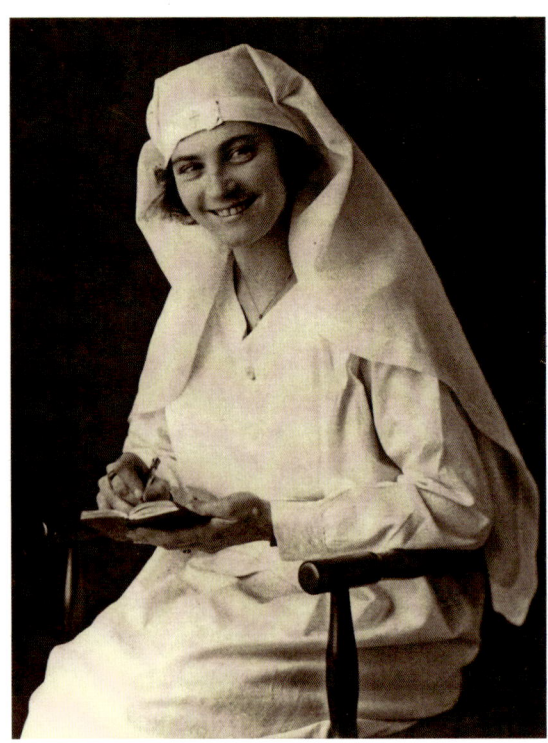

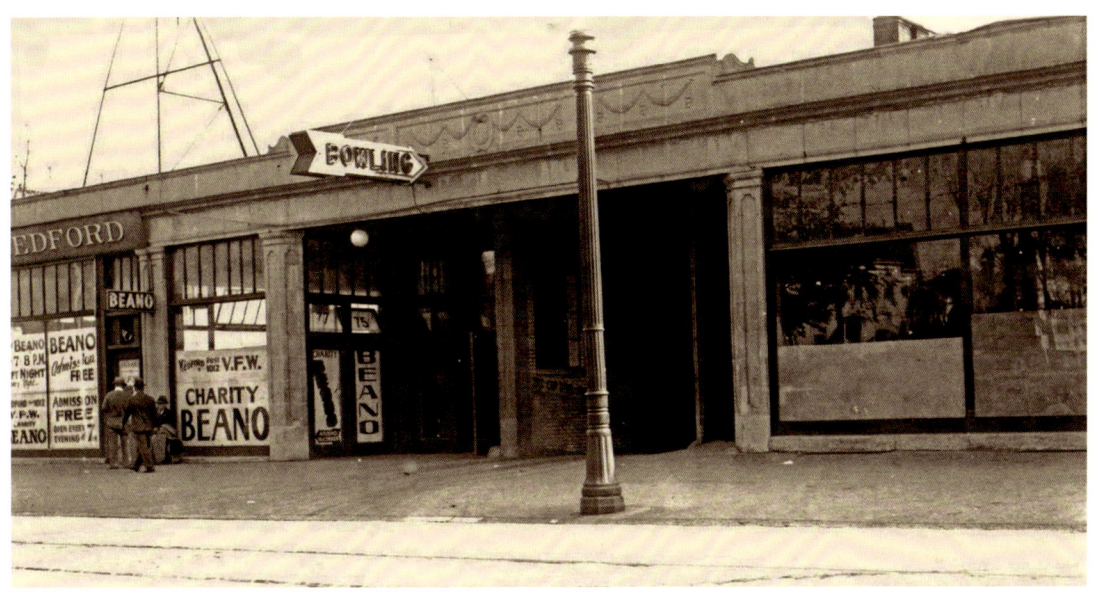

SALEM STREET BOWLING: In the 1930s, Medford Square offered both a pool hall and the Daylight Bowling Alley on Salem Street at the location of Harvard Vanguard in 2015. The candlepin bowling alley shared a border with the much more sedate Salem Street Cemetery, the older of Medford's two existing cemeteries. The earliest stone is marked 1683. The graves include those of many Revolutionary War veterans who are remembered at the city's Patriot's Day celebrations like this in 2014.

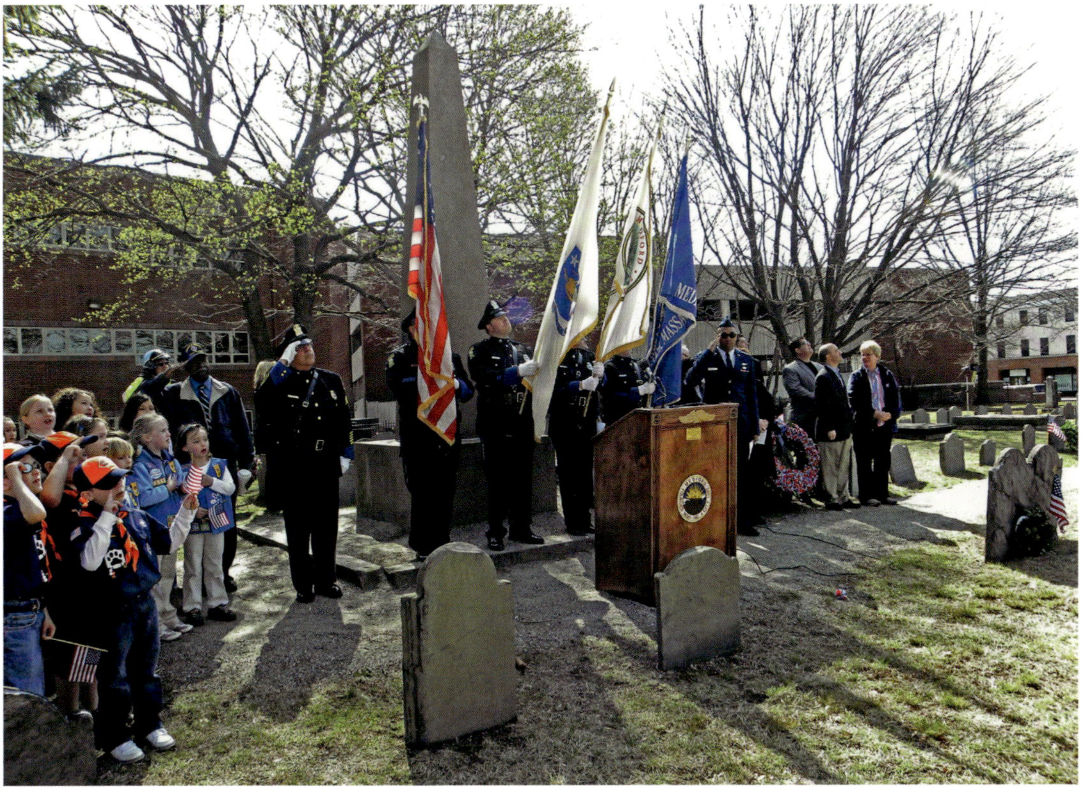

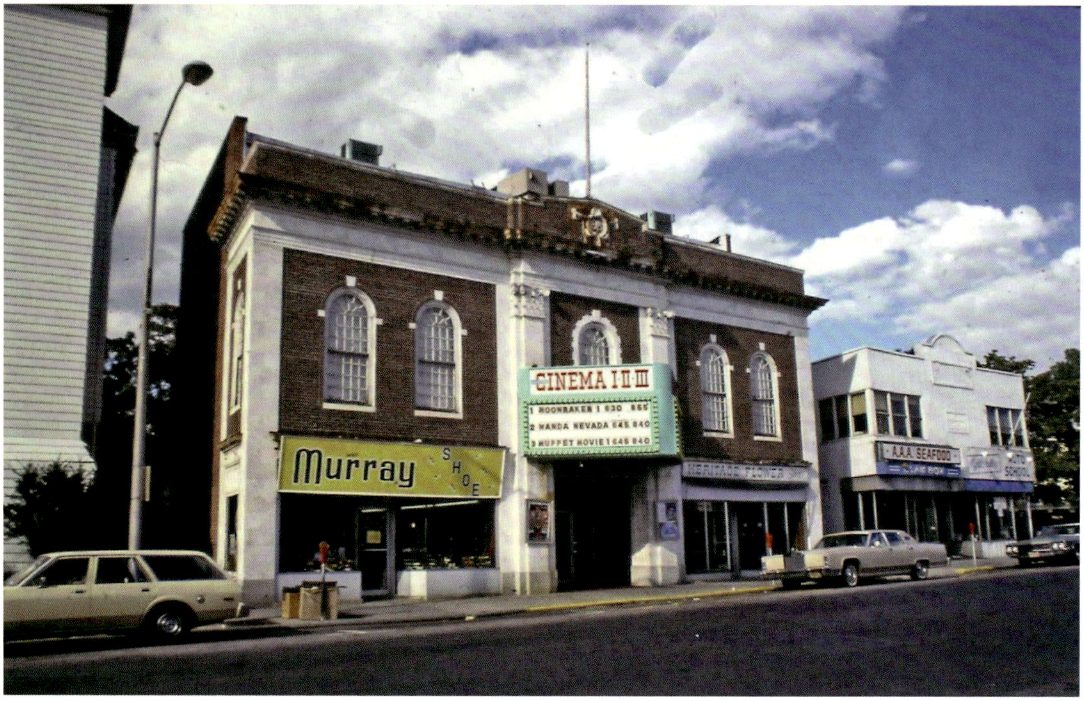

MEDFORD THEATRE: The Dyer Building at 36 Salem Street was built in 1915 as a movie theatre connected with the early film industry in Medford. Previously this was the site of the Withington Bakery. The cinema screened thousands of films in the next three quarters of a century and closed in 1983. The Elizabeth Grady salon has been a Salem Street institution at this location since 1981.

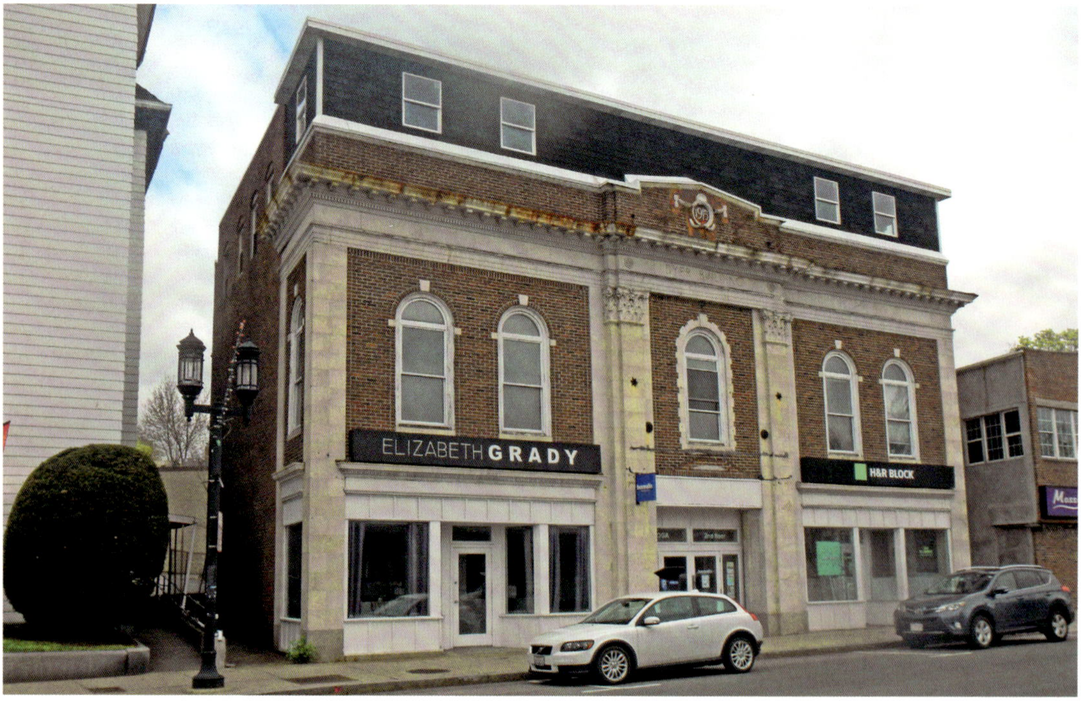

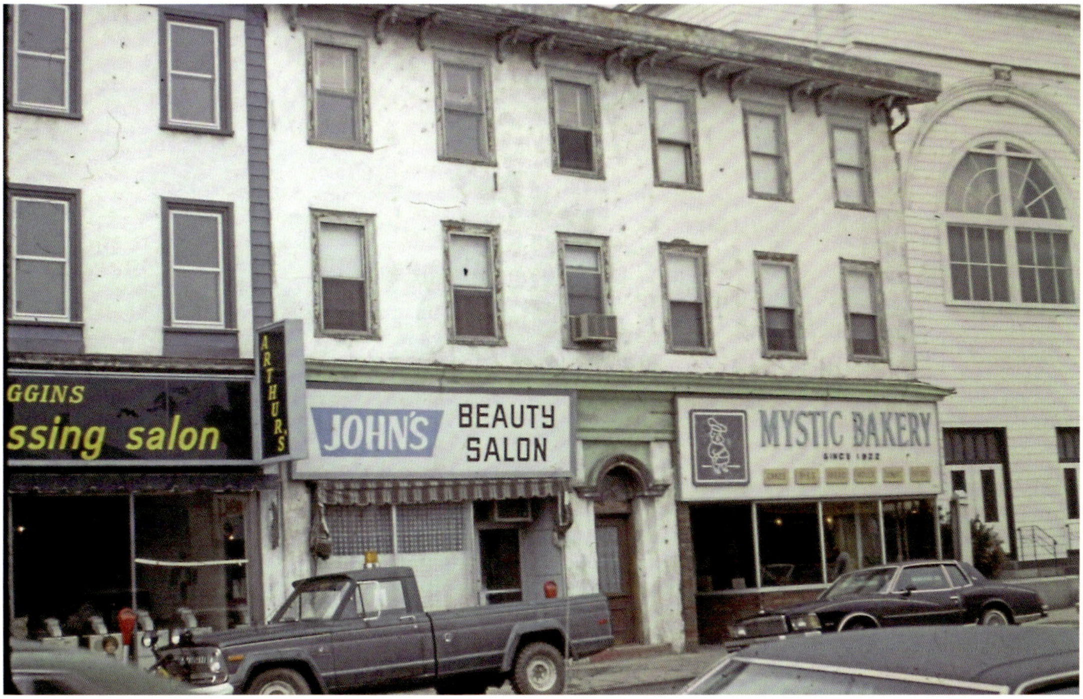

SALEM STREET BAKERIES: Maybe it's something about the location, but this block of Salem Street seems to attract bakeries. In the nineteenth century this was the block of the Withington Bakery, a beloved nineteenth century institution famous for Medford Crackers. In the 1970s, Mystic Bakery was a popular destination for treats. In 2015 we have Modern Bakery, the Medford branch of a North End favorite.

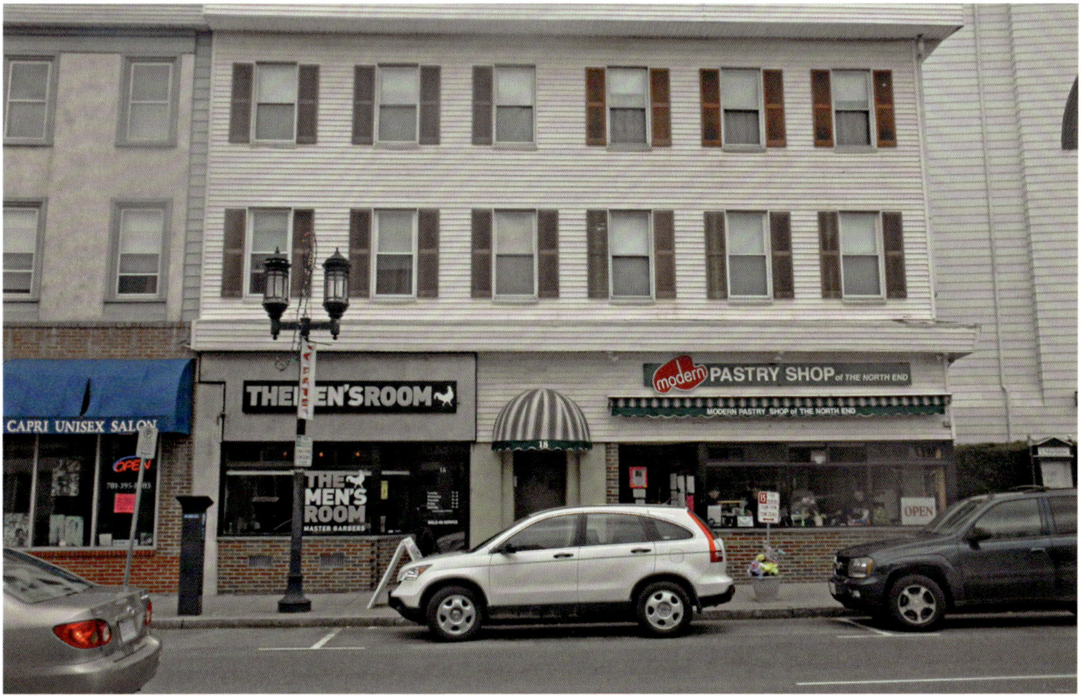

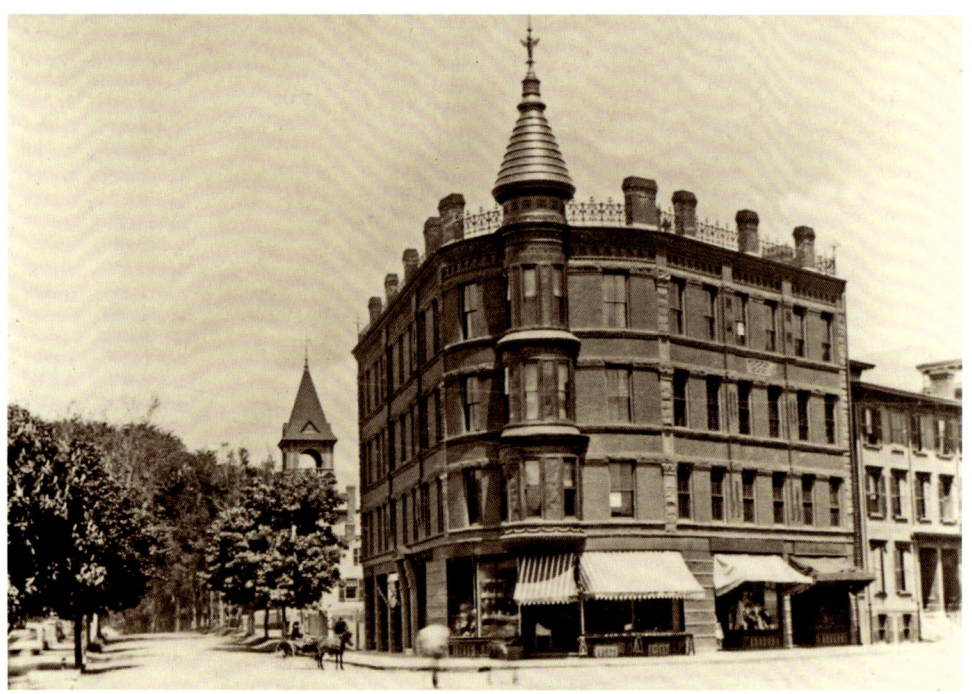

BIGELOW BUILDING: Medford Square would not be the same without the Bigelow Block on the corner of Forest and Salem Streets. The striking Victorian block was built in 1886. It is a four story brick building with sandstone trim, terra cotta plaques, and copper-clad turret at the corner. It is one of few surviving nineteenth century commercial buildings in the city. It is pictured here not long after its construction and as it is today, proudly housing Dunkin Donuts.

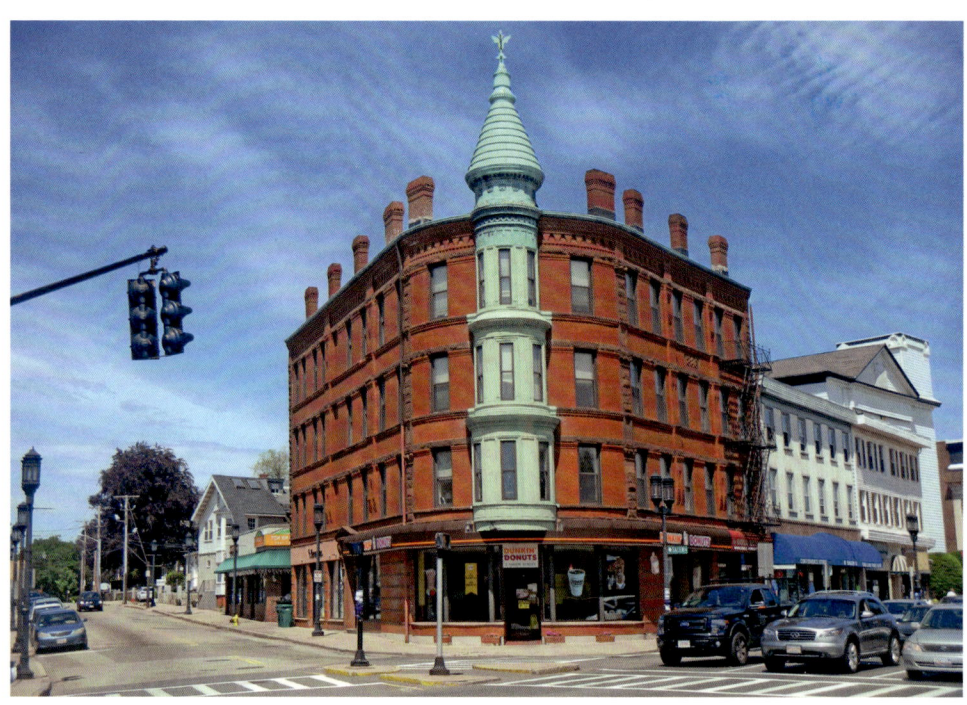

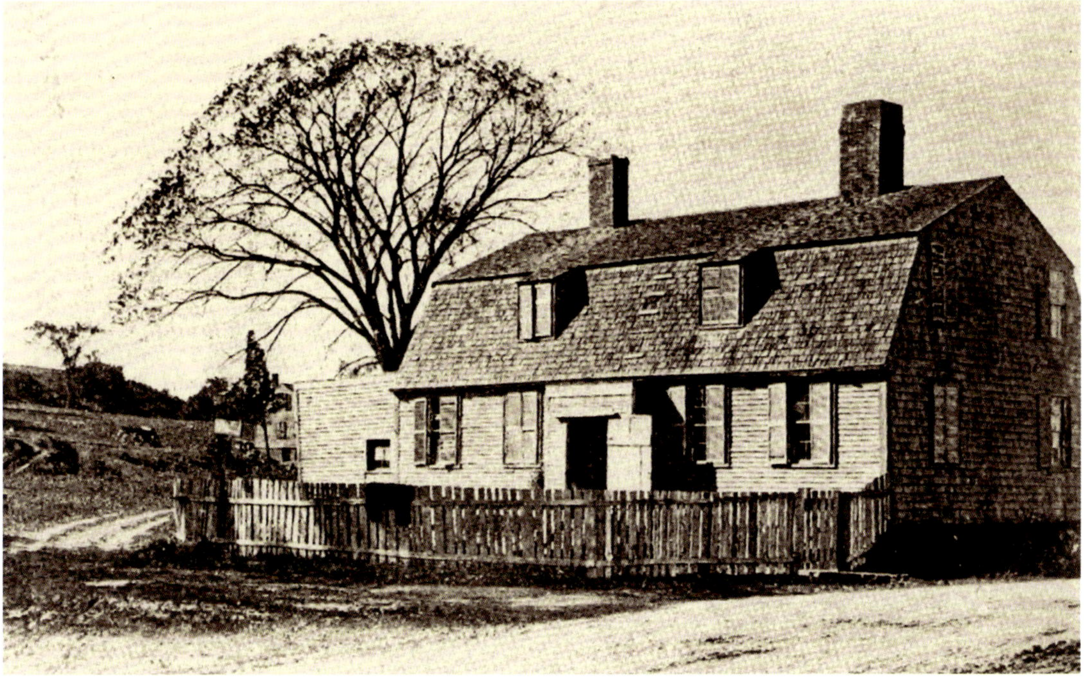

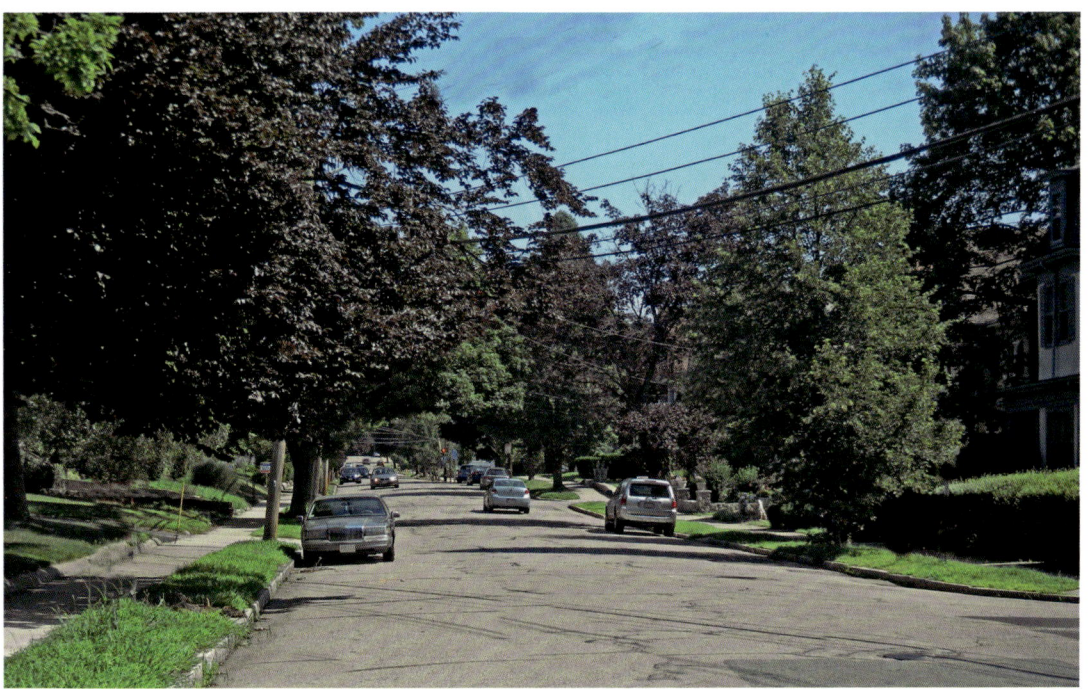

TOLL HOUSE: During the seventeenth century, a handful of major public roads – High Street, Main Street, Salem Street, "the road to Stoneham," and South Street – served the population around Medford Square. The Andover Turnpike Company was incorporated in 1805, but turned what is now Forest Street and Fellsway West over to Medford in 1830. When the Andover Turnpike was active, Forest Street was a toll road and travelers paused at this building to pay for their passage.

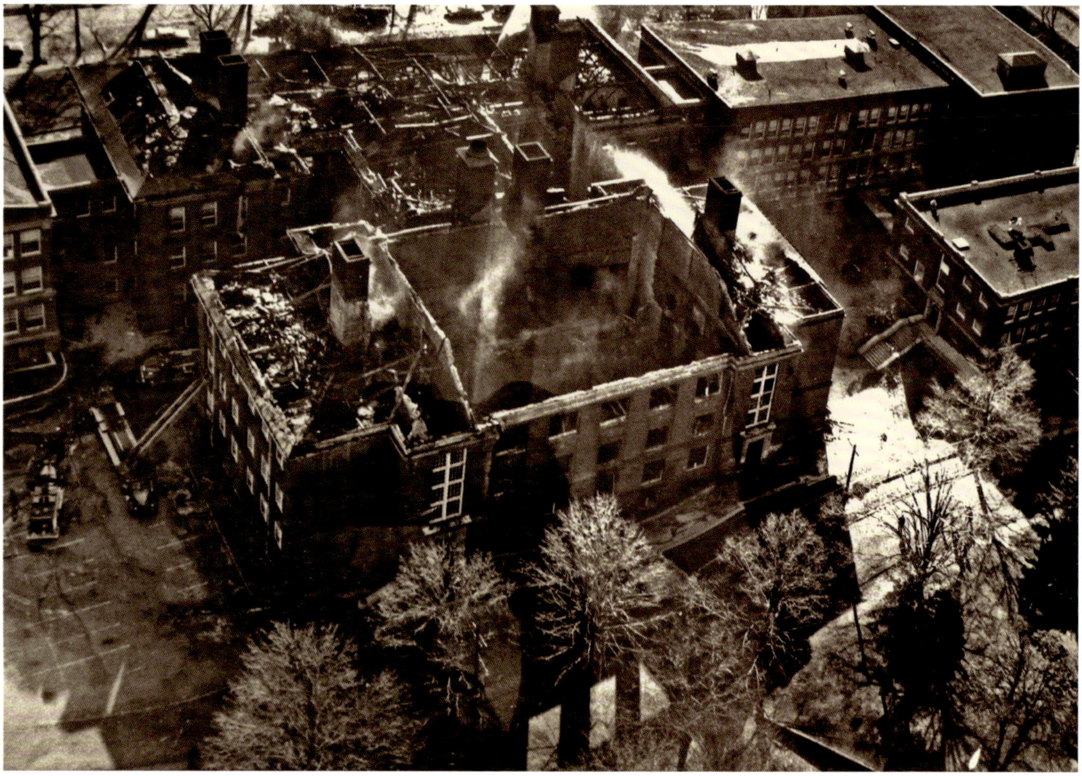

OLD HIGH SCHOOL: The central part of the old Medford High School building on Forest Street was destroyed by fire in 1965. School continued in the damaged building until the new high school was built in 1971. Another Medford Square fire took place on a freezing night in February of 1994. Several businesses on Main Street were destroyed in the blaze, and everything in sight, including trees wires, and this poor car were encased in ice from the fire hoses.

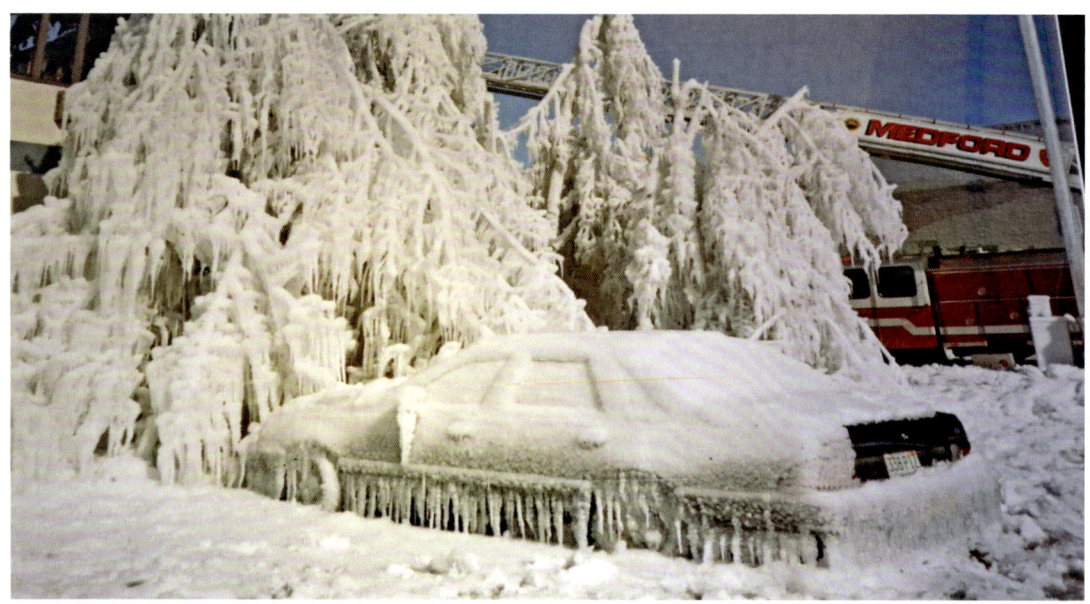

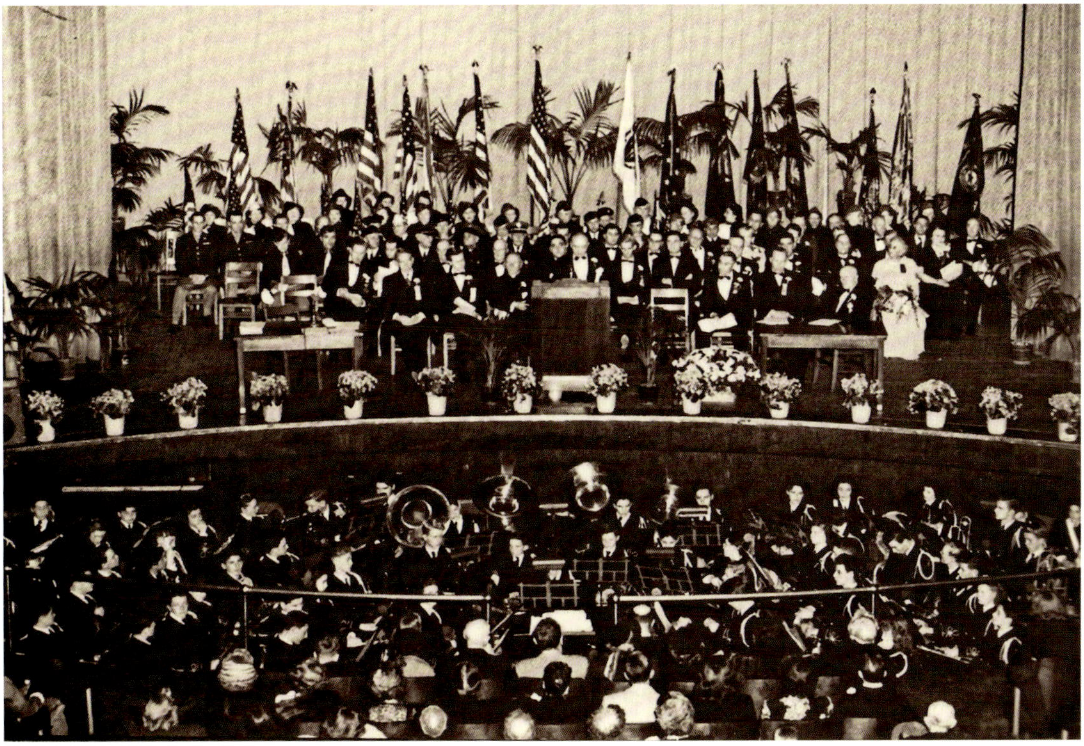

CHEVALIER AUDITORIUM: The Chevalier Theatre was built in 1939 by the Works Progress Administration as part of the Medford High School complex. The auditorium is the sixth largest theatre in Metropolitan Boston and is named after Medford native Godfrey Chevalier, a naval hero and aviation pioneer. The theater has been used for many a production from a 1940s black tie event to *Meet Me in St. Louis* in the 1990s.

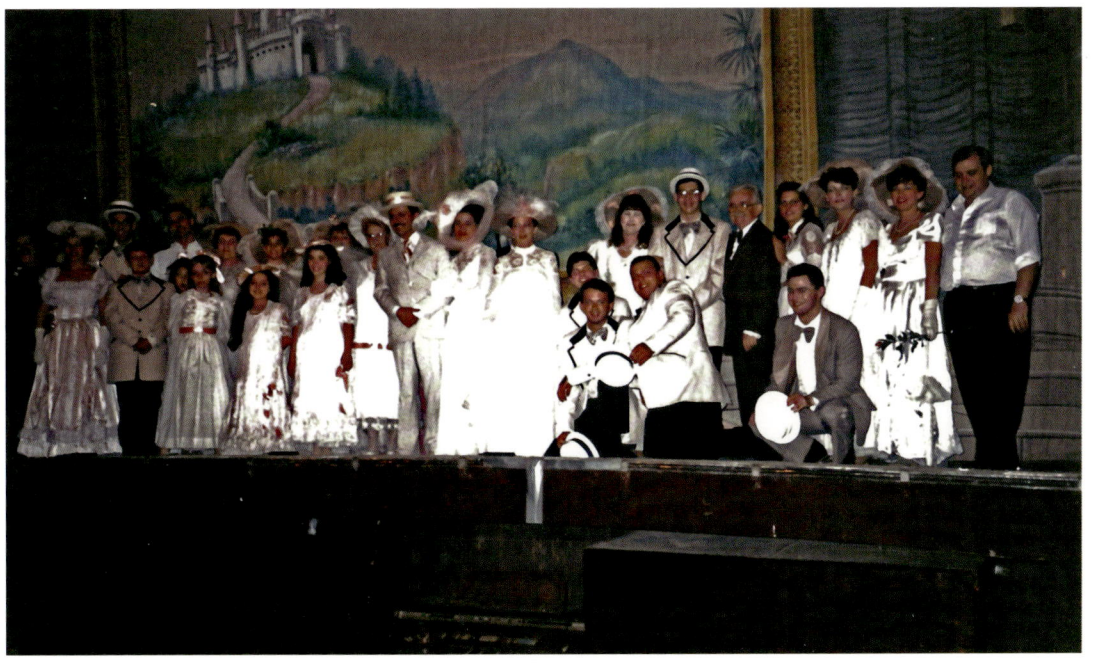

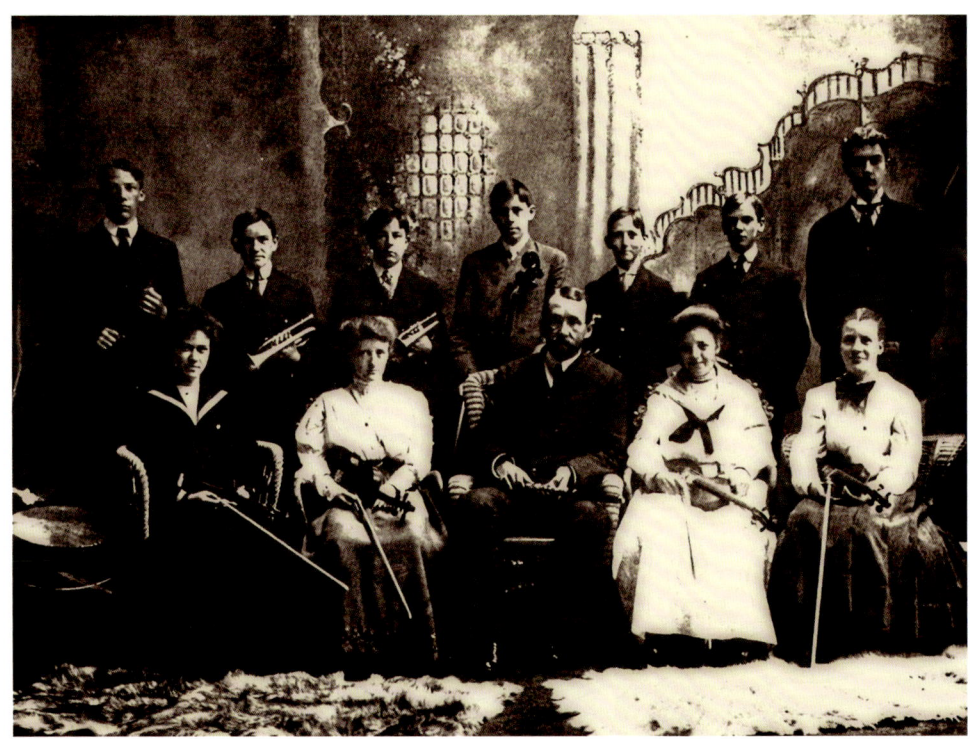

Musical Moments: Medford has always been a great place for musical performers. There were many musical groups in Medford's neighborhoods as well as musical ensembles in all the schools. In the early 1900s the unsmiling high school orchestra posed on the high school stage. In 2013, the alumni band played at celebration of the new veteran's monument in front of the high school.

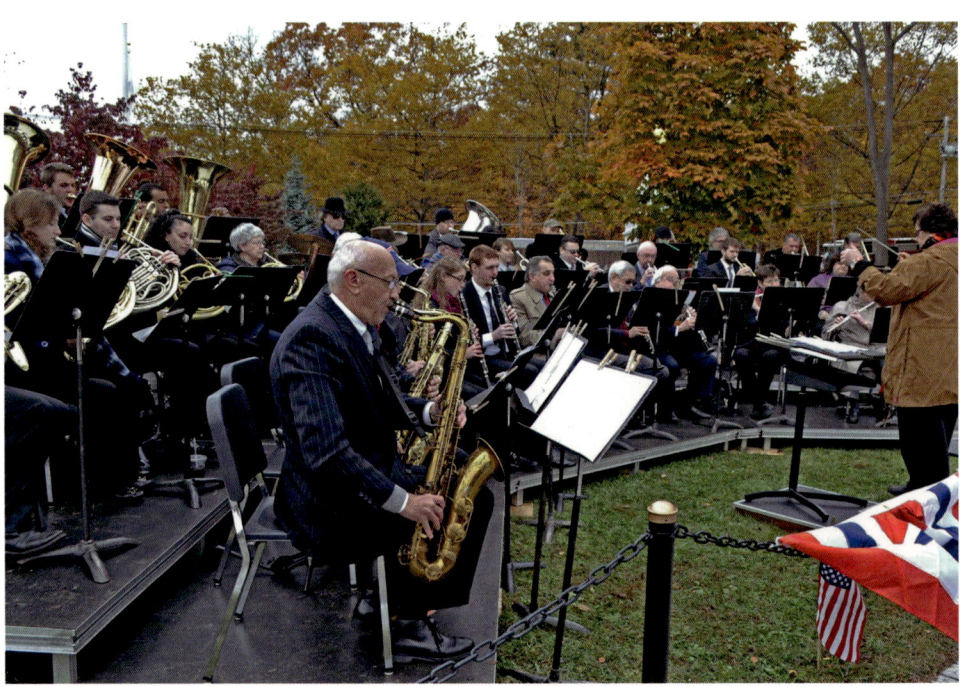

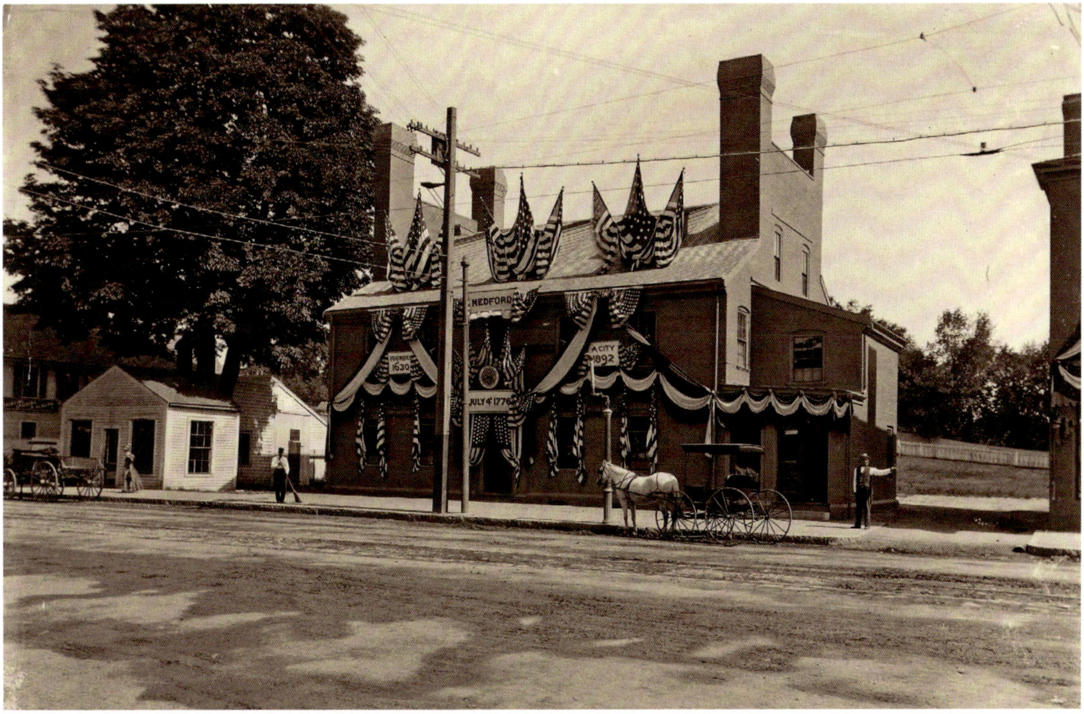

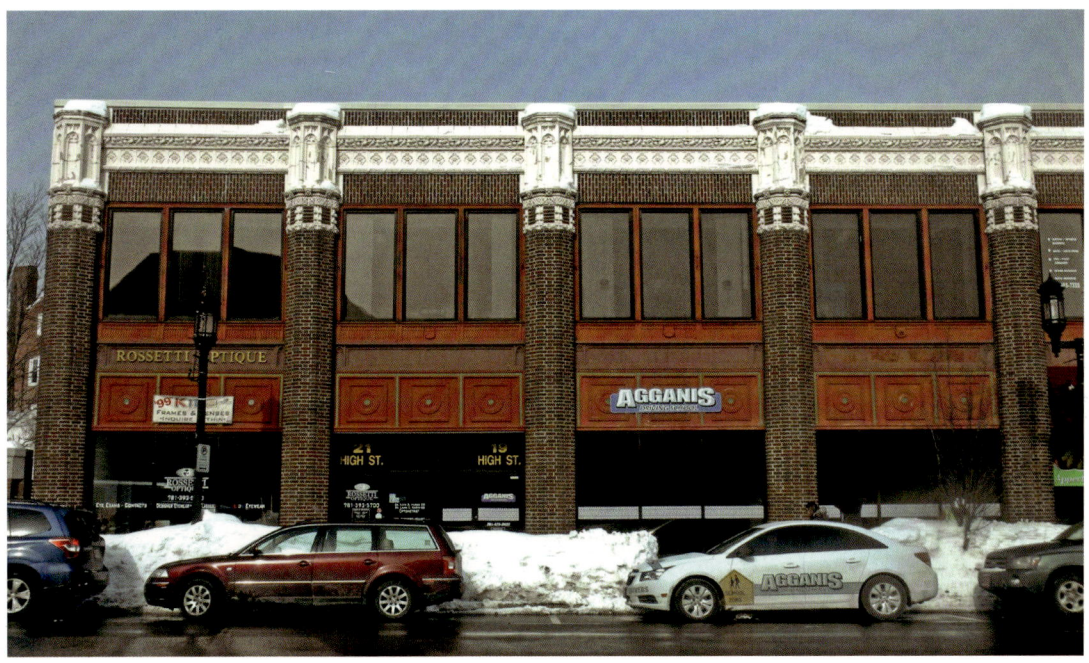

TOWN HALL ANNEX: In the nineteenth century, some town offices were housed in this building on High Street. Originally the Thomas Seccomb House, built in 1756, the building later became Simpson's Tavern where James Pierpont is rumored to have first played "Jingle Bells." The modern building once housed the Medford Café, a very popular spot in the 1930s and 1940s. A plaque commemorating "Jingle Bells" can be found on façade of the current office building.

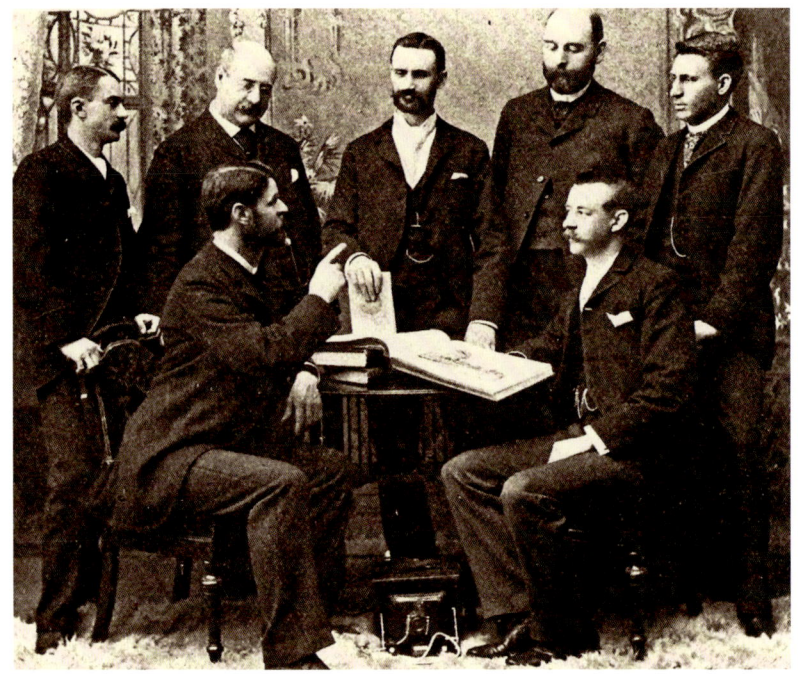

CREATIVE CITIZENS: The Mystic Camera Club was founded in 1889, with headquarters on Main Street. Many of the images that we have of early Medford were created by members of the MCC. In 2006 the arts group MACI (Medford Arts Center, Inc.) was established to encourage and support arts in the community. In 2012 these Tufts students volunteered to paint the interior of the Mystic Art Gallery. In 2015, MACI moved to a larger space at the Meadow Glen Mall.

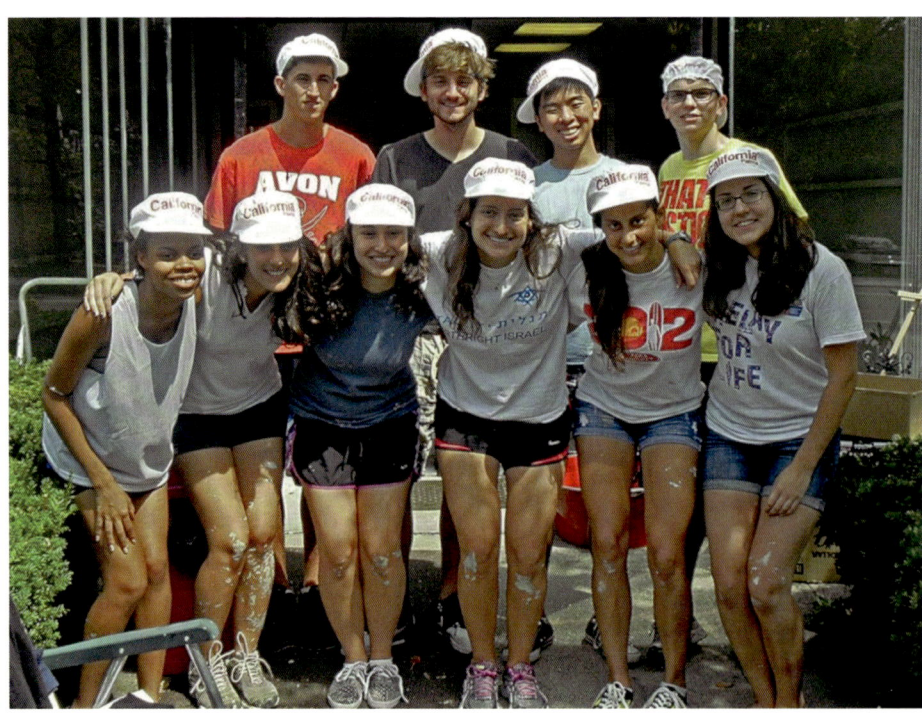

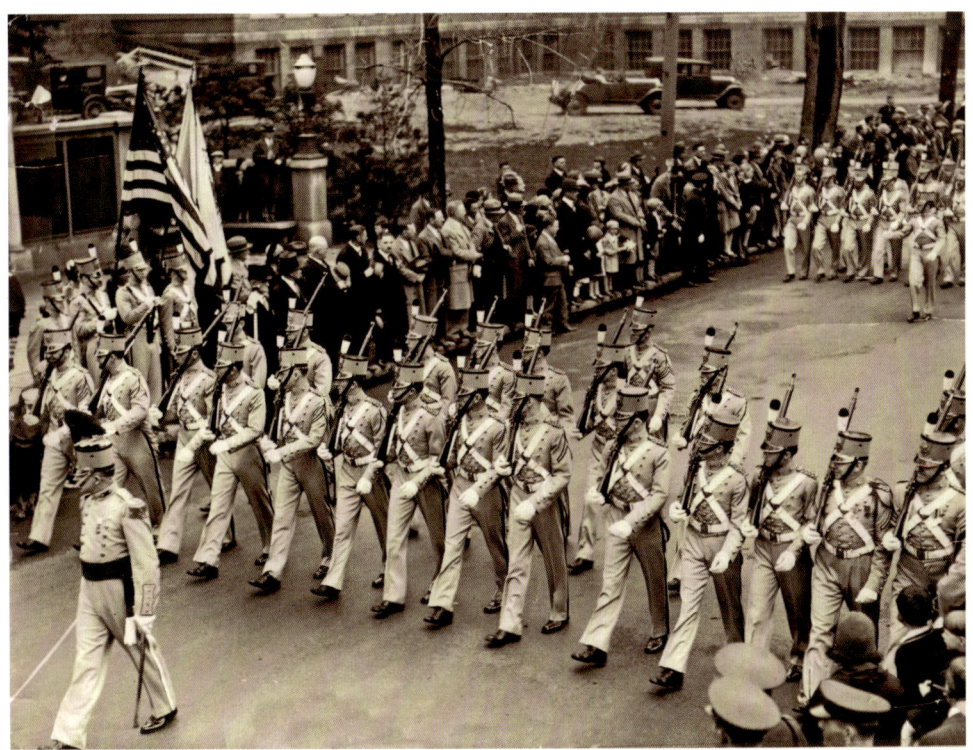

1930 Parade: Medford celebrated its 300th anniversary in 1930 with much pomp and circumstance. There were pageants, reenactments and dedications. The Medford Historical Register of that year called the parade "a four-mile, four-hour parade of cosmopolitan Medford that closed by the street lights and the crescent moon." This snappily dressed marching band took part in that extravagant anniversary. The snappily dressed State Police Pipe and Drum Corps continued the parade tradition at the 2005 Arts Festival at the Royall House.

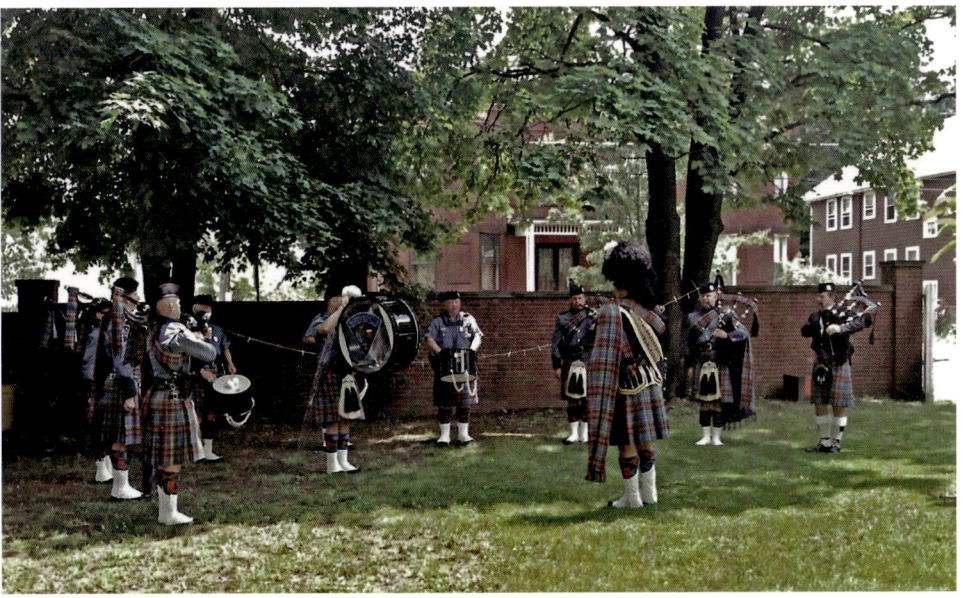

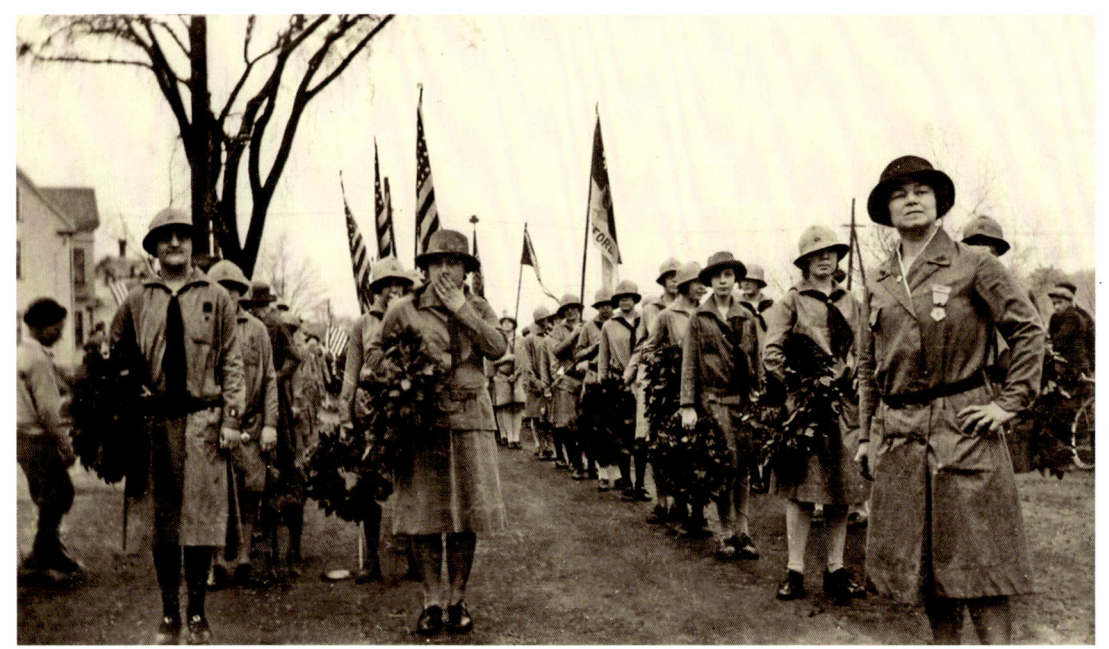

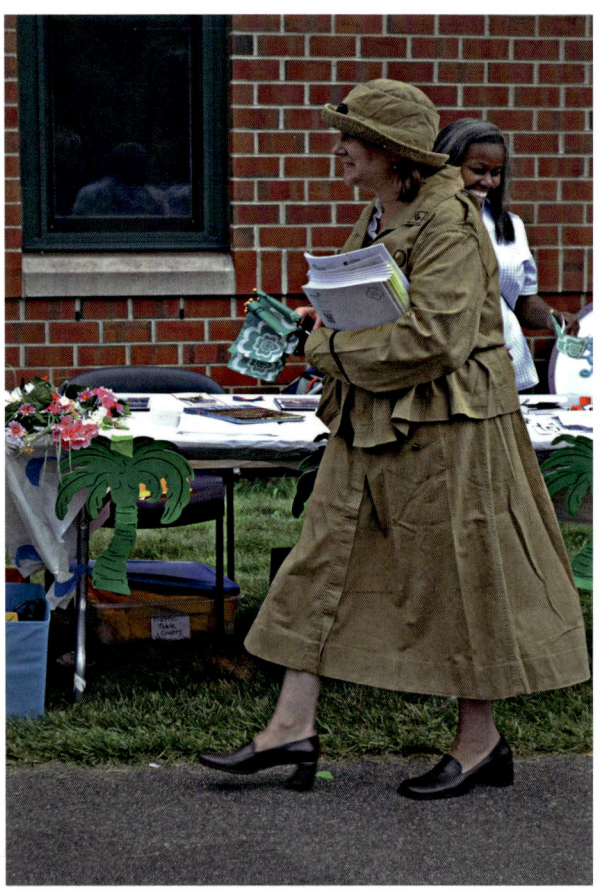

GIRL SCOUTS: Among the many other groups that marched in the 1930 parade were Medford's girl scouts. There have been Girl Scout troops in Medford since the early twentieth century. In 2014 troop leaders modelled historic uniforms at Medford's Community Day.

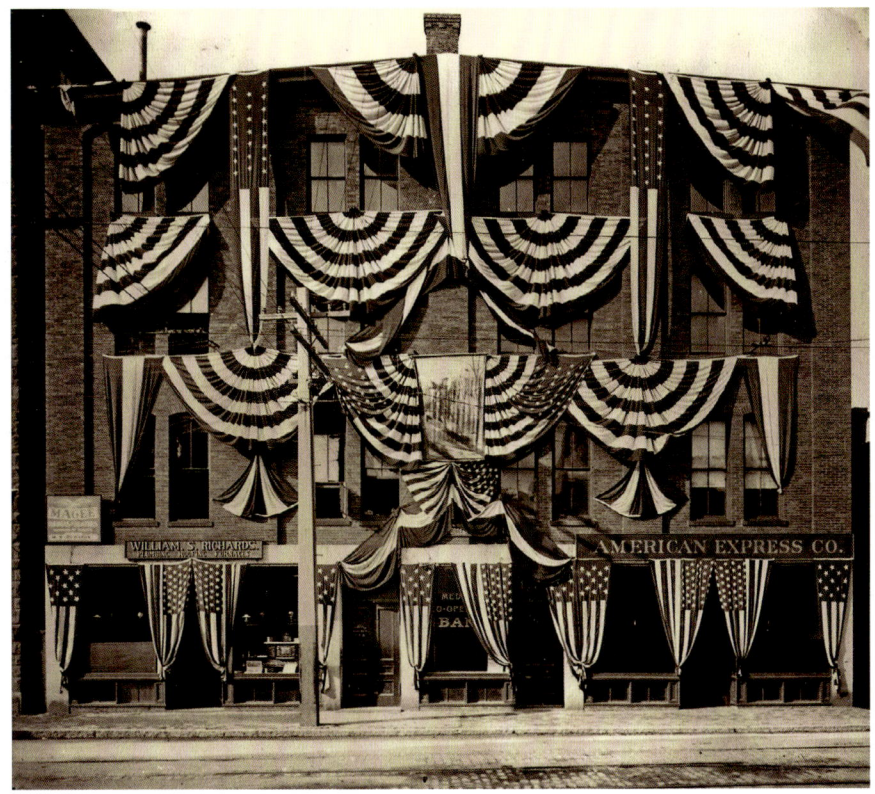

MASONIC APARTMENTS: This familiar red brick building has been the home of many Medford Square businesses since its construction in the mid-nineteenth century. It was originally the property of James M. Usher who also owned the Usher Block in West Medford. In addition to commercial tenants, like Ward's Gifts, the building was used by the Masons after 1925 when an addition was added to the original structure.

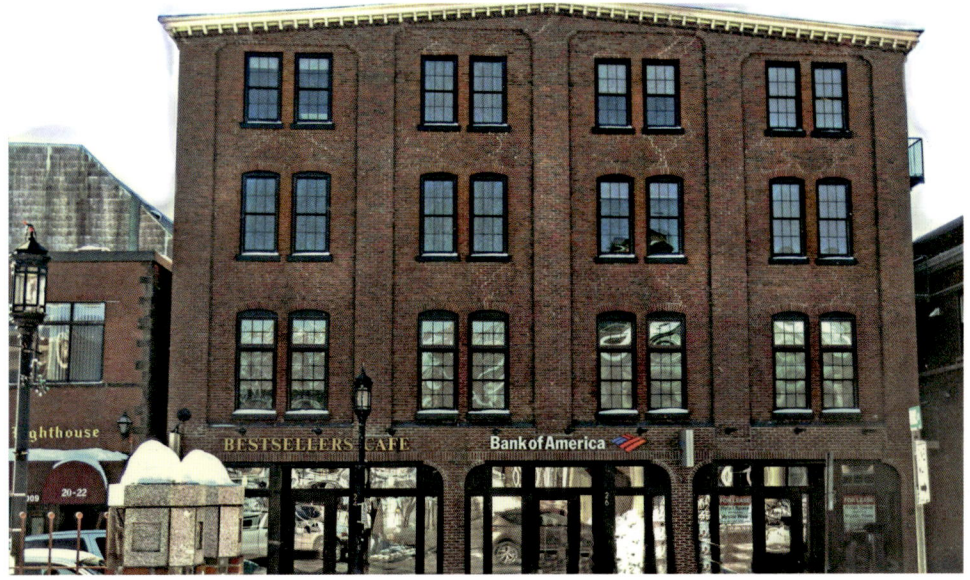

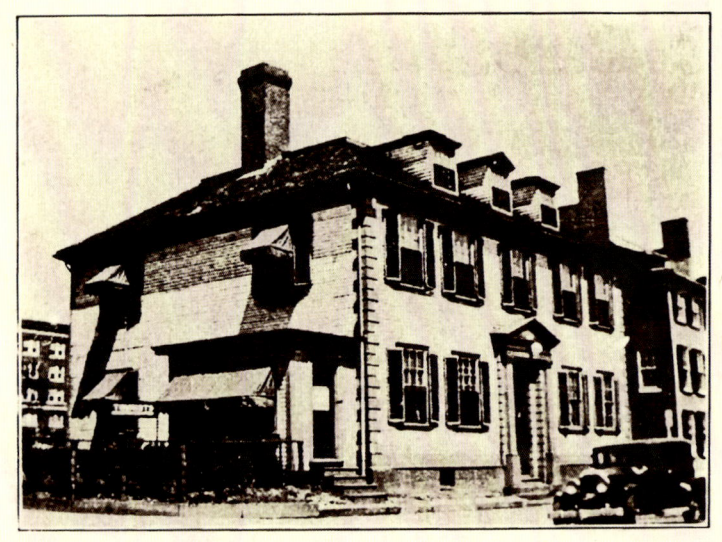

57 High Street: In the 1920s and 1930s Medford, with its historical houses and natural spaces, was a tourist destination of sorts. Colby's at 57 High Street offered rooms for visitors and also was home to some long term boarders. The building was originally the Benjamin Hall House, one of several Hall family houses on High Street. The only remaining Hall house is Gaffey's Funeral Home.

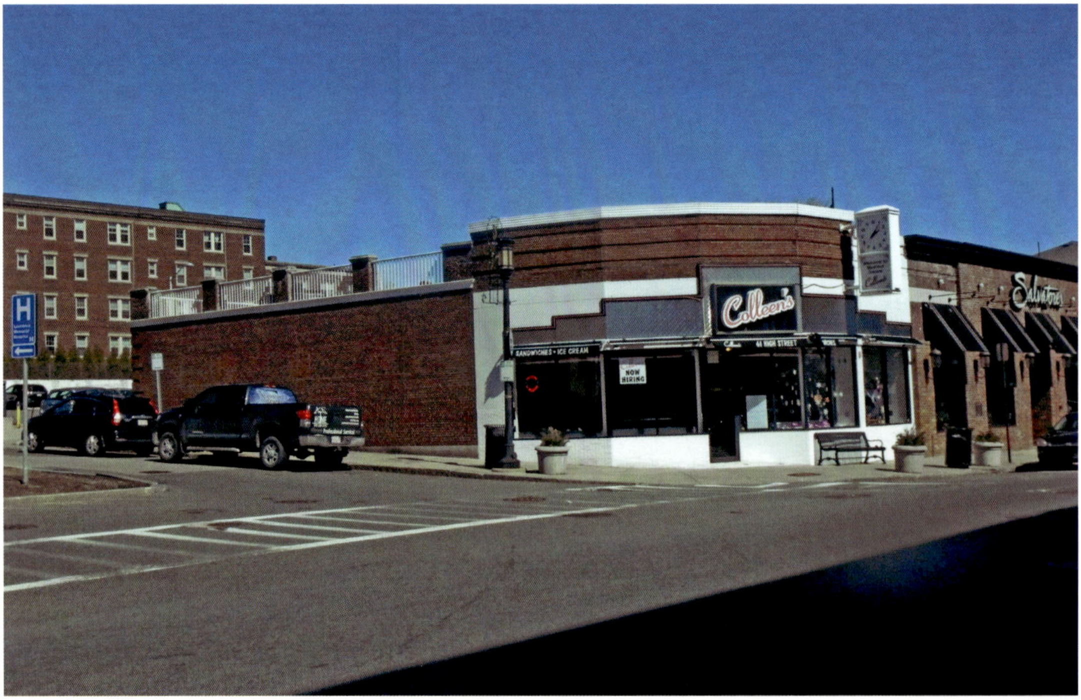

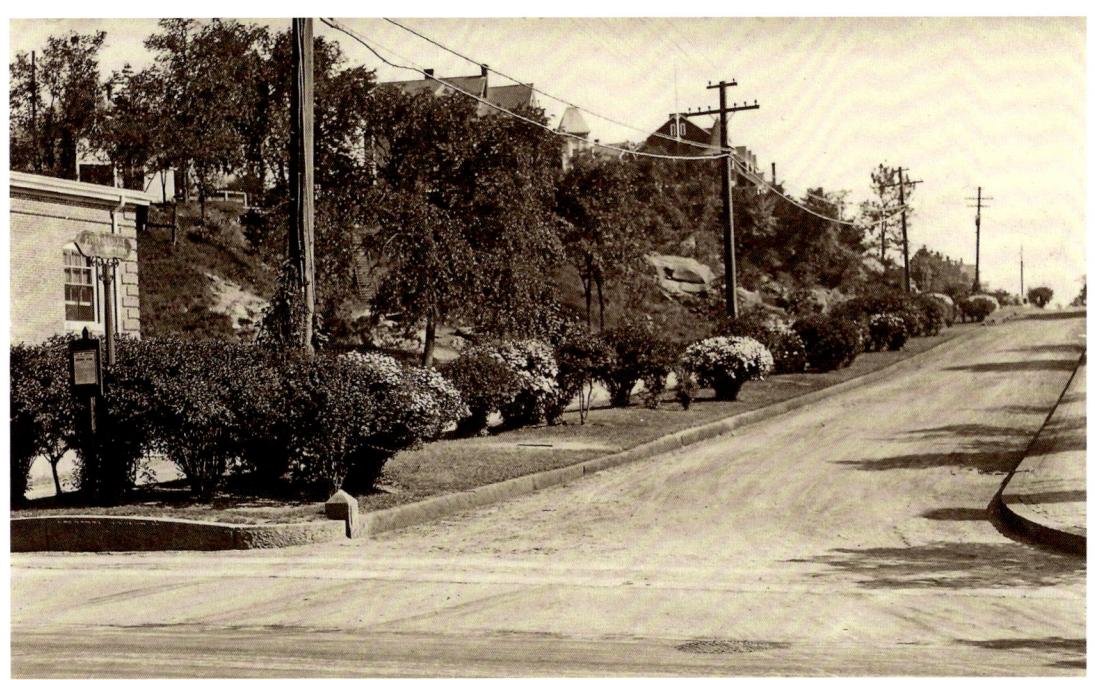

GOVERNORS AVE: Named after eighteenth century Governor John Brooks, Governors Avenue reaches from Medford Square up to Pasture Hill in the Middlesex Fells. The street was laid out as a double street with a grass plot in the middle. The grass covers a water main that led from Spot Pond which was the city's water supply in the late nineteenth century. The older photograph shows the street before 1916 when the Medford Historical Society was constructed at 10 Governors Avenue.

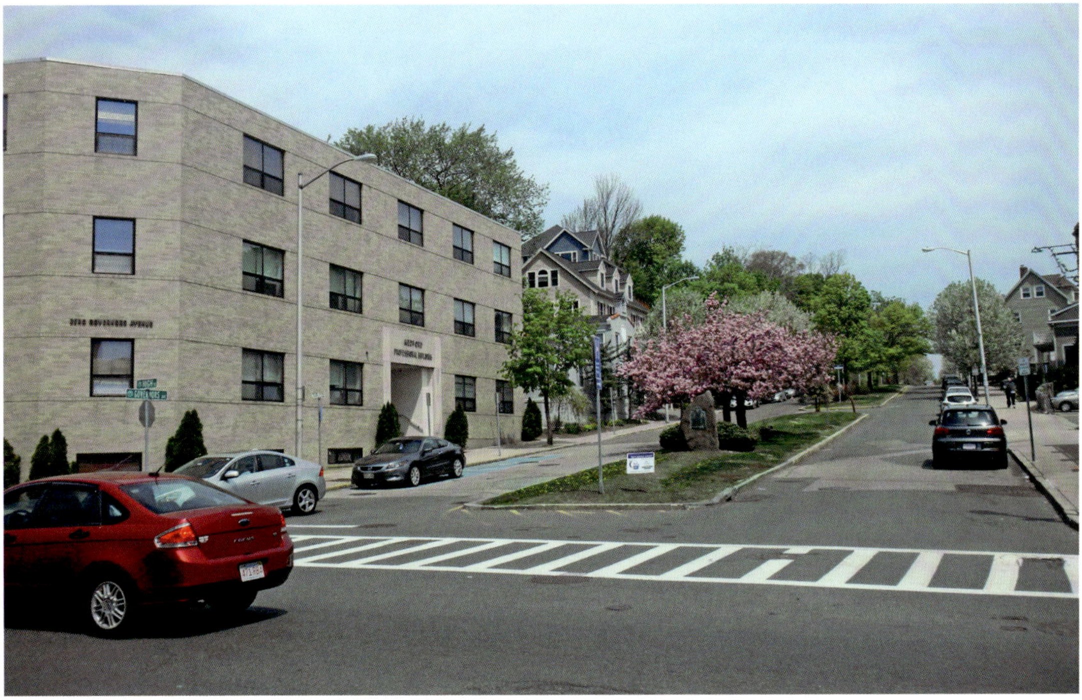

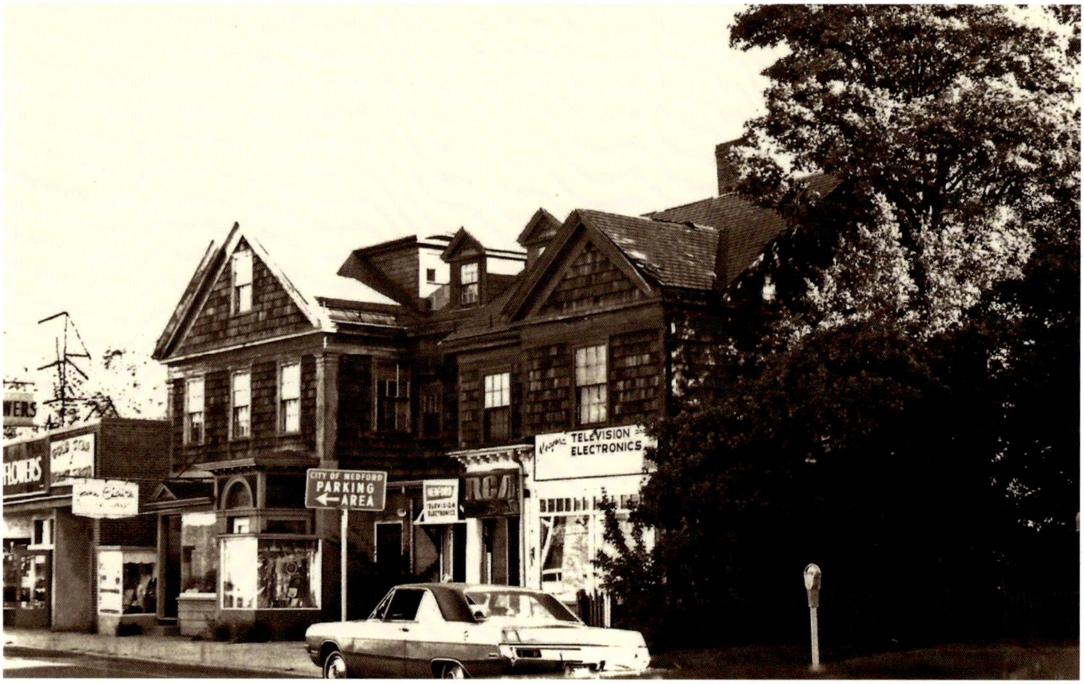

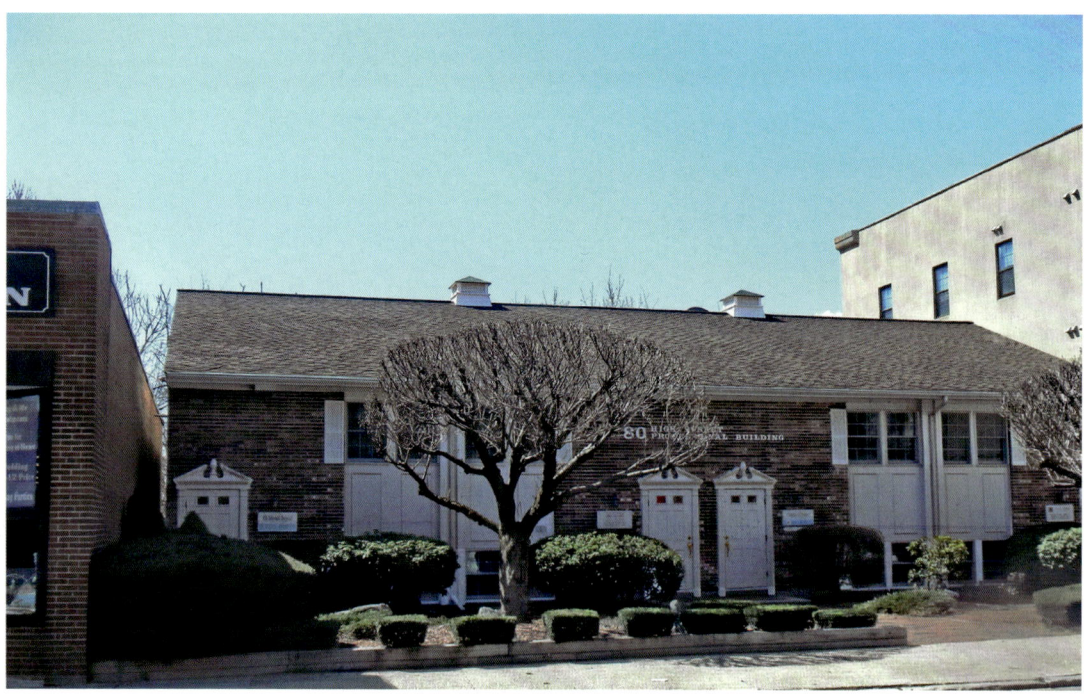

80 High Street: This office building is also known as the Swan-Bemis House. The house was built in 1839 in the Greek revival style, by local doctor Daniel Swan who lived across the street. His colleague Dr. Charles Vose Bemis lived there from 1839-1906. It was renovated in the early twentieth century and eventually became a commercial property as can be seen in the 1974 image. In 2015 it houses a number of medical and dental offices.

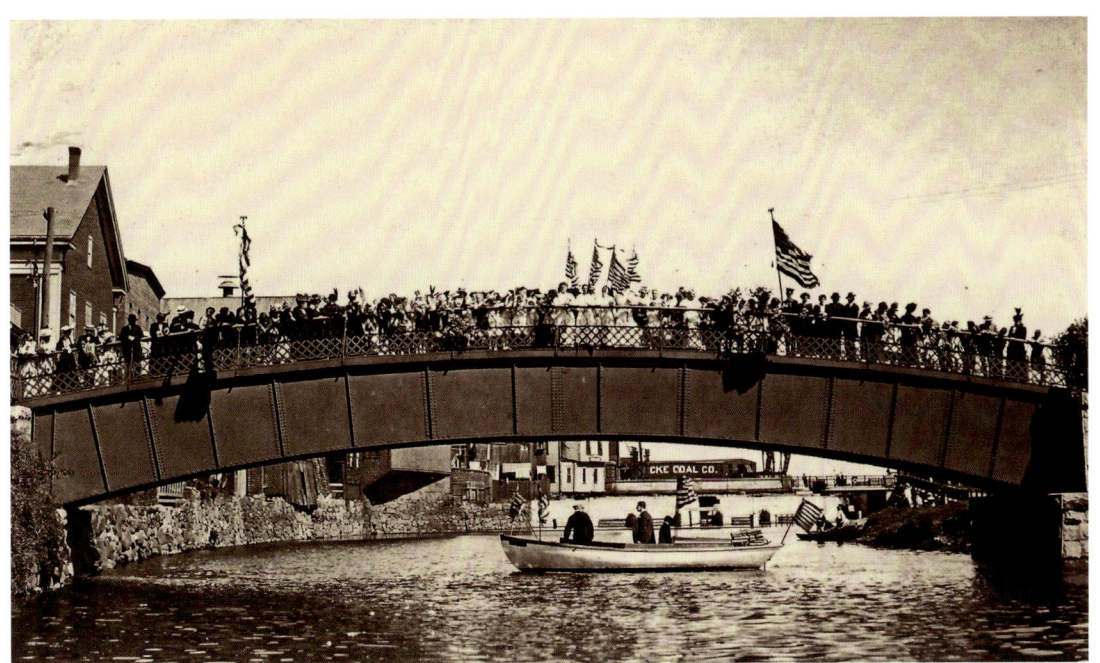

MEDFORD PIPE BRIDGE: During the city's 275th anniversary celebration in 1905, everyone who could fit lined the pedestrian bridge over the Mystic to have their picture taken. The bridge was fairly new in those days, having been built in 1897 by the Metropolitan Water Board. In addition to foot traffic the bridge was designed to carry water pipes between the Chestnut Hill Reservoir and Spot Pond that were cross connected with the Mystic Water Works pumping station in Somerville.

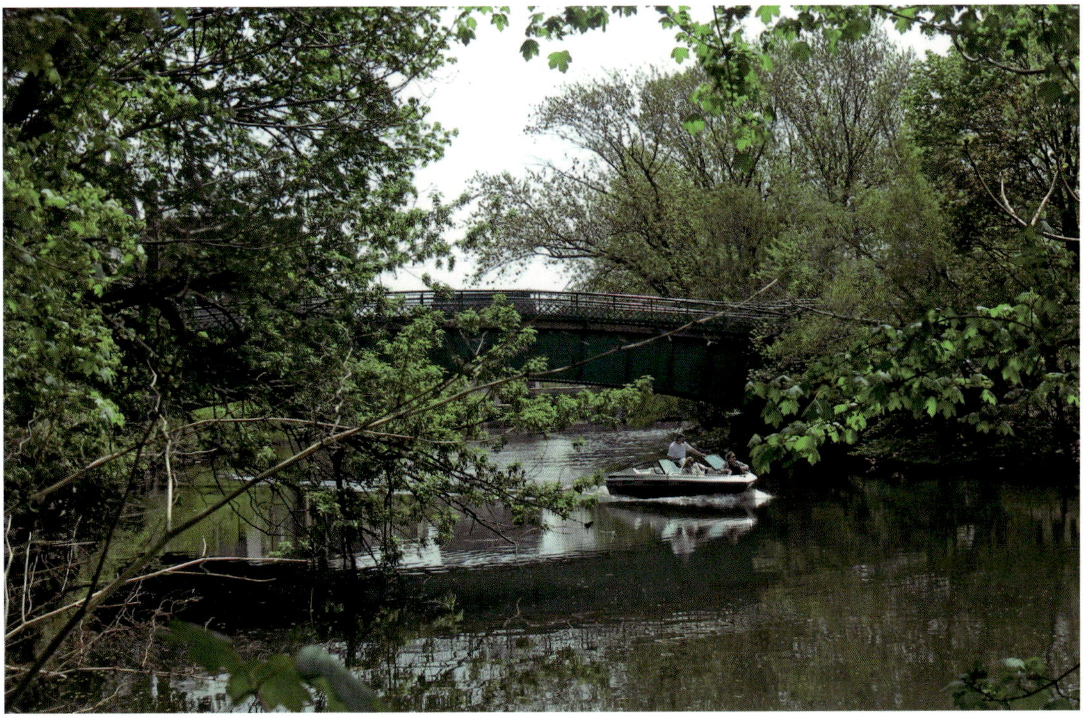

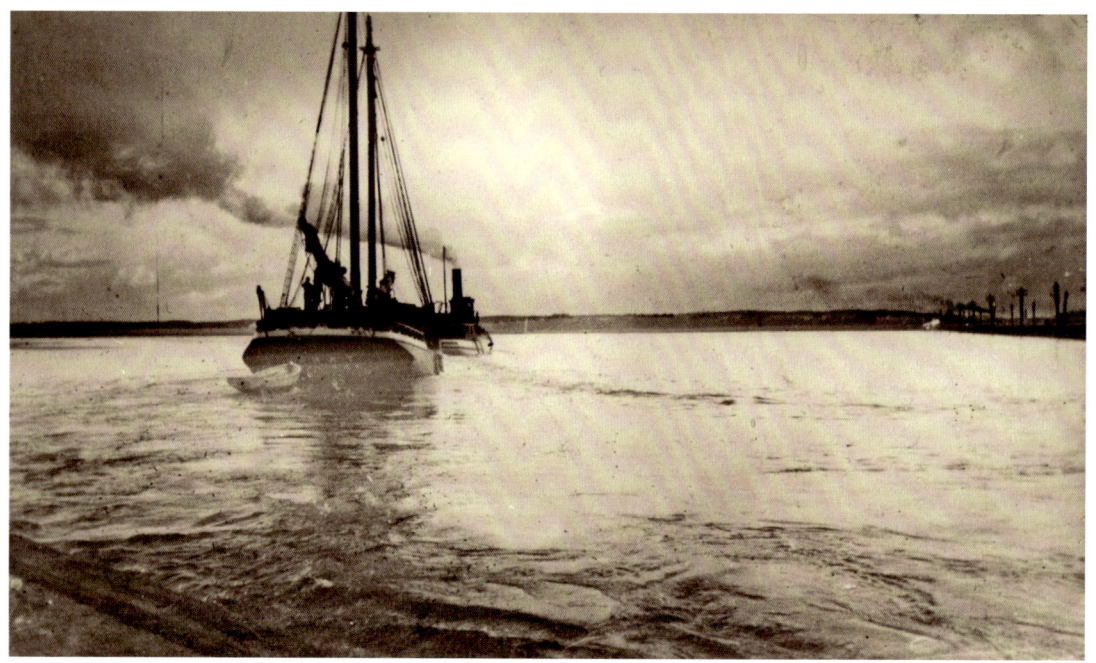

MYSTIC RIVER RECREATION: Since Medford's early days, the Mystic River has been a site for recreation as well as commerce. Pleasure boats like those in this late nineteenth century photo were plentiful on the river and boatyards flourished well into the twentieth century. In recent years those who enjoy the river also take care of it through organizations like the Mystic Watershed Association. The kayakers in this modern photos gathered to remove invasive water chestnuts from Medford's natural treasure.

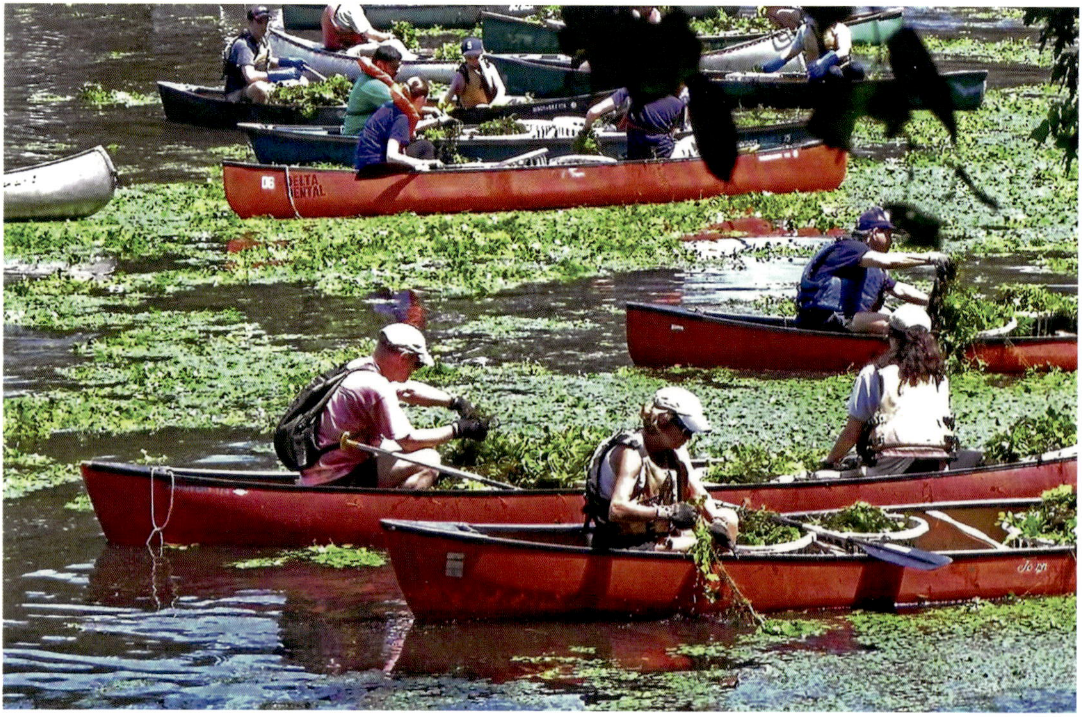

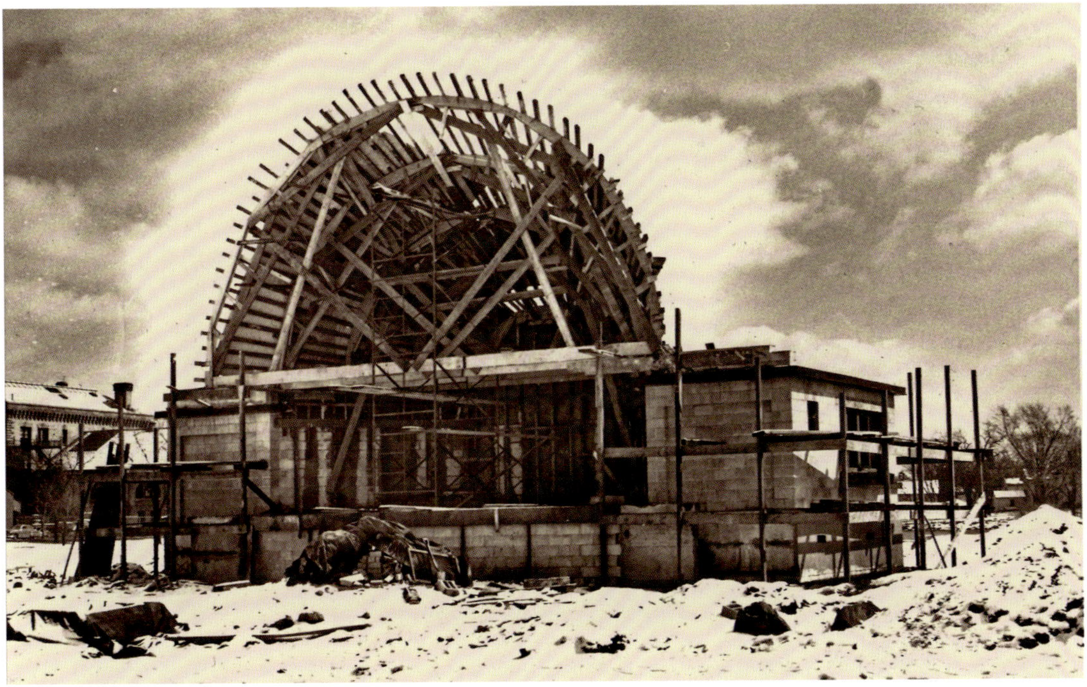

CONDON SHELL: In 1956 the MDC hired the Tassinari Construction Corporation to build a concert shell by the Mystic River, close to where the Medford Band held outdoor concerts for many years. In 1959 the shell was named after Monsignor John B. Condon. Although smaller than Boston's Hatch Shell, Medford's shell boasts similar acoustics and has hosted many a musical event over the years, including the Porch Party Mamas who rocked it out at the Medford Arts festival in 2007.

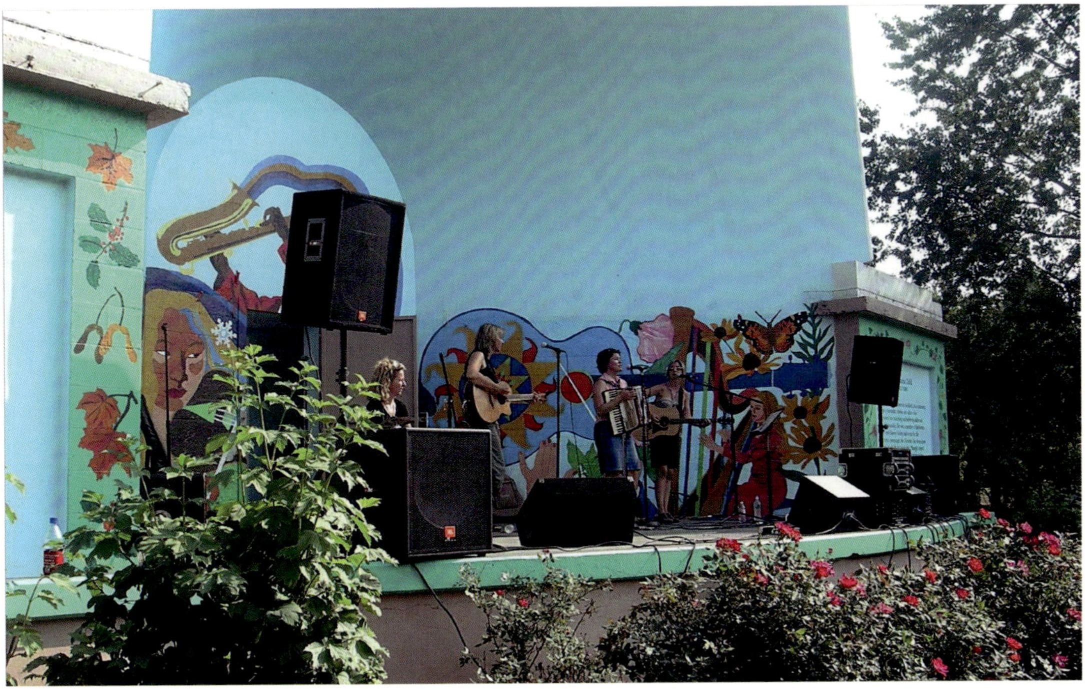

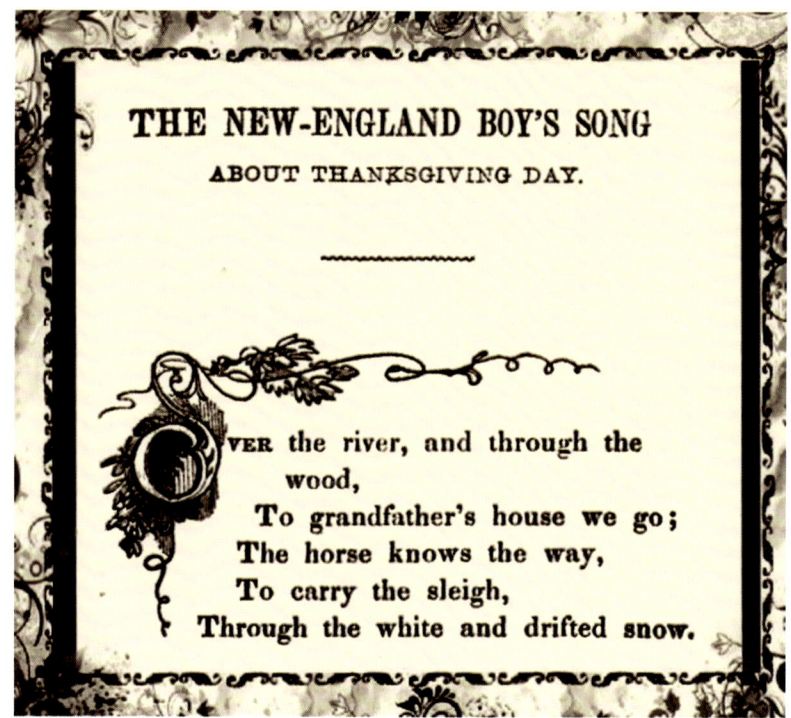

GRANDFATHER'S HOUSE: The house at 114 South Street is better known as Grandfather's house from the song "Over the River and Through the Woods" by Lydia Maria Child. The first version of "Over the River" was a poem called *The New-England Boy's Song about Thanksgiving Day* (1844). The poem was later set to music by an unknown composer. The house did indeed belong to Child's grandfather and her family would cross the river in a sleigh at the holidays.

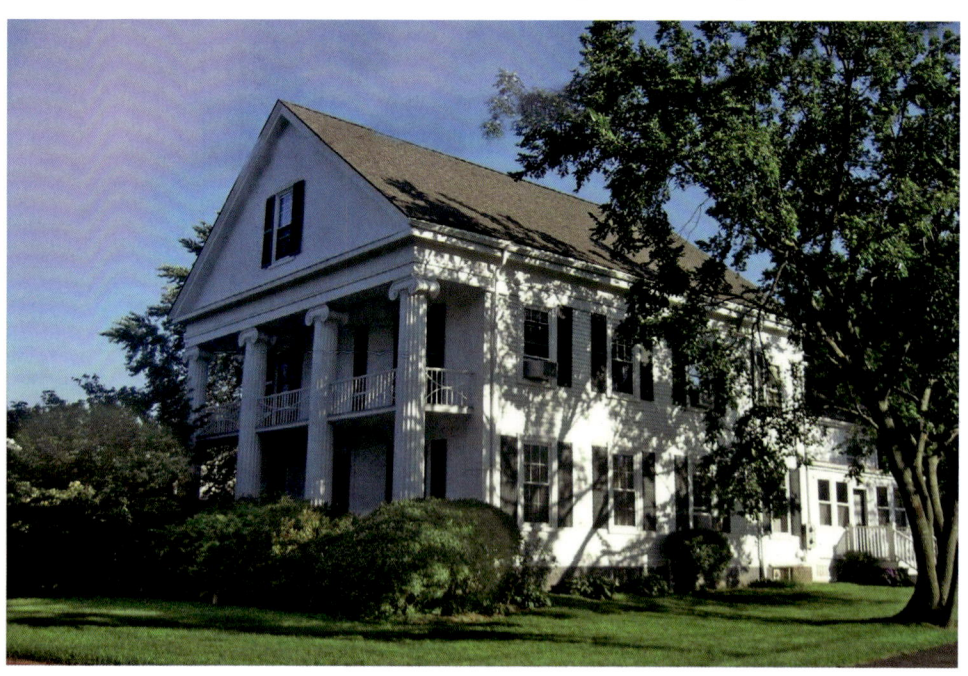

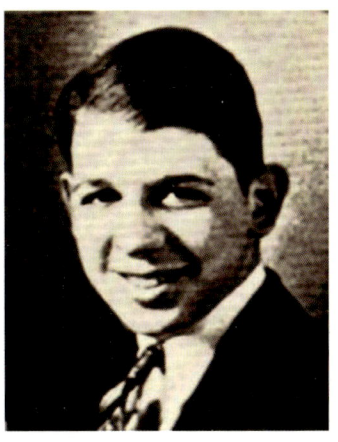
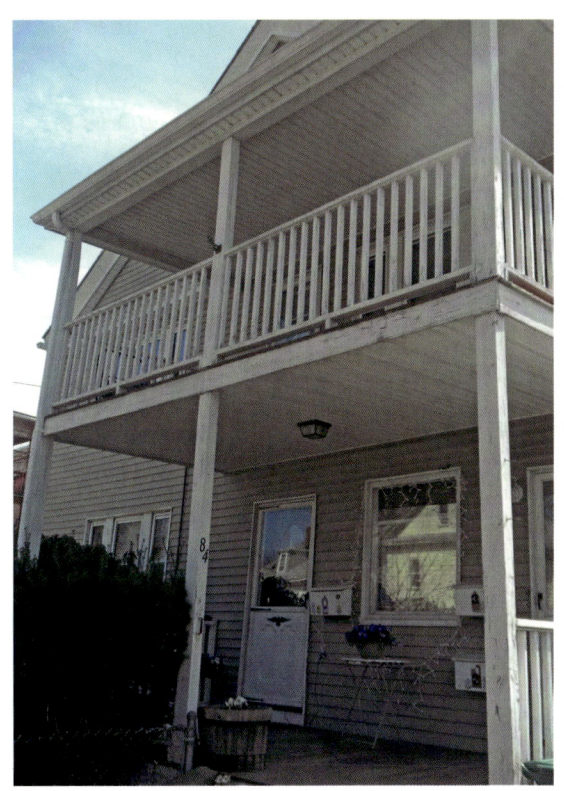

84 South Street: Poet John Ciardi grew up on South Street. He attended Medford High School, and Tufts University. After serving in World War II he lived in the family home while teaching at Harvard. In 1961 he accepted a job at Rutgers and bid Medford goodbye. He died in 1986. Many of Ciardi's poems mention his life in Medford. In 2004 the Friends of the Medford Public Library sponsored a literary landmark plaque in honor of Medford's poet.

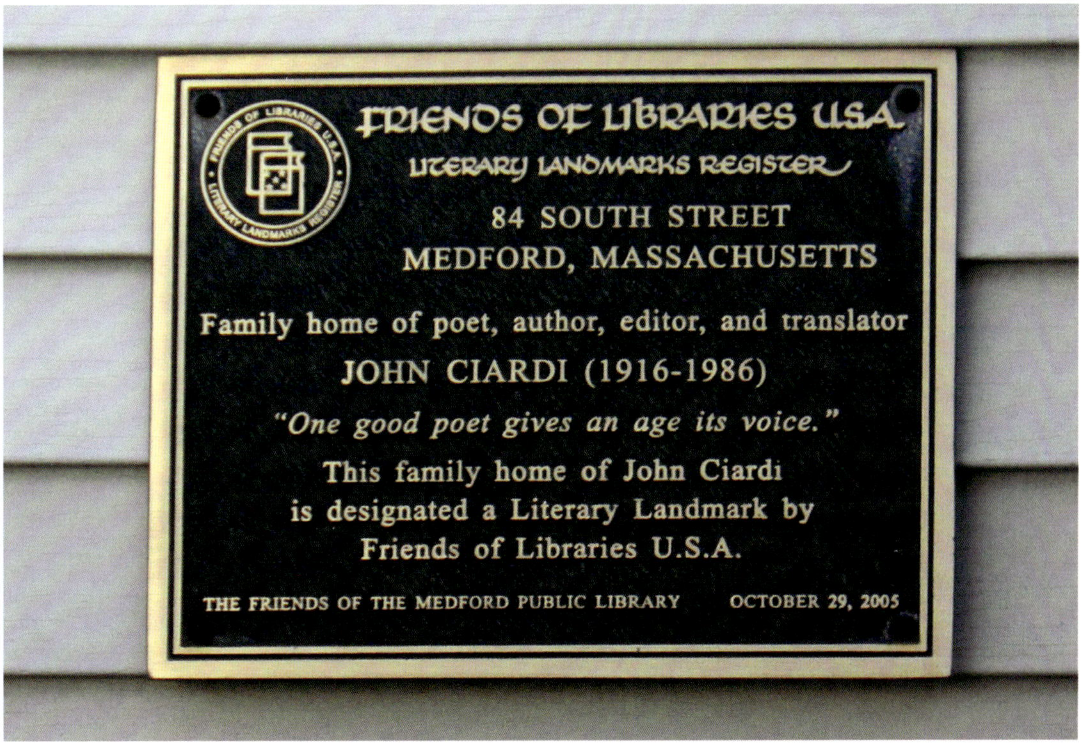

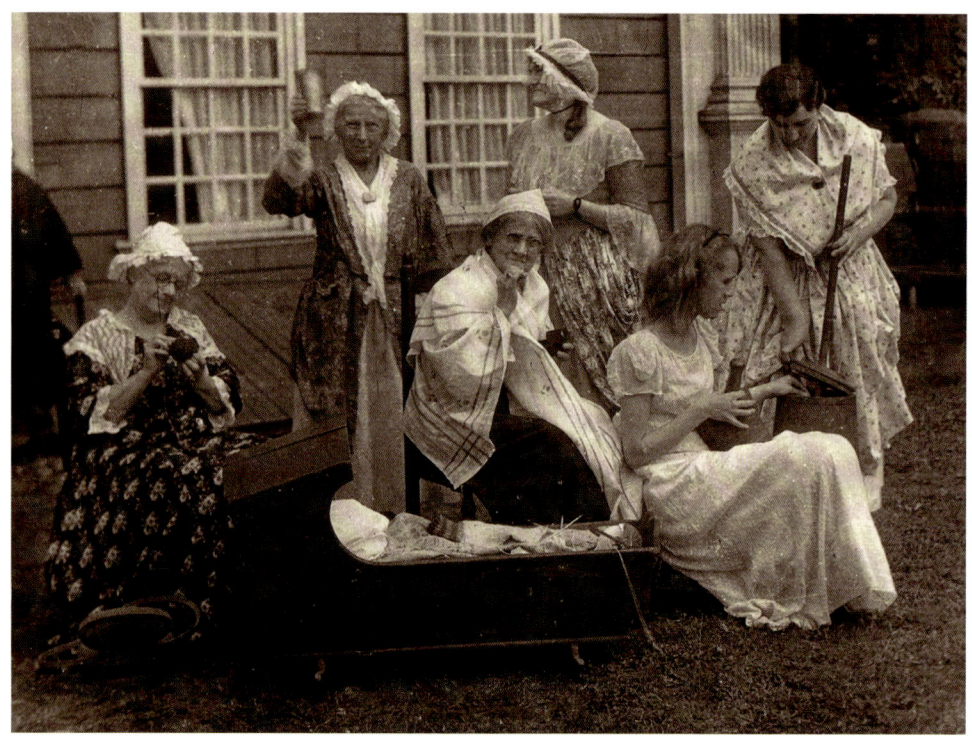

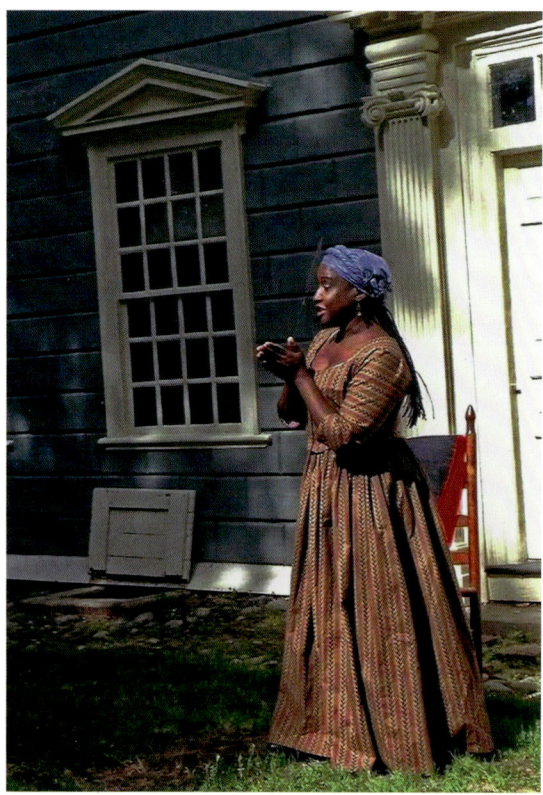

ROYALL HOUSE: In the eighteenth century, the Royall House and Slave Quarters belonged to the largest slaveholding family in Massachusetts. For many years, the Museum interpreted the history of the colonial era. In 1930 these "colonial" ladies participated in a pageant. In recent years, the Museum has focused on the legacy of Northern slavery. In 2015, storyteller Tammy Denease presented a performance as Belinda, a Royall slave who sued for a pension from the state of Massachusetts.

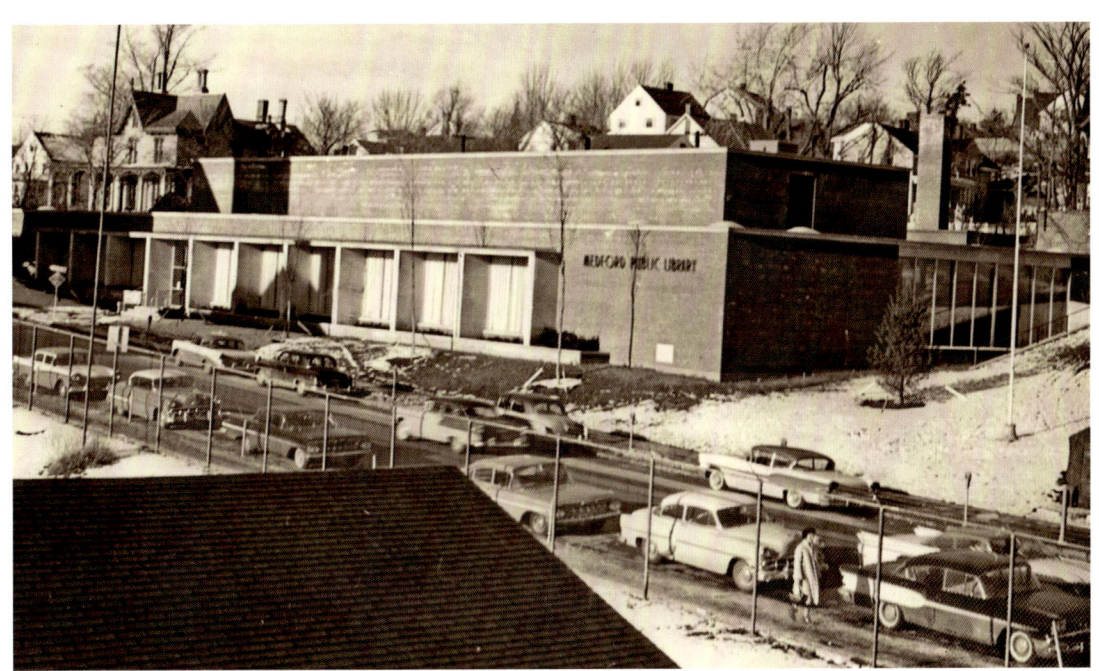

MEDFORD PUBLIC LIBRARY: From 1875 to 1959, the Medford Public Library was housed in the former mansion of shipbuilder Thatcher Magoun. In the late nineteenth century a separate building was added for children's services. By the 1950s the buildings were razed, and a new library opened in 1960. Fifty-plus years and hundreds of thousands of circulations later, the structure may be dated but it has never run out of shelf space!

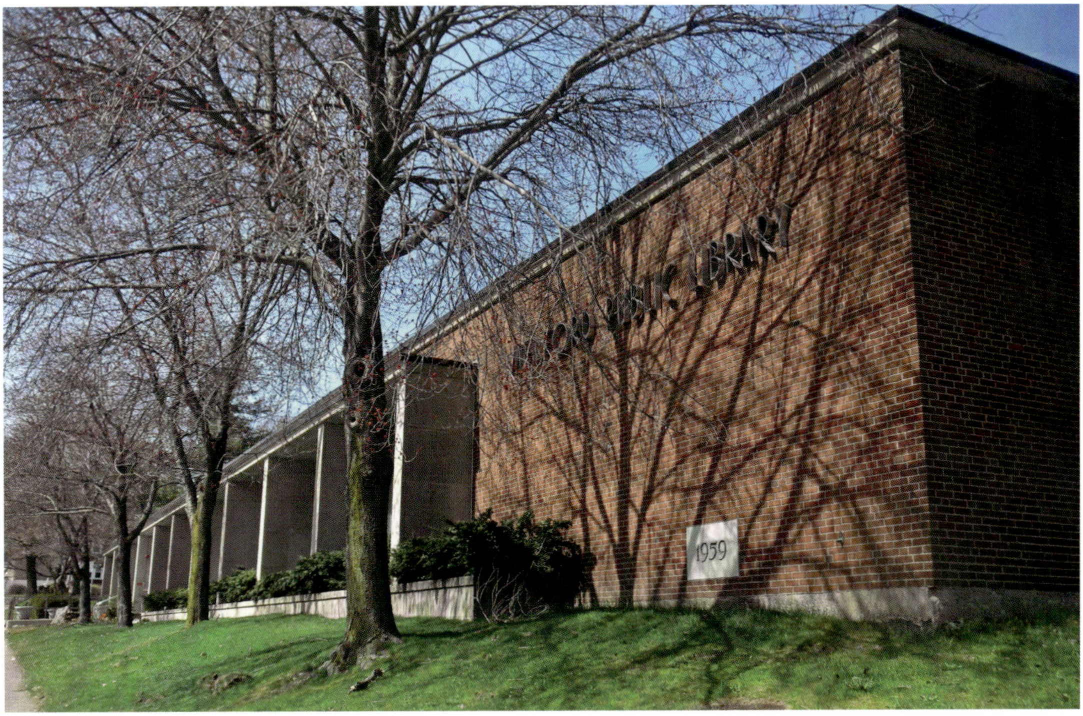

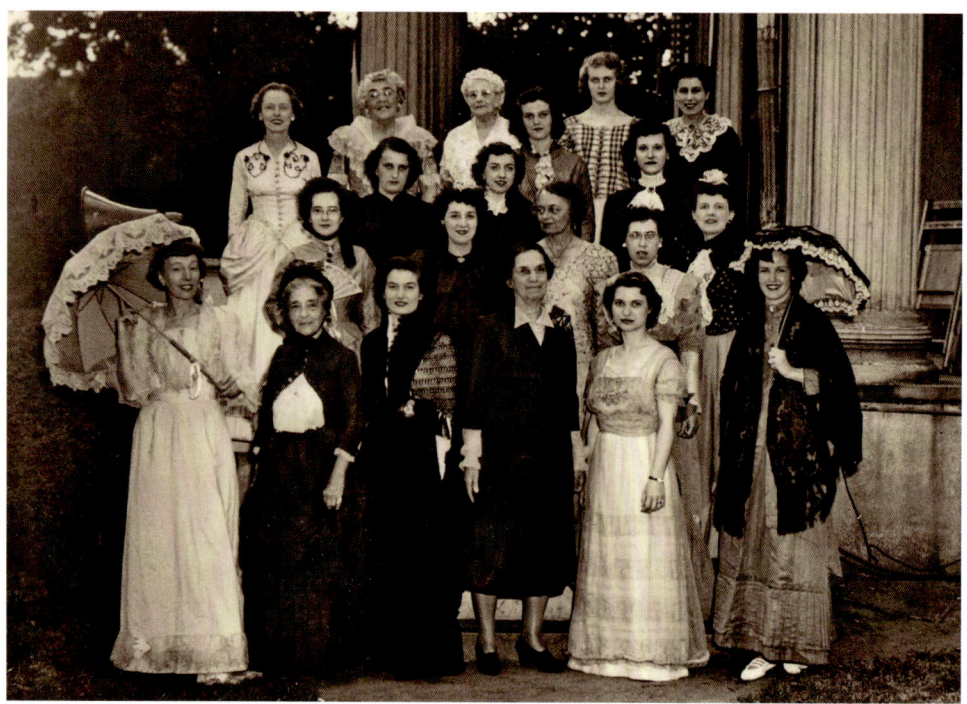

LIBRARIANS: In 1955 the city celebrated the 100th anniversary of the Medford Public Library. During the celebration, the library staff posed up in their best Victorian costumes on the steps of the building. In 2004, librarians and friends celebrated the 150th anniversary with a pirate-themed Seven Seas Ball. The swashbuckling library crew posed on the steps at Medford City Hal during the ball.

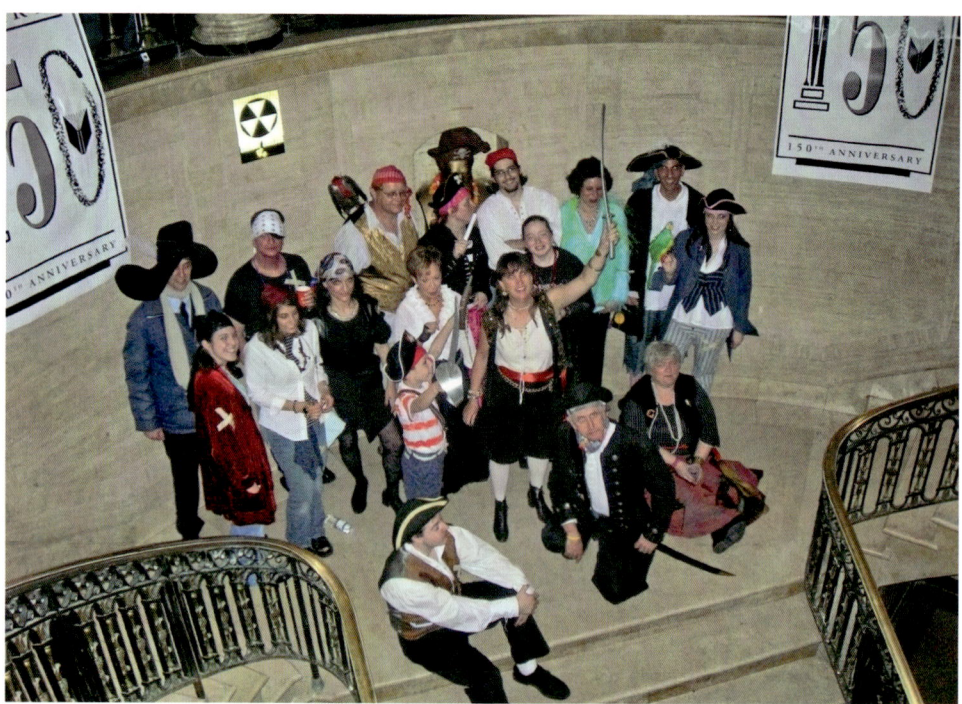

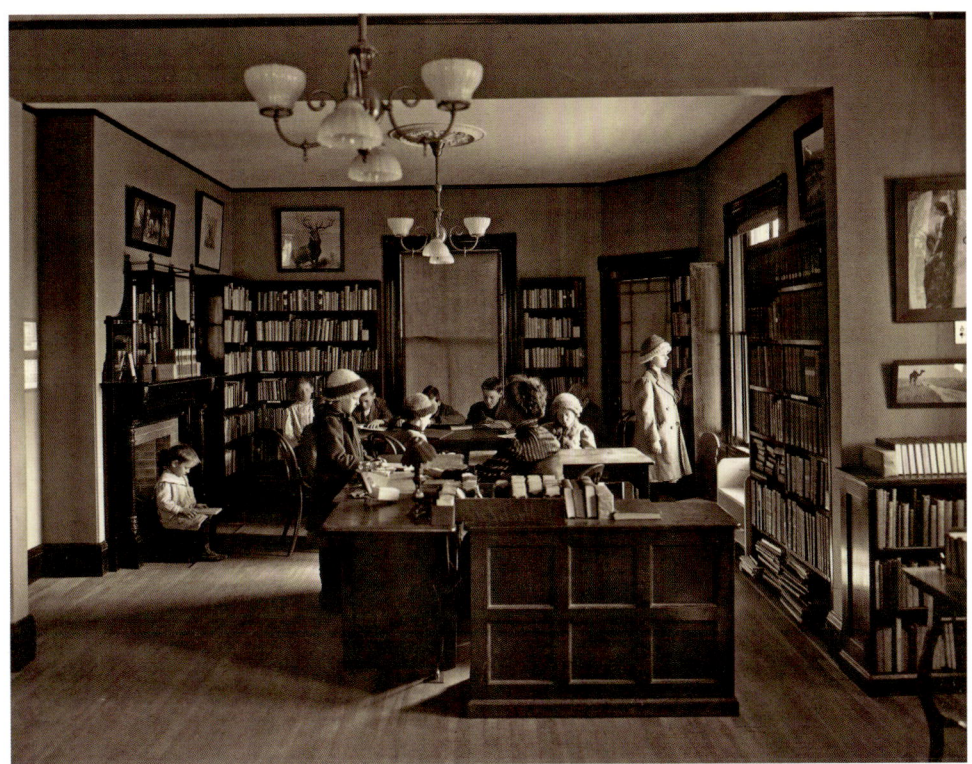

CHILDREN'S ROOMS: In the late nineteenth century, a separate children's building was added to the main library. The Victorian children's room was rather a cheerless place, but separate children's facilities were new to American libraries at that time. Today's children's departments are bright and cheerful places designed to engage young readers. The sculptural bookcase pieces were donated in memory of Charlotte Bloomberg, the mother of former New York mayor Michael Bloomberg.

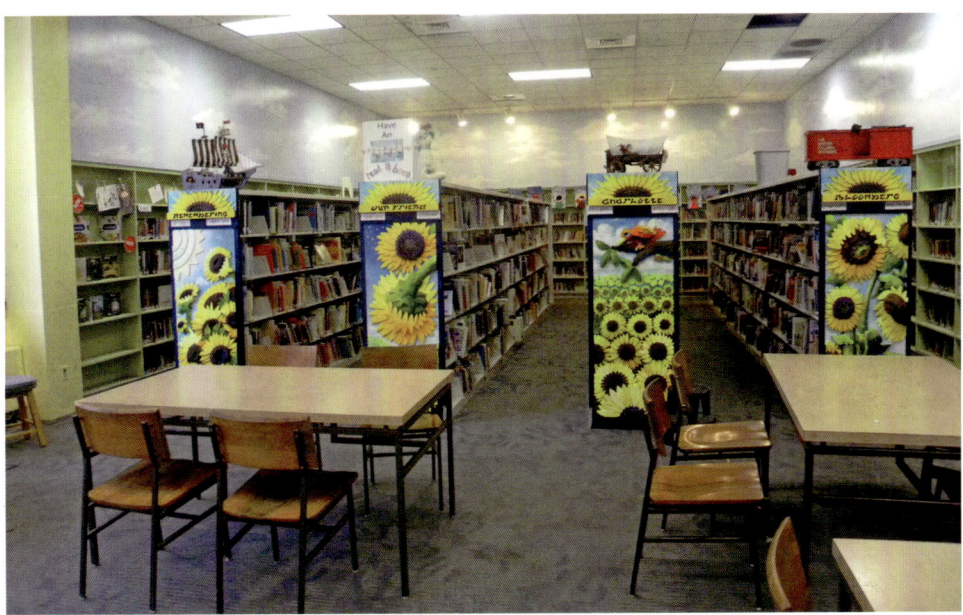

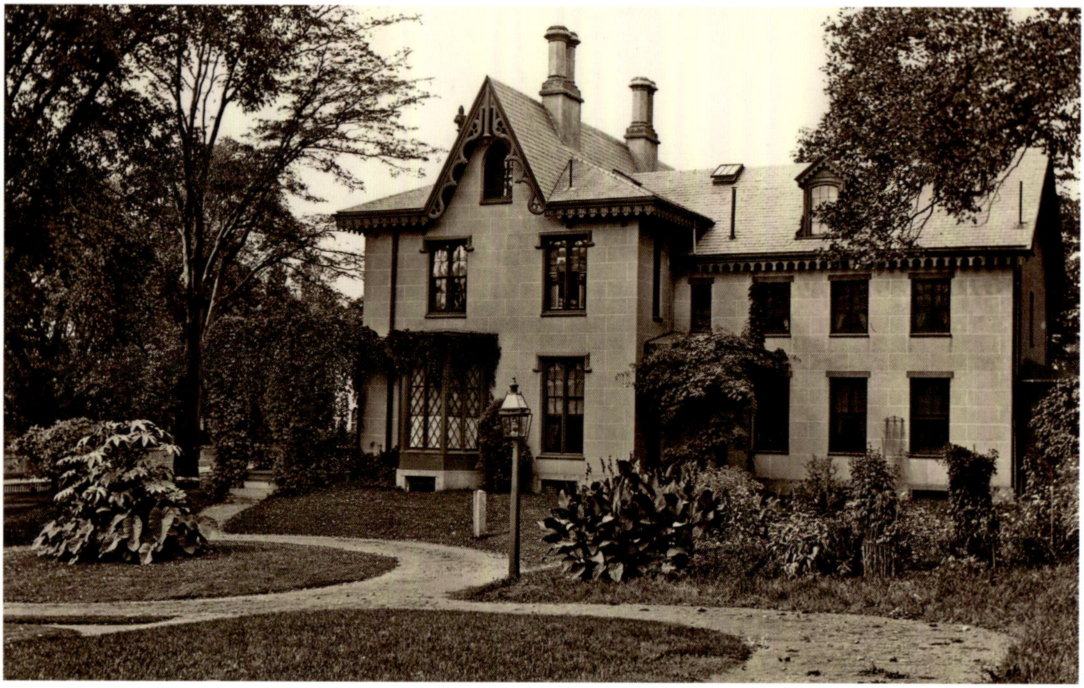

129 High Street: Gothic Revival house was commissioned in 1842 by schoolmaster John Angier and his wife Abby Adams, a granddaughter of John Adams. The house is more commonly associated with the family of Eleazar Boynton. The house was designed by New York architect Alexander Jackson Downing who also designed the Custom House of New York City. The house is a rare Massachusetts example of Gothic Revival styling more commonly found along the Hudson River.

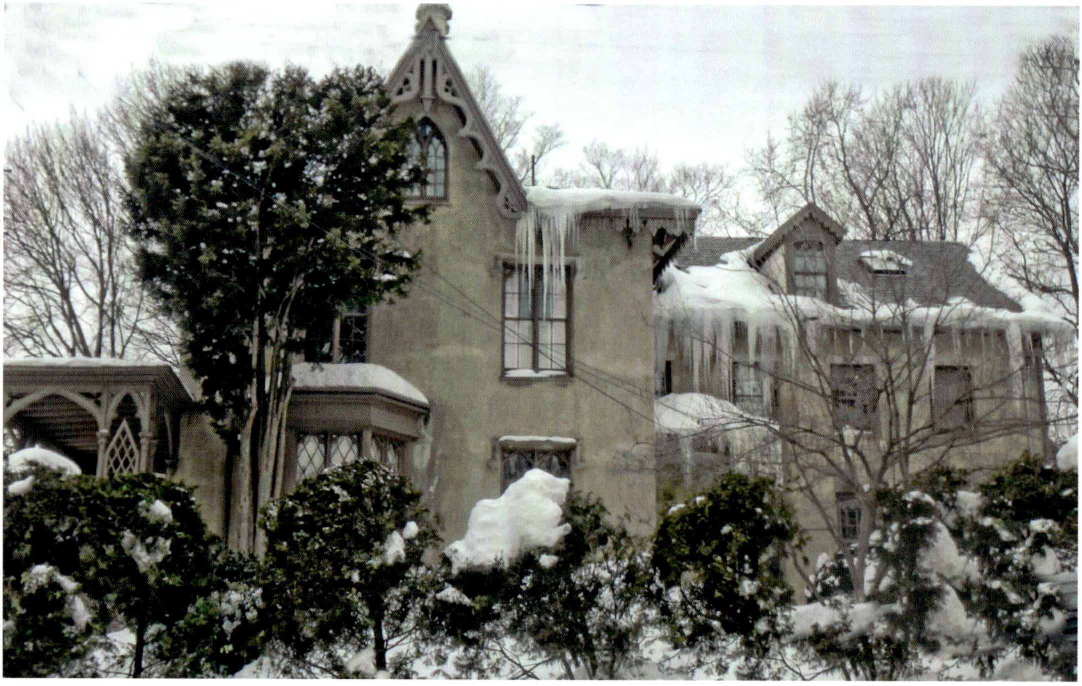

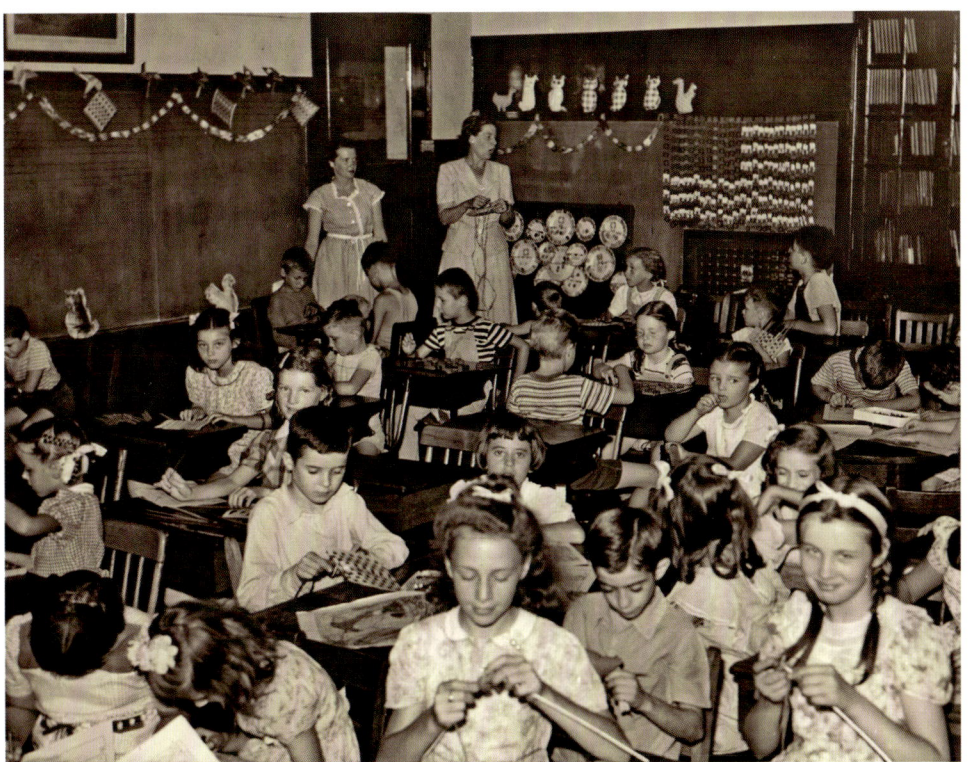

WAIT SCHOOL: Built in 1939, the William Cushing Wait Elementary School on Powder House Road had 181 students enrolled in its first year. The school also offered summer classes. Students are pictured at the school in the 1940s learning to knit. William Cushing Wait was an associate justice of the Massachusetts Supreme Judicial Court, and an active member of the Medford Historical Society. He died in 1935.

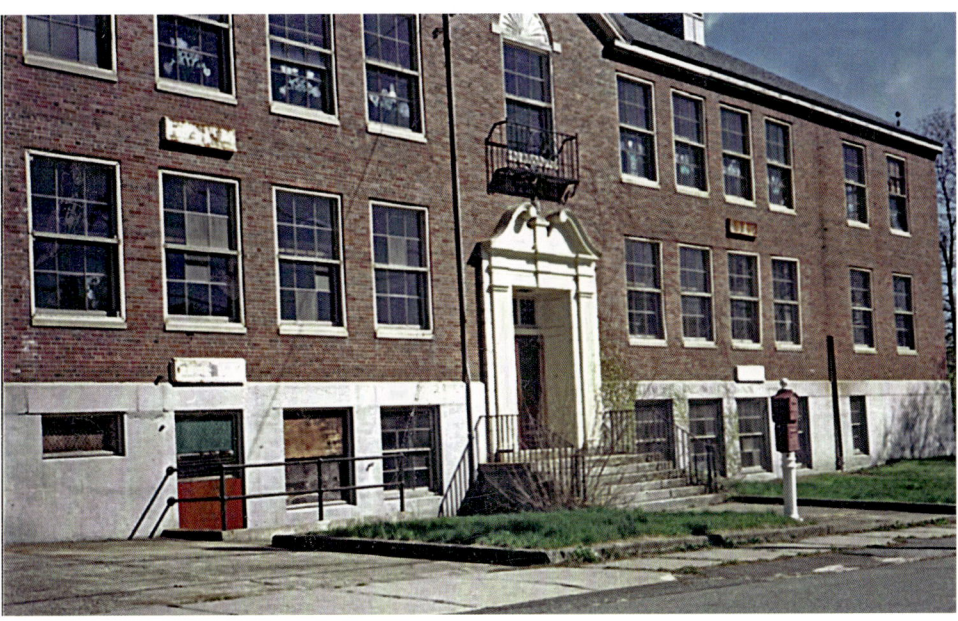

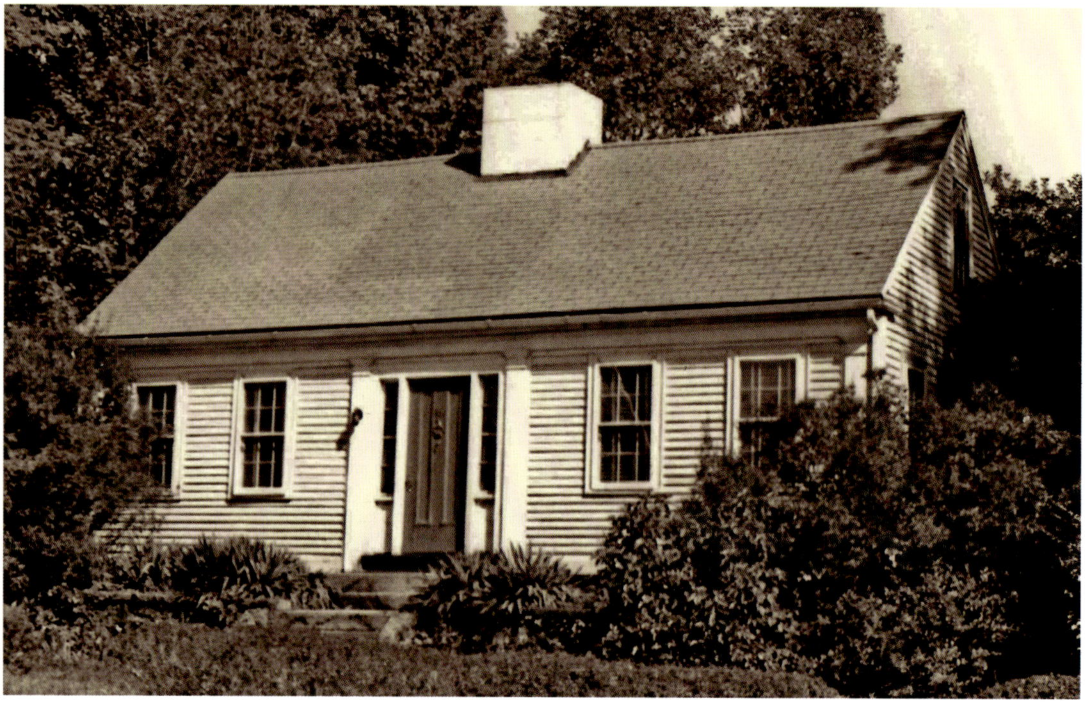

253 High Street: The John Wade House is one of only two early Cape style houses in the city. The house was built *c.* 1784 by John Wade, a tanner. The one and a half story wood frame house has a side gable roof, a large central chimney, and a granite foundation. The house is sometimes referred to locally as the Pierce Tavern, although it was never used as such, and probably stood next door to a tavern.

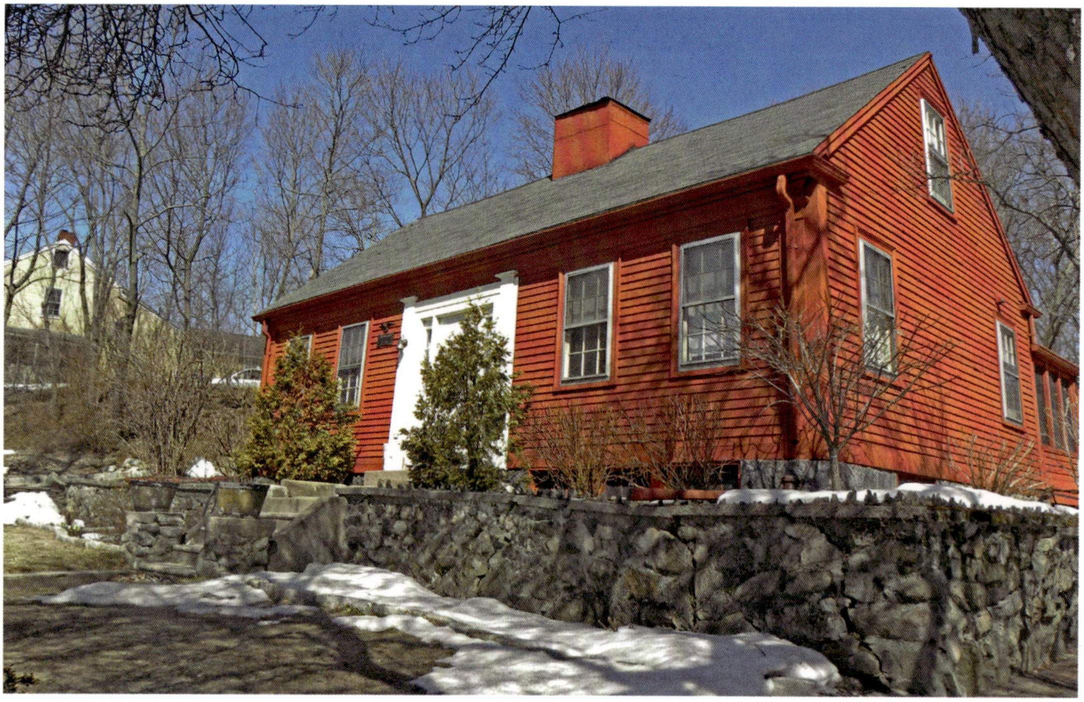

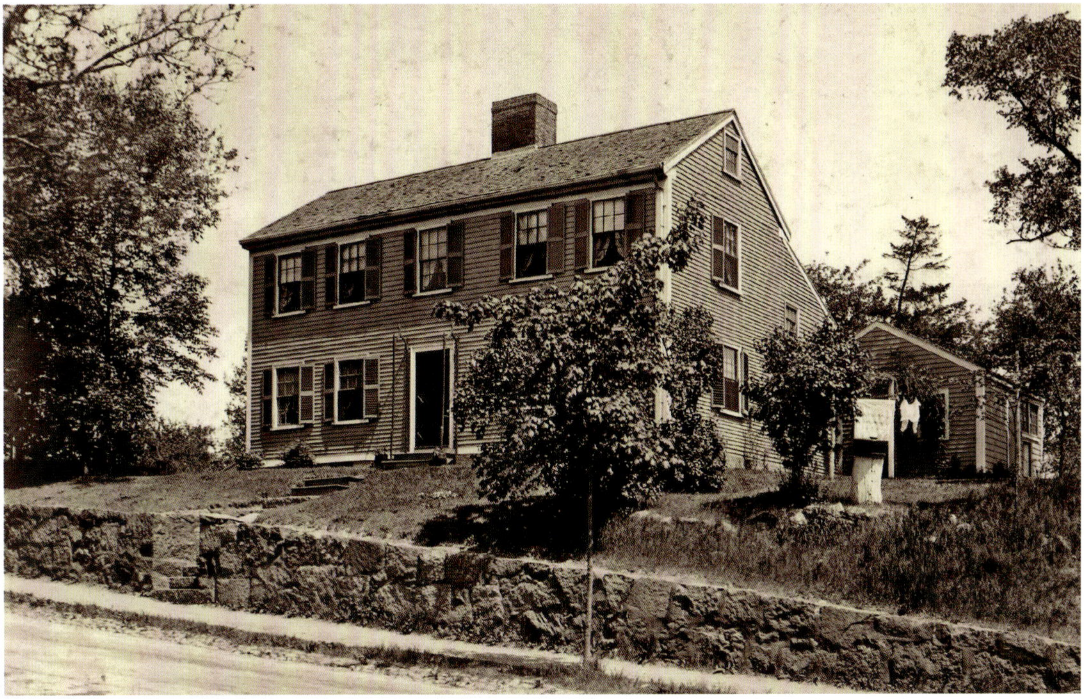

MARM SIMONDS HOUSE: The house at 265 High Street was built between 1810 and 1820 for Abigail "Marm" Simonds, a Medford "schoolmarm" who taught in the early 1800s. Simonds was a private school teacher paid by the town for the tuition of local students. Many nineteenth century history sources refer to that part of High Street as Marm Simonds Hill.

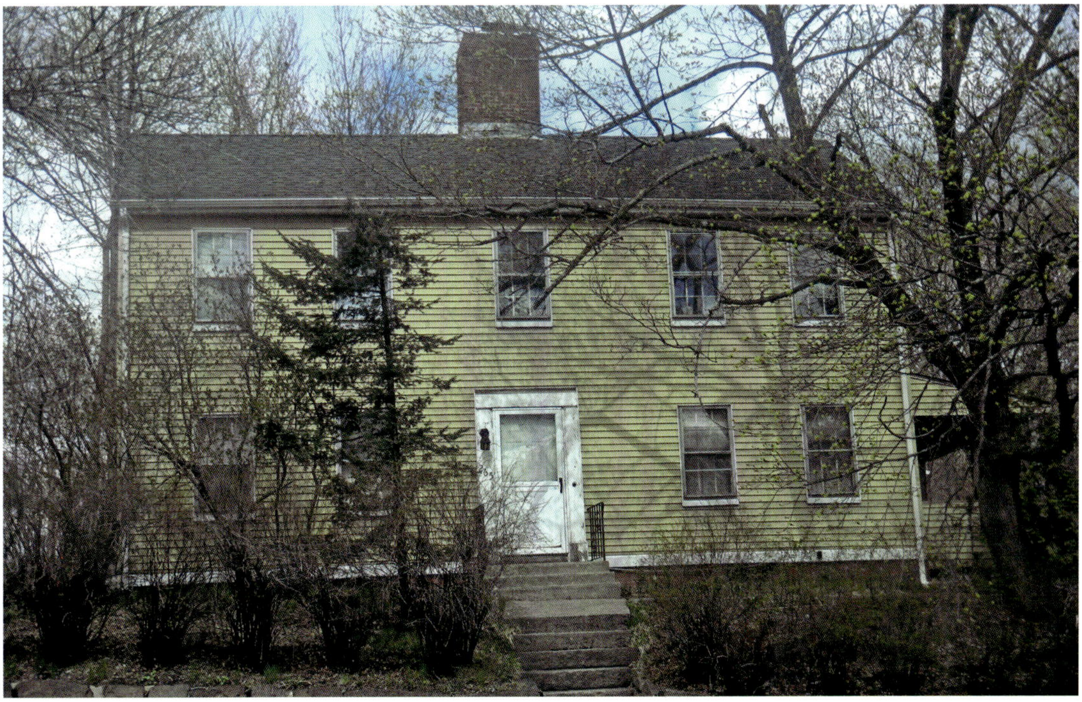

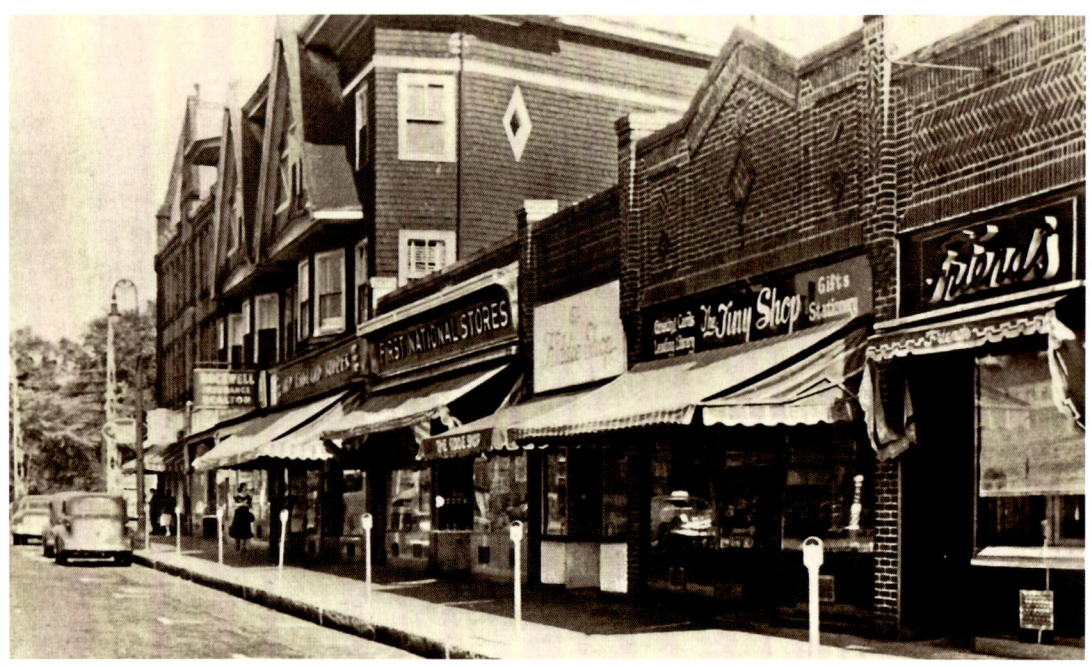

WEST MEDFORD SQUARE: In the 1870s large estates in the West Medford area were divided up into house lots and West Medford grew quickly. Like the larger Medford Square, West Medford's business area was a mix of local businesses and national chains. At one point there were three grocery stores in the Square including the First National which can be seen in this 1940s photo.

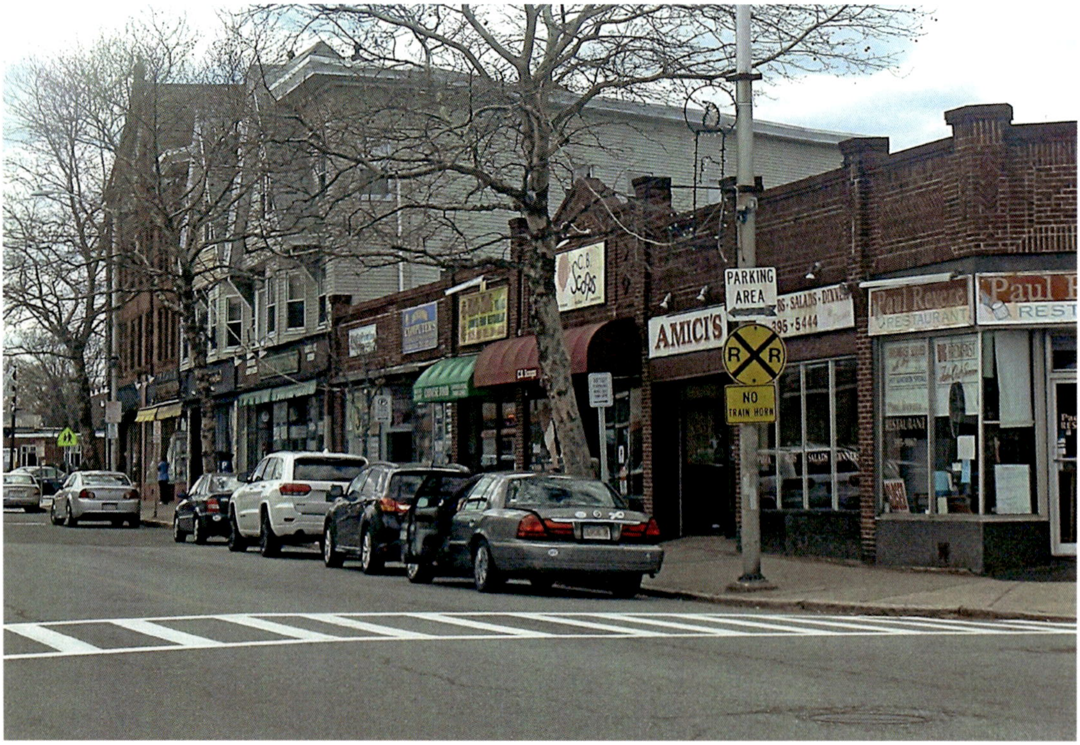

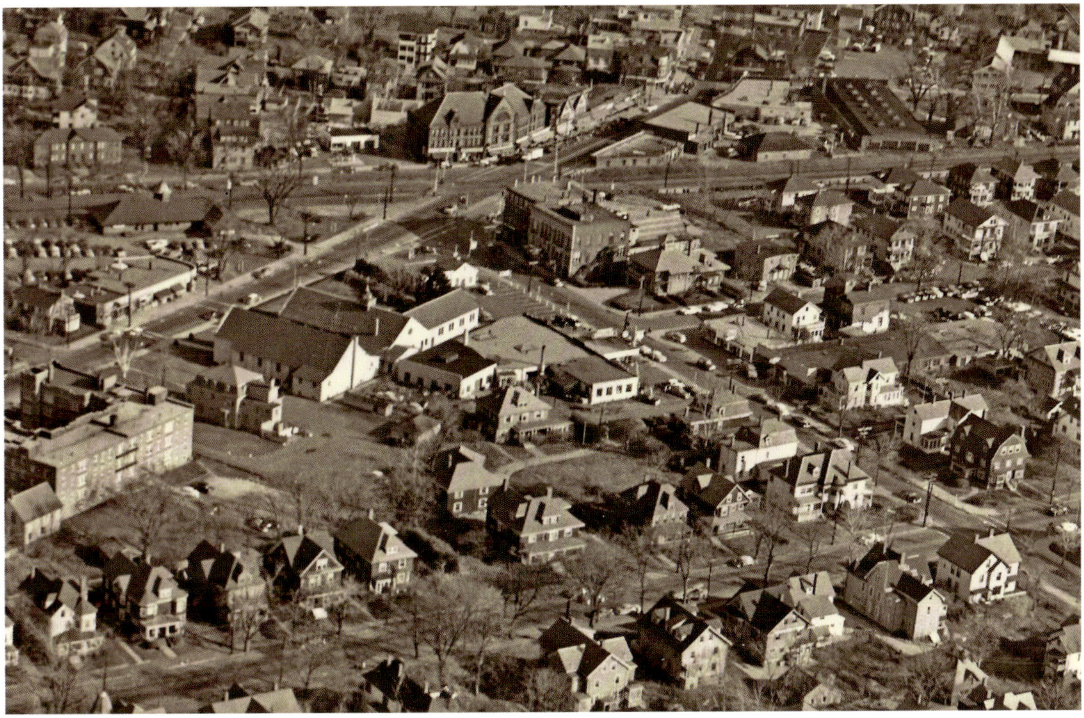

USHER BUILDING: Built in 1893, this Romanesque style commercial building is the centerpiece of West Medford Square. The brick and sandstone block was constructed by local businessman James Usher. Usher was a very busy Victorian with a reputation for eccentricity. In addition to his businesses, Usher was a local historian, Unitarian clergyman, and the publisher of Medford's first newspaper *The Medford Journal* (1870).

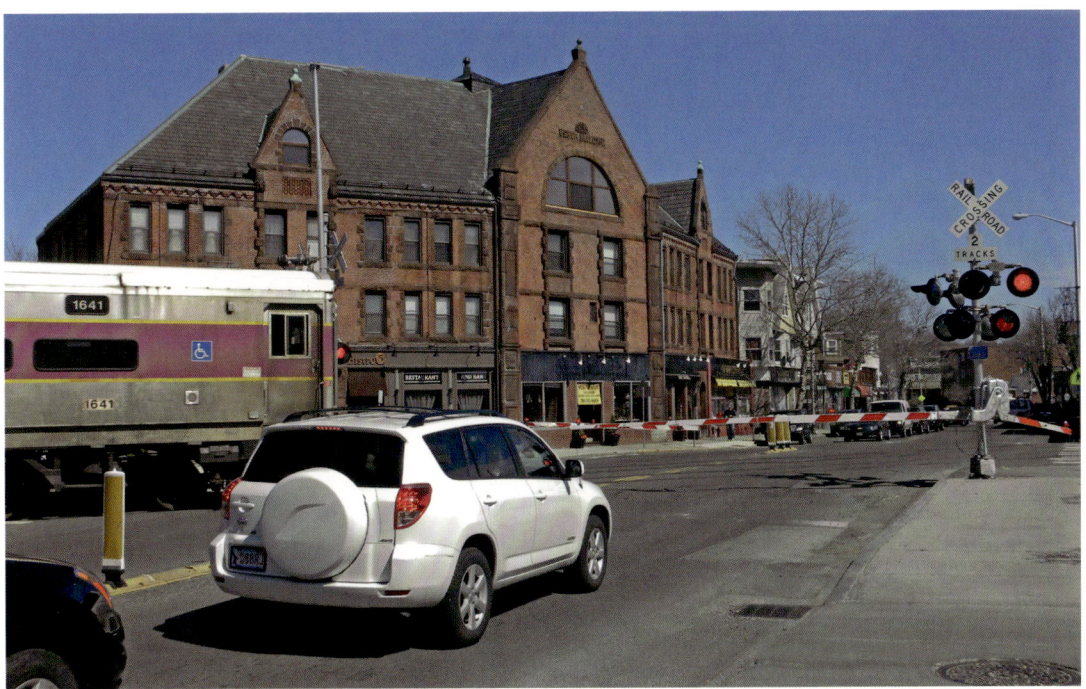

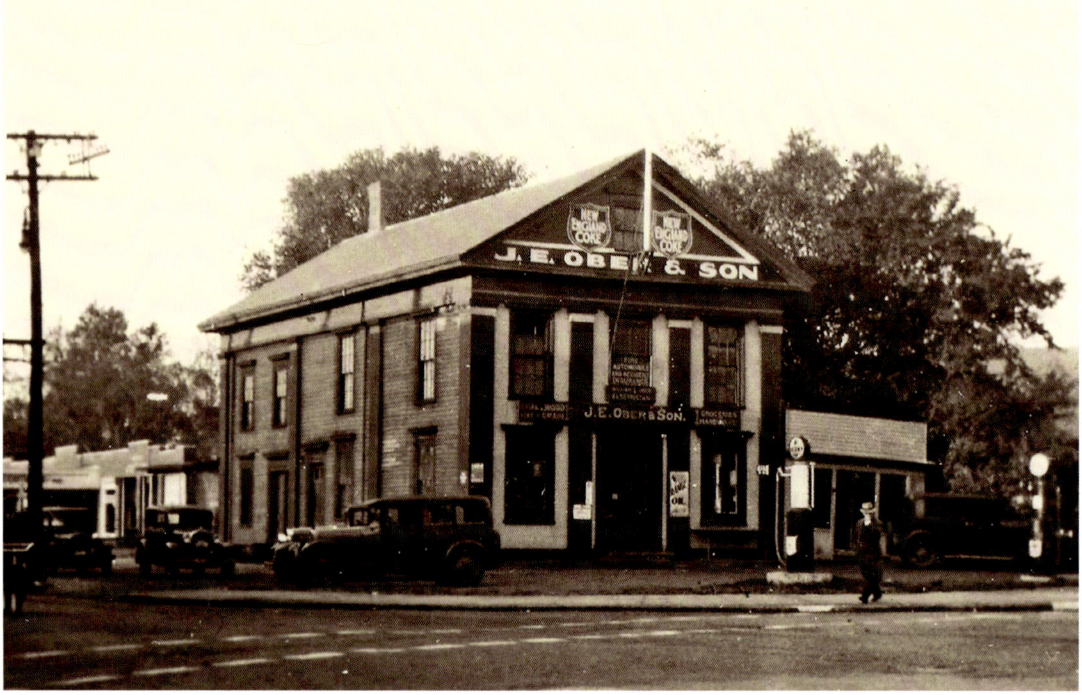

COUNTRY STORE: Ober's Store was a fixture in West Medford Square from the 1870s to the 1950s. Until 1935, Ober's was an old-fashioned general store carrying everything from lamp oil to dress fabric to ice skates. In 1935, the owner William Ober shocked the city by changing the premises into a modern hardware store. The store served West Medford well for several more decades. William Ober died in 1951.

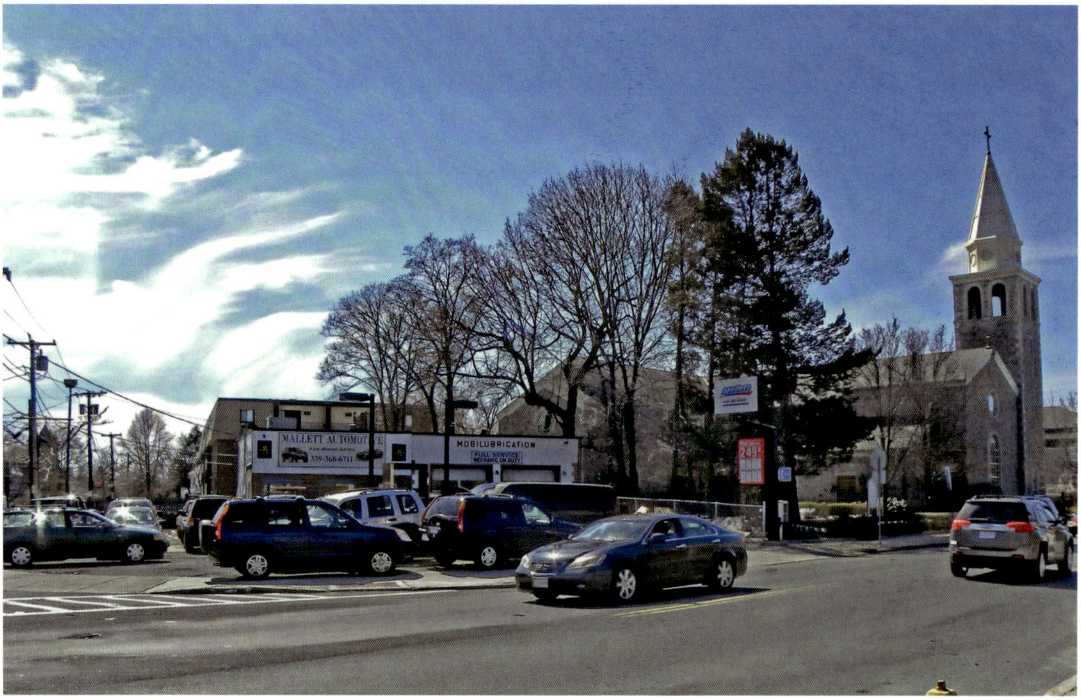

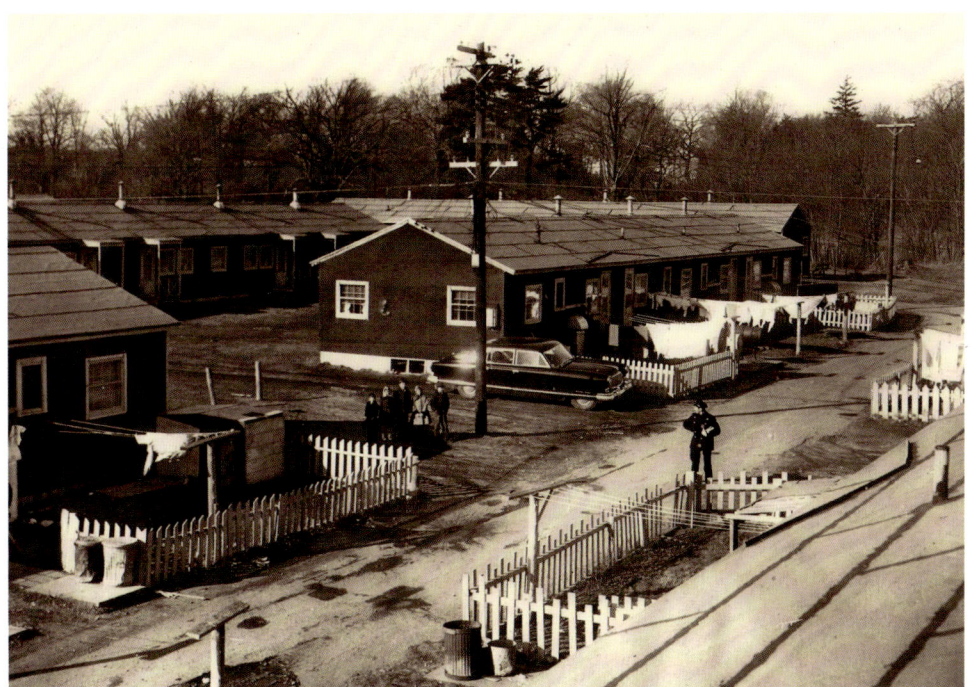

BROOKS VILLAGE: After World War II Medford was one of the first Massachusetts communities to create a veterans housing village. Using federal funds, Medford created Brooks Village, consisting of 200 "temporary" housing units at the Brooks Estate off Grove Street. Ten families were housed in the Shepherd Brooks Manor as well. The development served as the first home for hundreds of Medford families from 1946–1954. A Brooks Village Fiftieth Reunion was held in 1996.

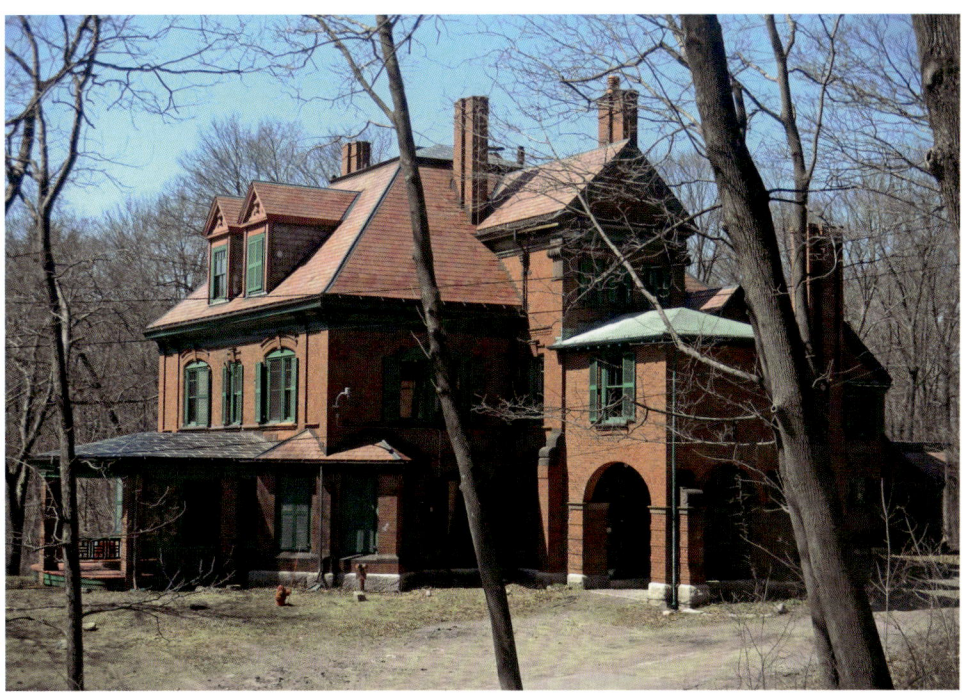

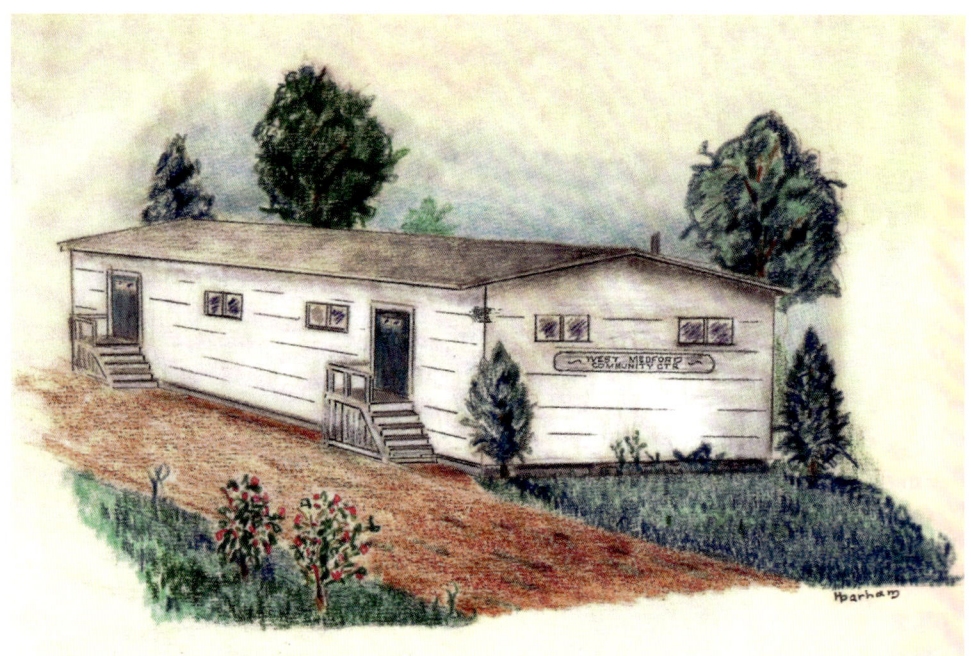

WMCC: In the 1940s, West Medford community leaders took a surplus Army barracks and reassembled it in West Medford's Dugger Park. It became the West Medford Community Center. The WMCC became the nucleus of social and family life in the predominantly African-American community. The most recent WMCC building was rebuilt in 2007. The Center continues to offer many experiences including dance classes with instructor Joanna Matthews who posed in front of the Center in 2015.

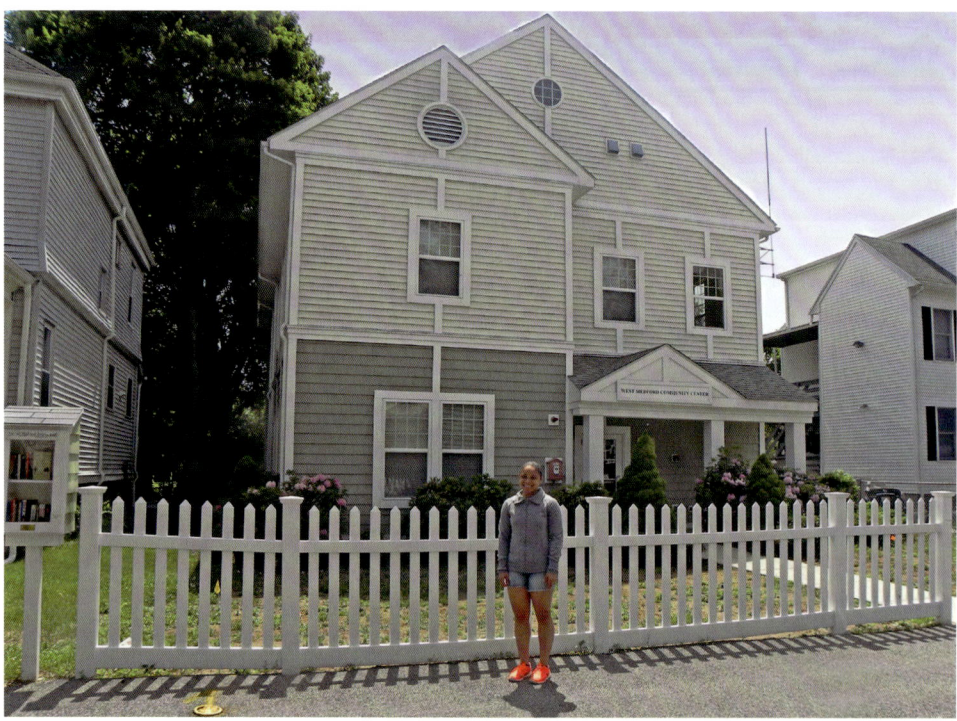

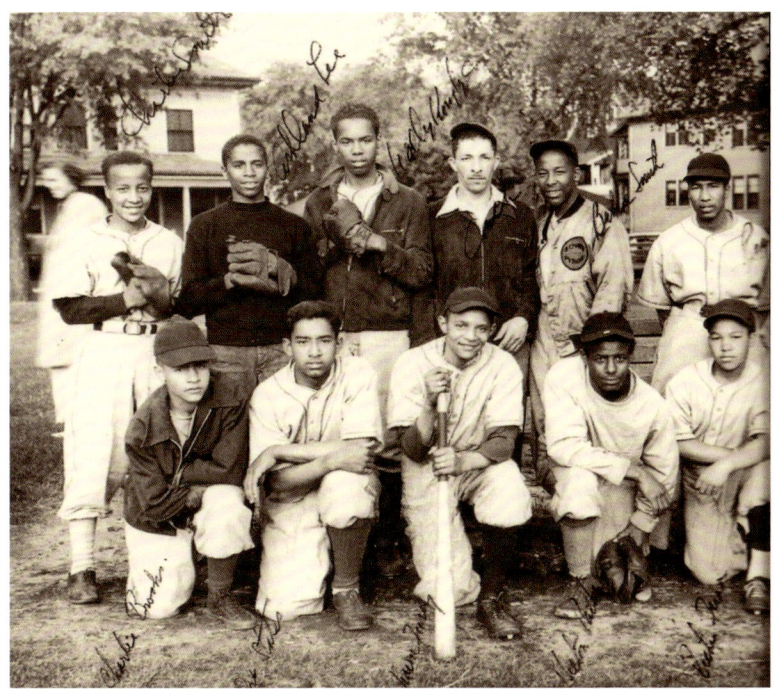

WEST MEDFORD BASEBALL: Starting in the 1930s, West Medford community leader Walter Isaacs coached the children of the predominantly African-American neighborhood in baseball, tennis, and bowling. The 1947 team included Wallace Kountze, third from the left in the second row. Mr. Kountze pursued a career in public service on the federal, state and local levels. He is seen here at the 2009 Citizen of the Year banquet with Dom Camarra and John Lonergan. Mr. Kountze passed away in August 2015.

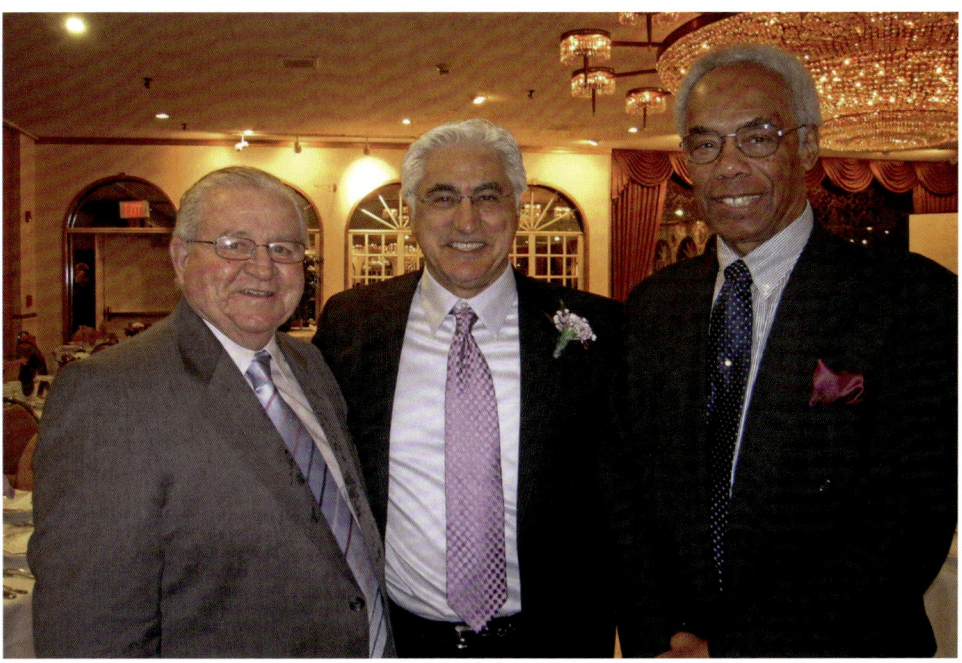

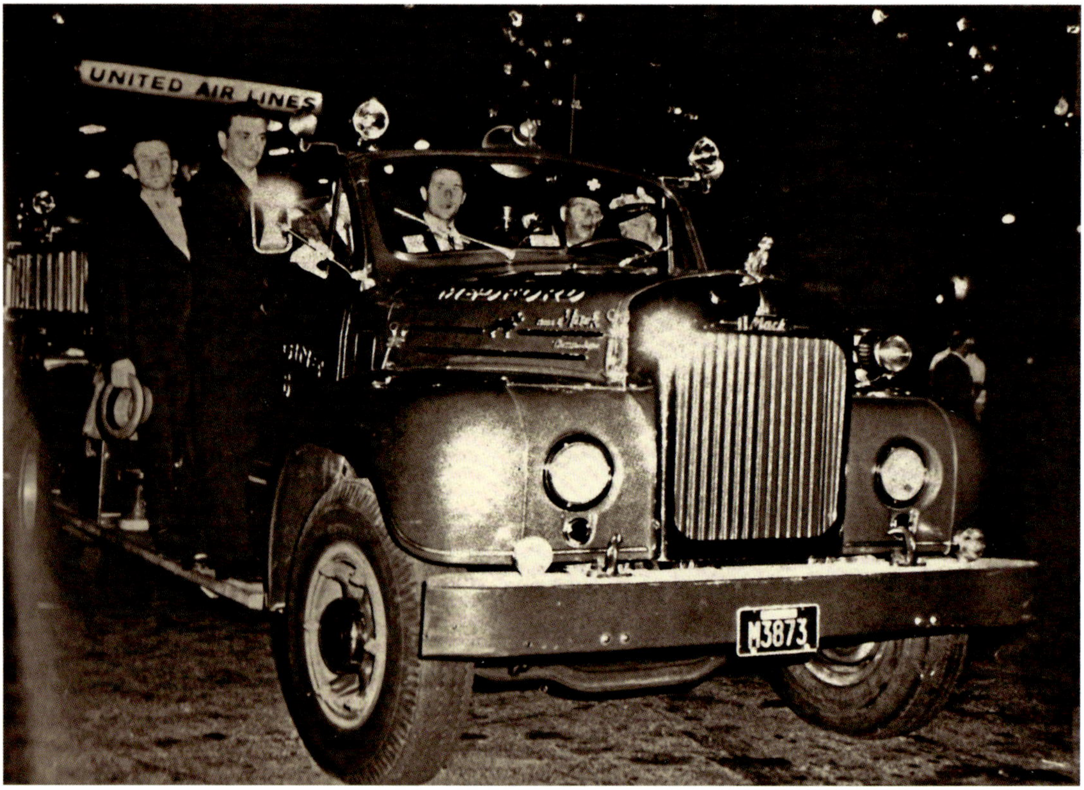

BASEBALL STARS: Born on August 1936, Medford native Bill Monboquette. He pitched for the Boston Red Sox, Detroit Tigers, New York Yankees, and the San Francisco Giants. He graduated from Medford High School and was signed by the Red Sox in 1955. He was welcomed back to West Medford in style during a celebration in the 1960s. Celebration was also in order in 2015, when the Medford High School Girls Softball Team became the regional champions.

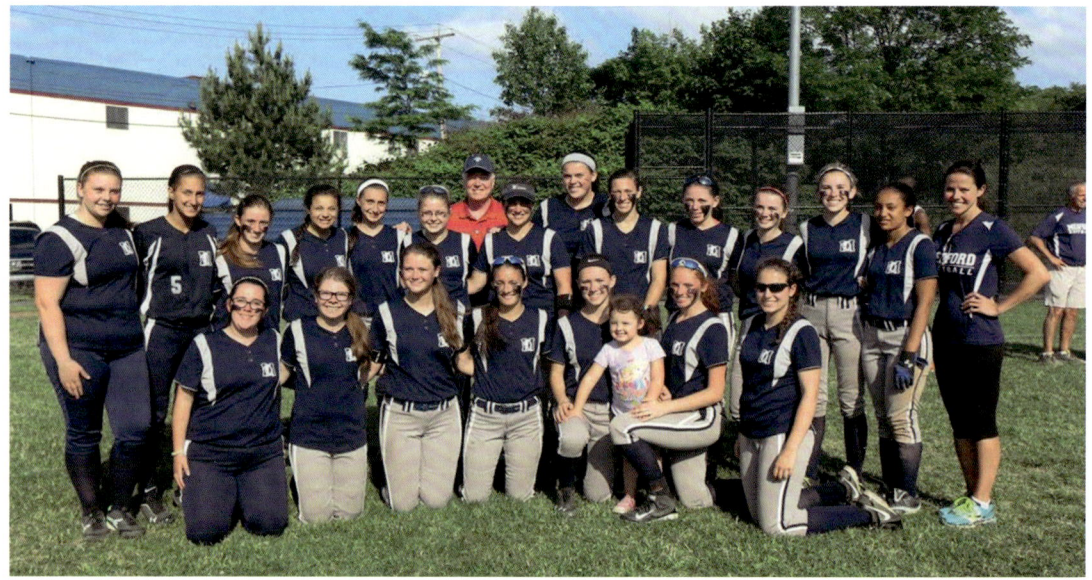

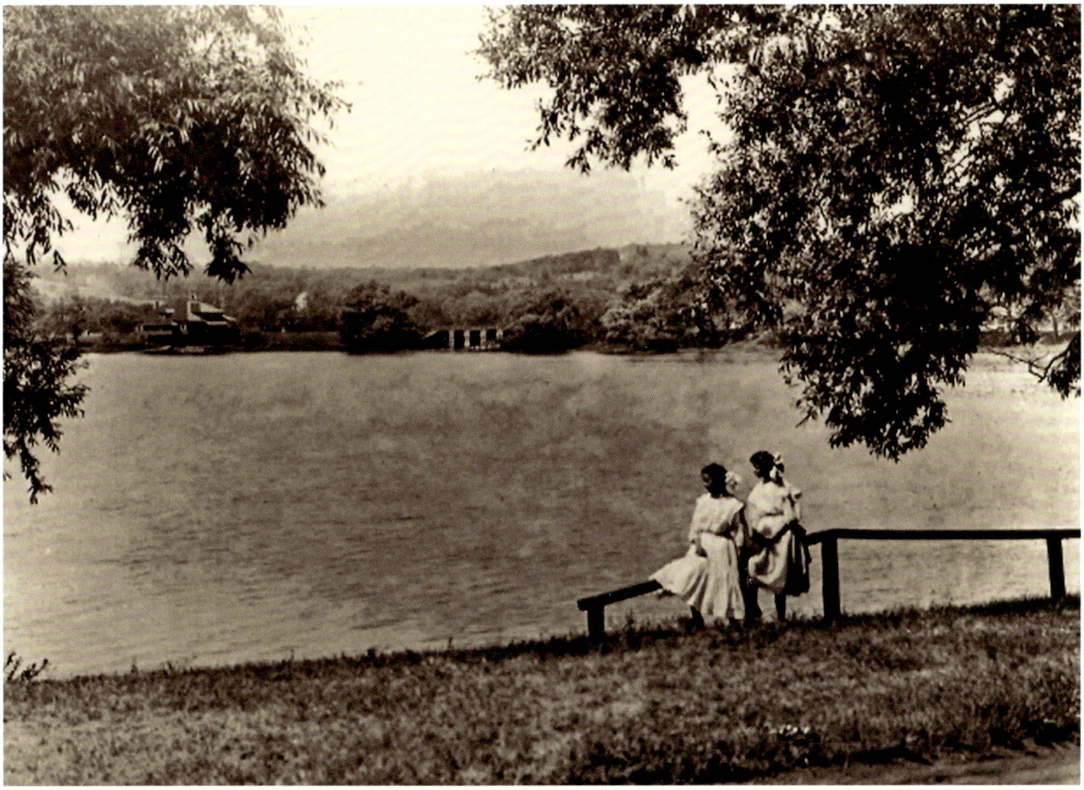

MEDFORD BOAT CLUB:
The Mystic Lakes were once a single body of water known as Medford Pond. In 1863 the Pond became a water source for Charlestown and a dam divided the Pond. The Medford Boat Club chartered in 1898, is located on the earthen dam between the Upper and Lower Lakes. Since its opening, the Club has been a happy retreat for boat lovers and water loving families like cousins Ronan, Alexander and Adeline Saunders, and Nathan McCarthy.

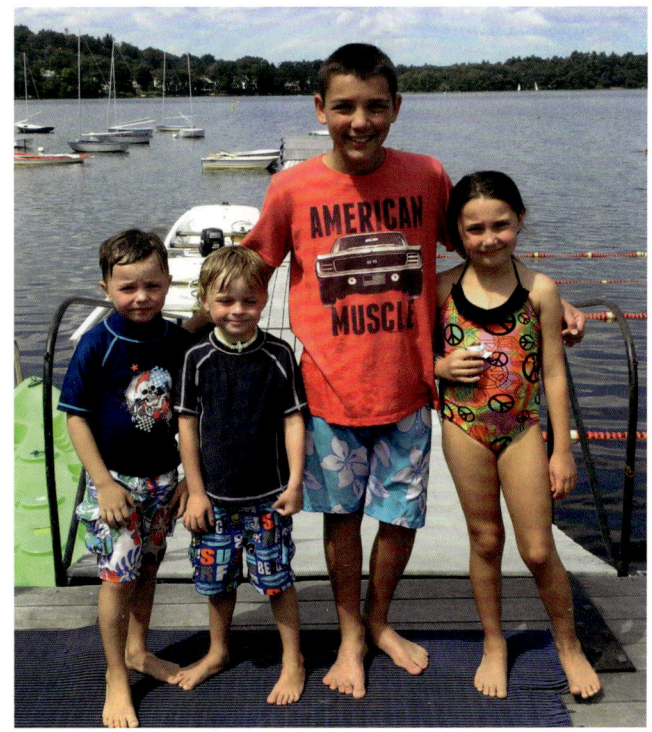

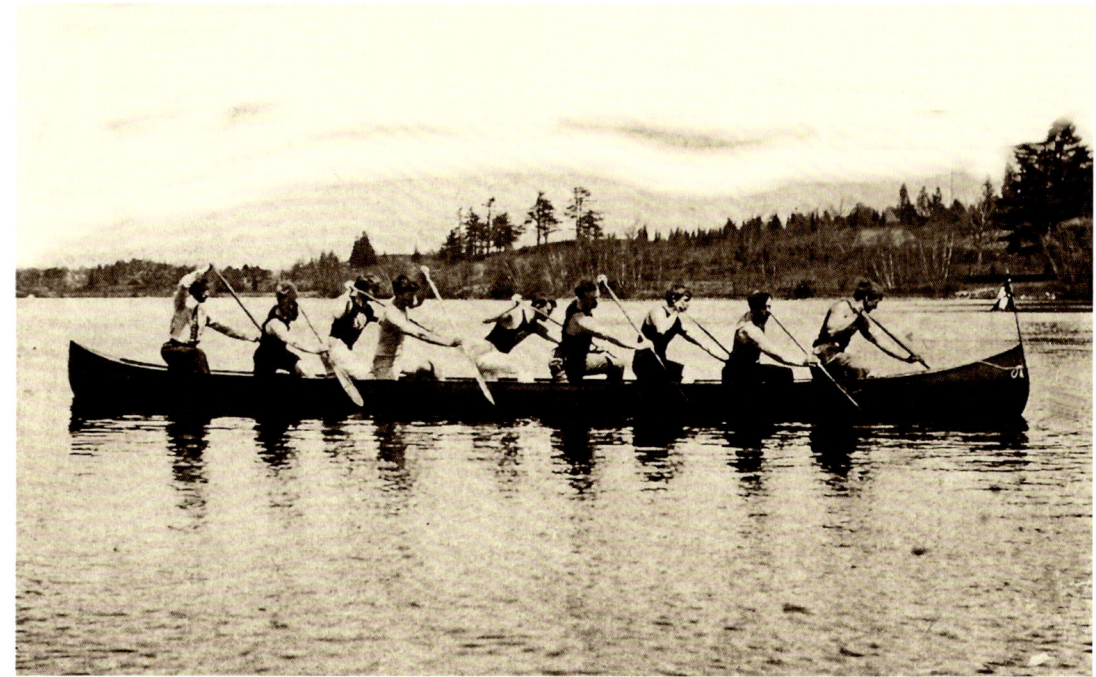

CANOES: During the city's 275th anniversary in 1905, the Eastern division of the American Canoe Association held their meet on the Mystic Lakes. The canoe team of the Medford Boat Club won the Eastern championship that day and members of the other teams camped overnight on the shores of the lake. Canoeing remains a popular Medford sport. This bright pink canoe took to the water near River's Edge on the Medford/Malden Line during the 2014 Arts Festival.

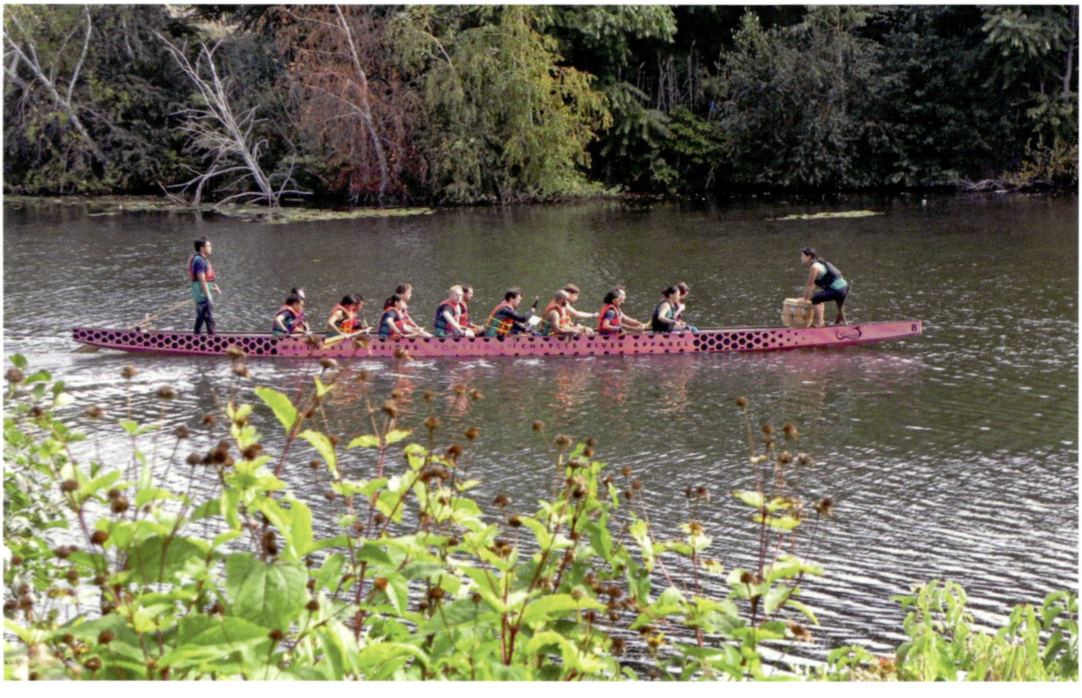

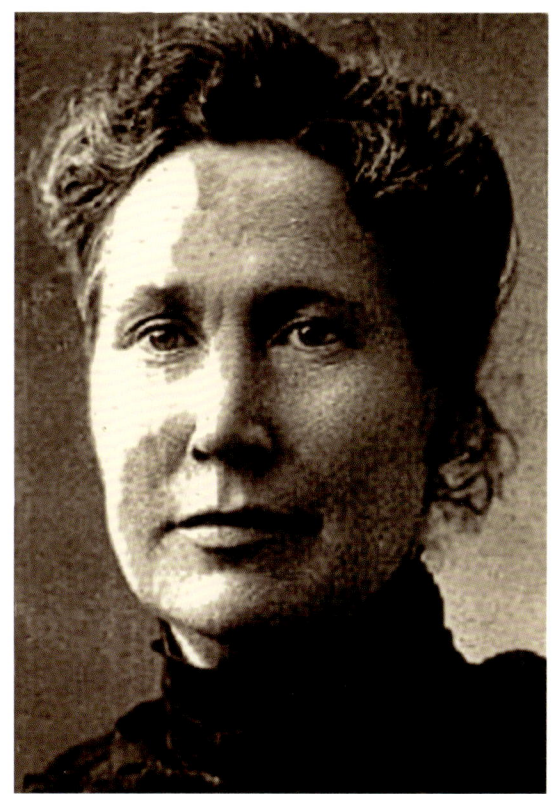

541 Winthrop Street: Mary Kenney O'Sullivan was a labor leader and advocate for workers' rights. She married John O'Sullivan, the labor editor of the *Boston Globe* and became the director of the Women's Educational and Industrial Union. After the death of her husband in 1902, O'Sullivan moved her family to 541 Winthrop Street. O'Sullivan worked in the State's Department of Labor and Industries and fought for workers' and women's rights until her death in 1943.

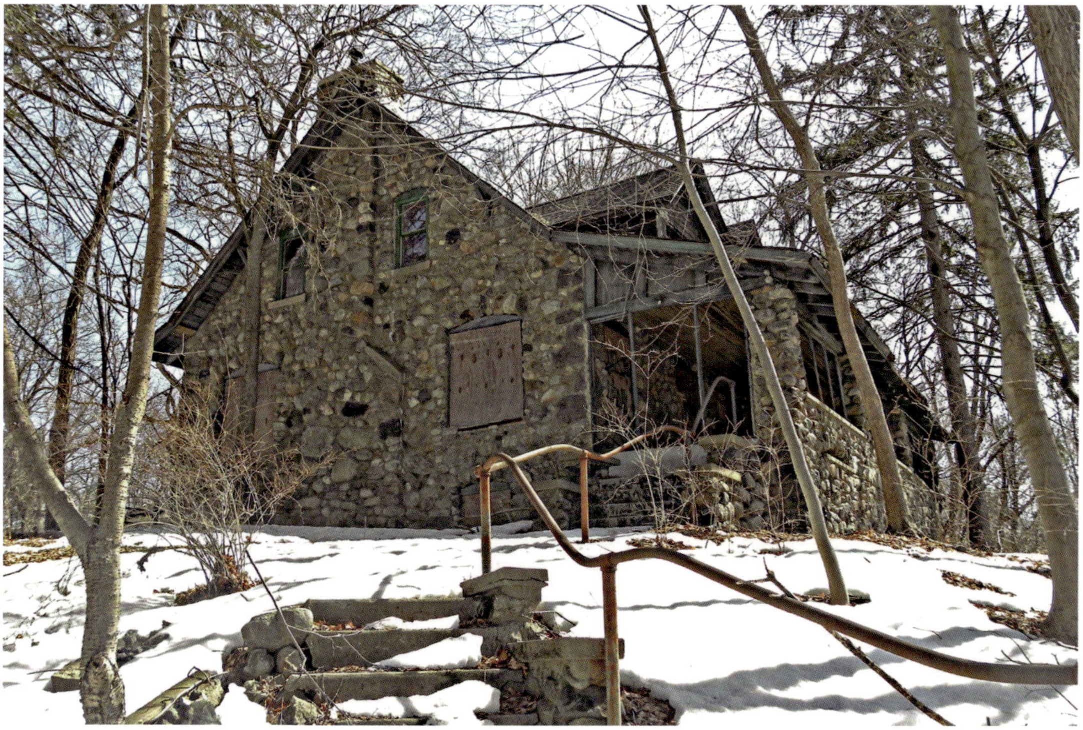

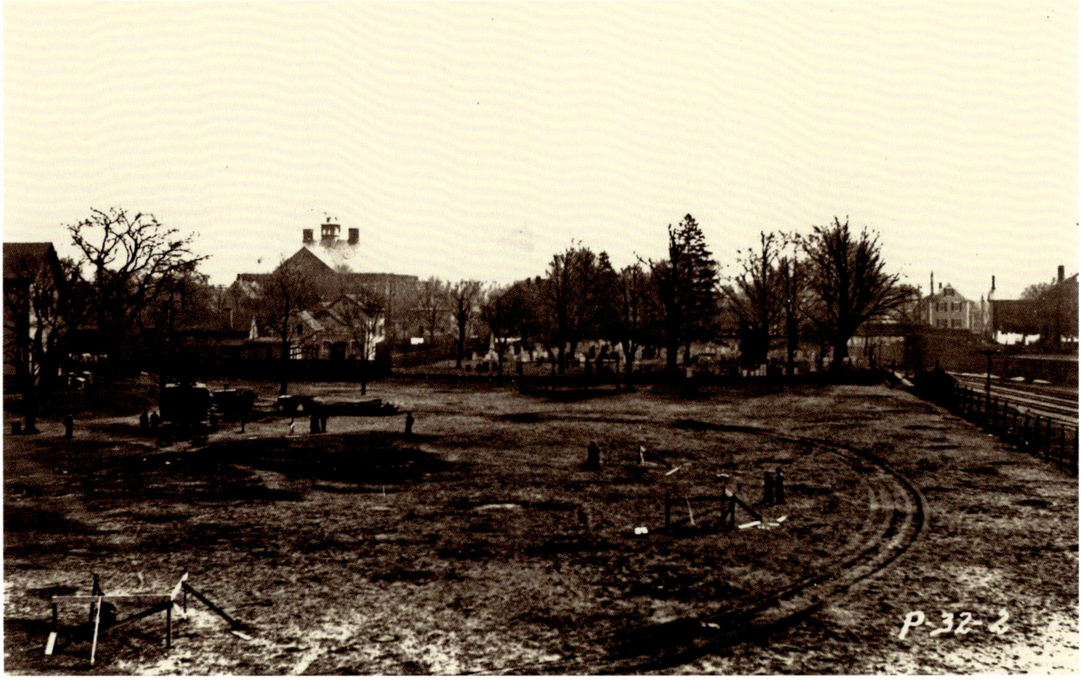

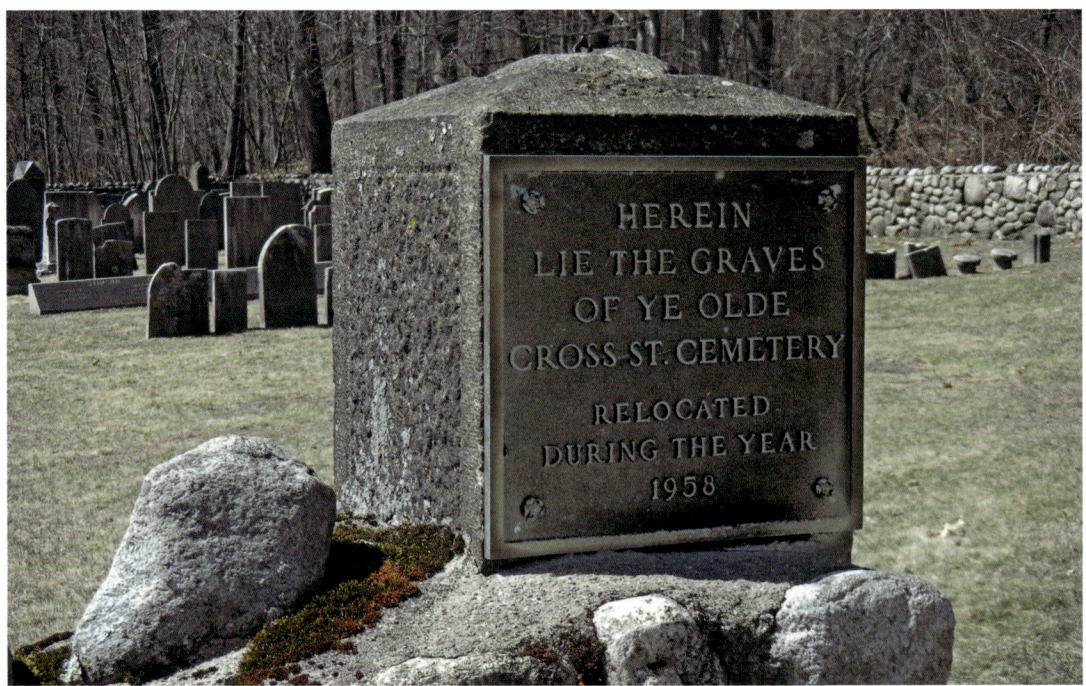

CROSS STREET: At one time, Medford had three cemeteries. The Cross Street cemetery was the city's second oldest burial ground and was in use between 1816 and the early 1900s. The cemetery can be seen in the background of this 1930s photo which also shows the start of construction of the City Hall. In 1958, the graves were moved and reinterred in a fenced off section of Oak Grove Cemetery during the construction of Route 93.

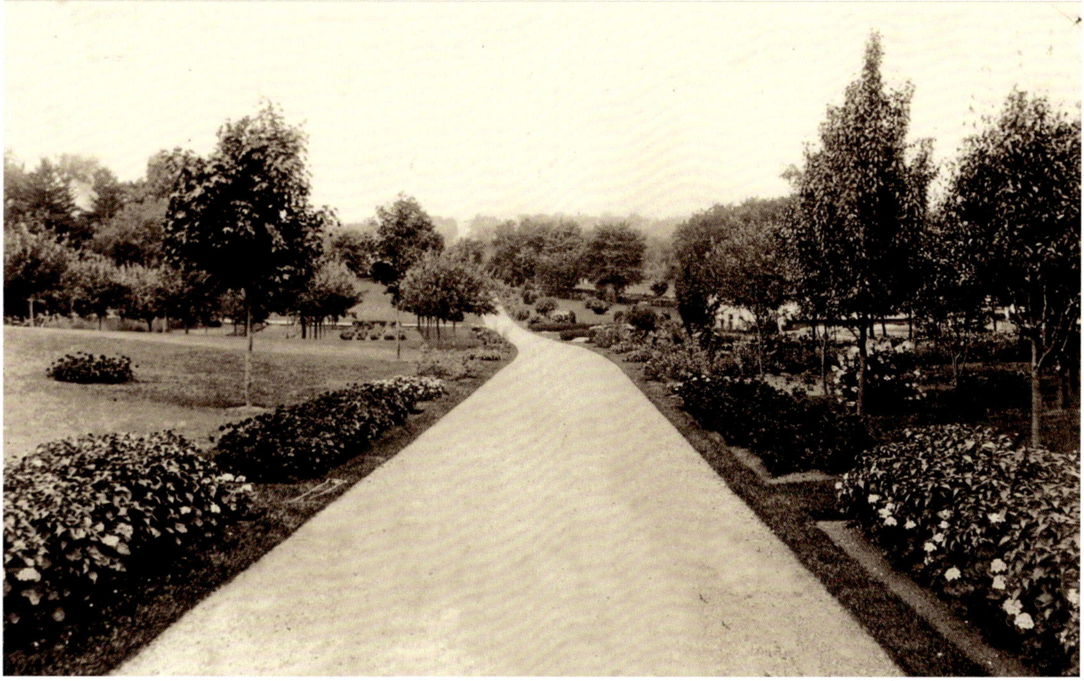

LAWRENCE ESTATES: The Albree-Hall-Lawrence House is an historic eighteenth century farmhouse house at 353 Lawrence Road. The house was once owned by Peter Chardon Brooks, and the farm was later purchased by Samuel C. Lawrence, the first mayor of Medford, and incorporated into his estate. Lawrence's land was turned into house lots in the 1920s. The neighborhood was called the Lawrence Estates and was marketed as "the" place to live for young modern families.

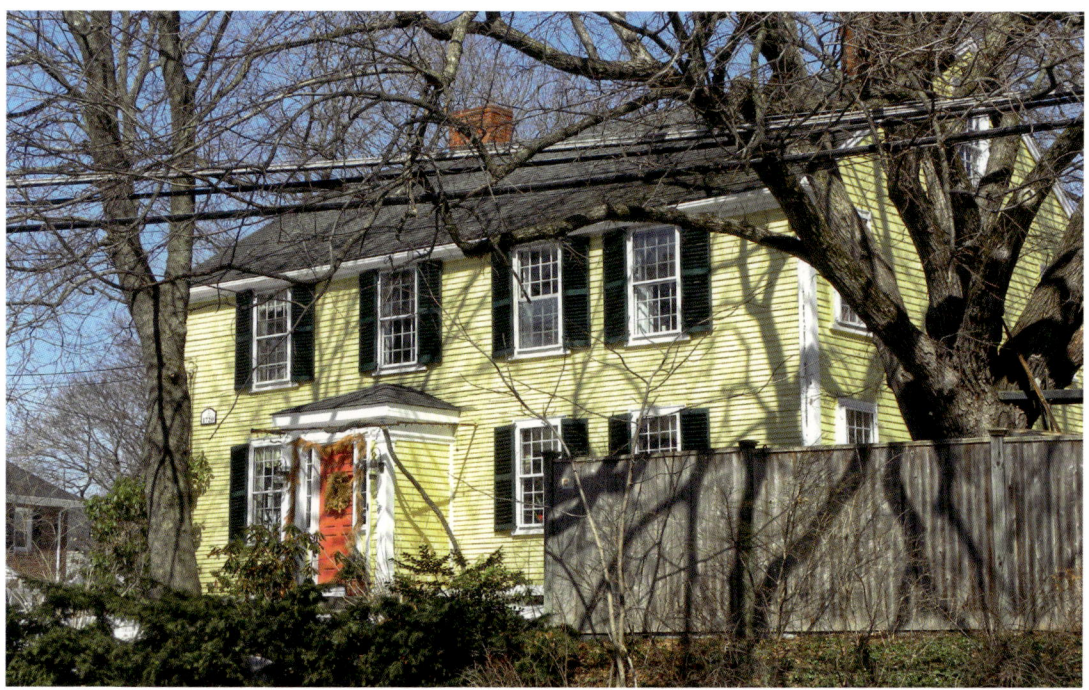

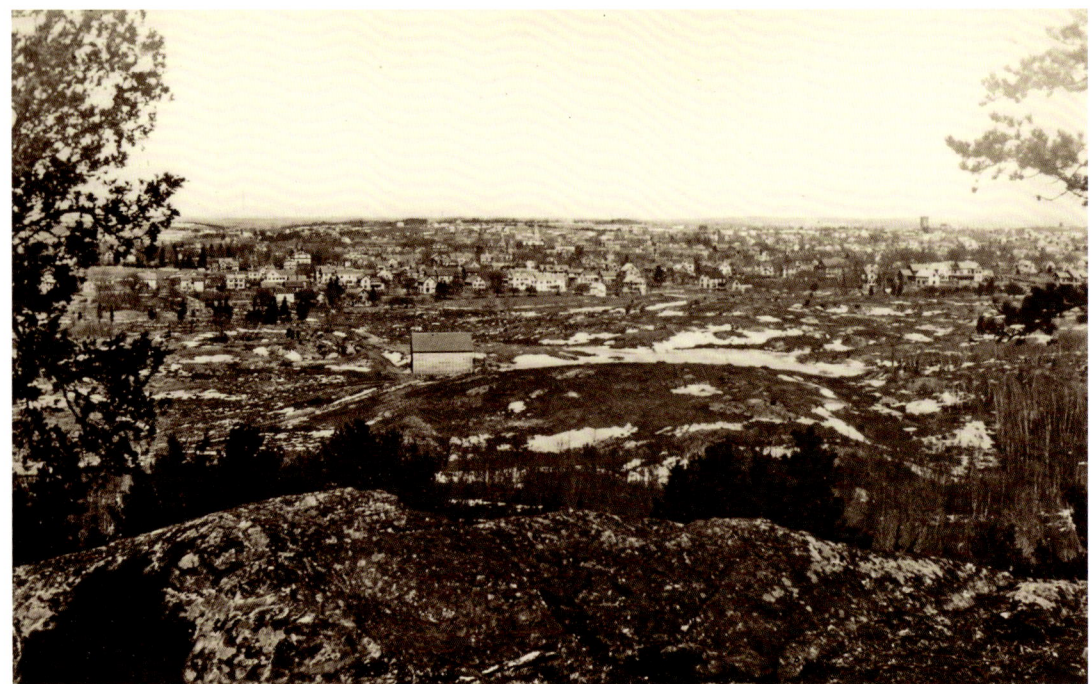

BEAR HILL: According to tradition, John Winthrop ate lunch on Bear Hill when he visited Medford in 1632. Bear Hill has the highest elevation in the Fells. The location has provided great photographic views of the surrounding towns in the nineteenth century and today. The Fells became a protected area during the late nineteenth century largely due to the preservation efforts of local residents Elizur Wright and George Davenport.

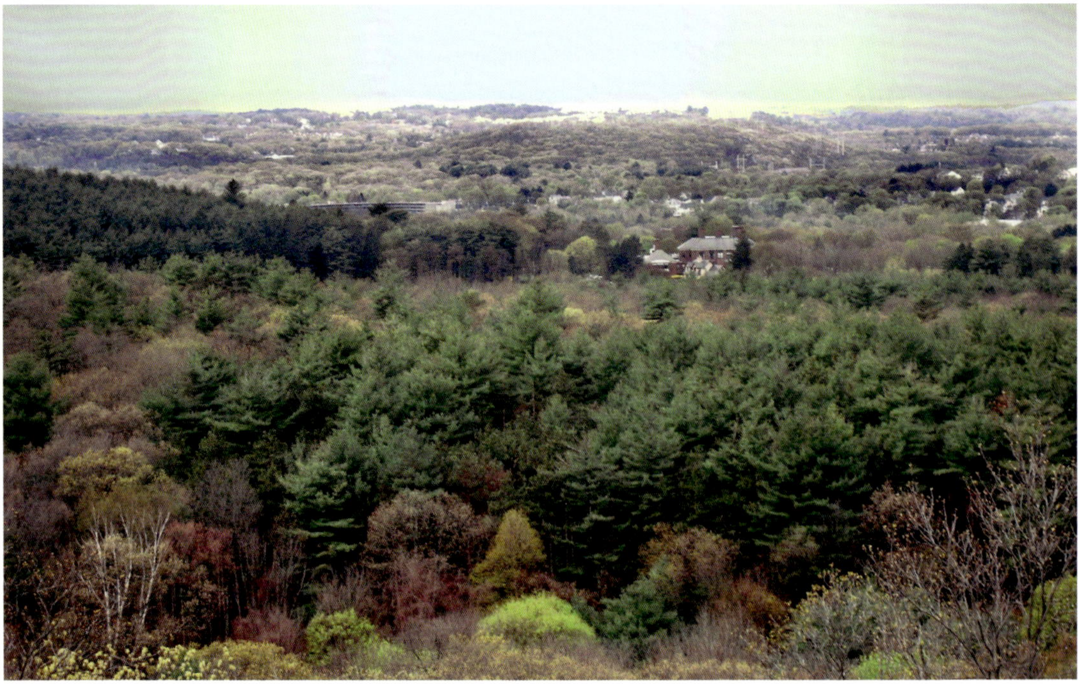

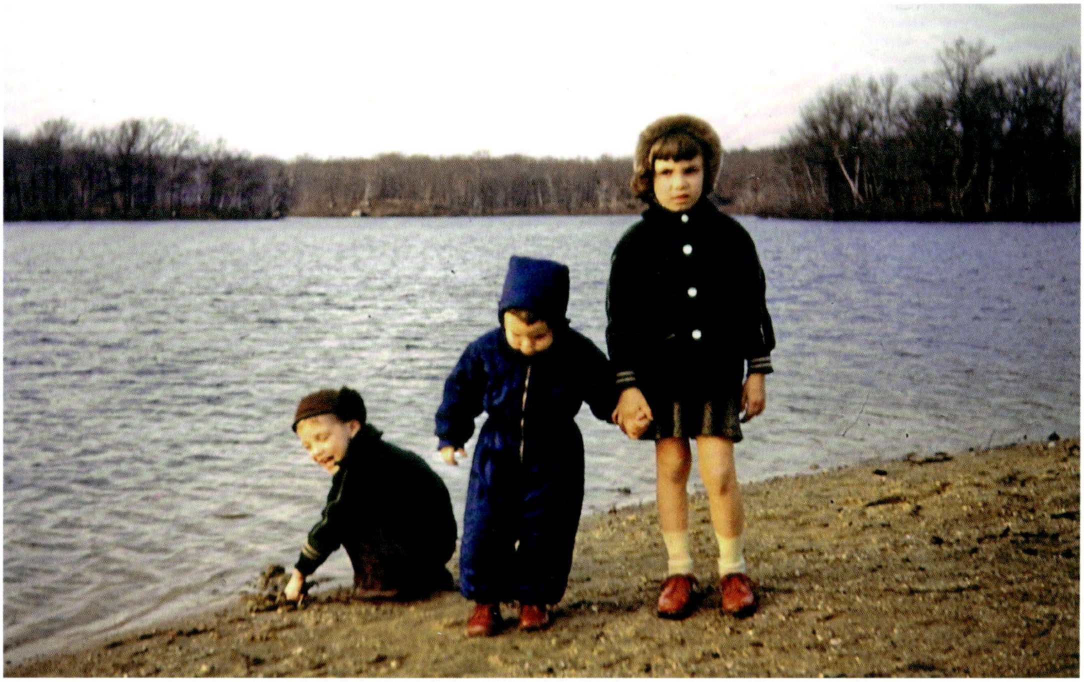

WRIGHT'S POND: Although part of the Middlesex Fells, Wright's Pond is an artificial body of water, constructed in 1888. It was once part of the water supply, but became Medford's favorite beach in the early twentieth century. Fulton Heights was a summer vacation destination because of its proximity to the Pond. Families have enjoyed the Pond for generations from 1954, when the great grandchildren of Mayor Larkin visited, to today, when it is a welcome summer retreat.

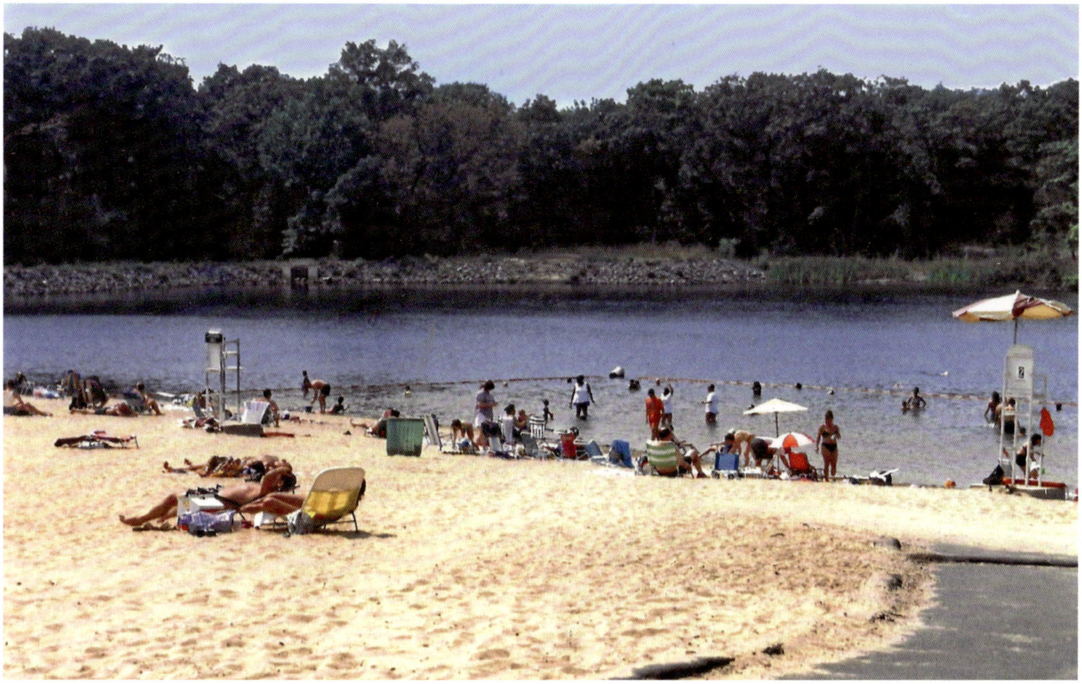

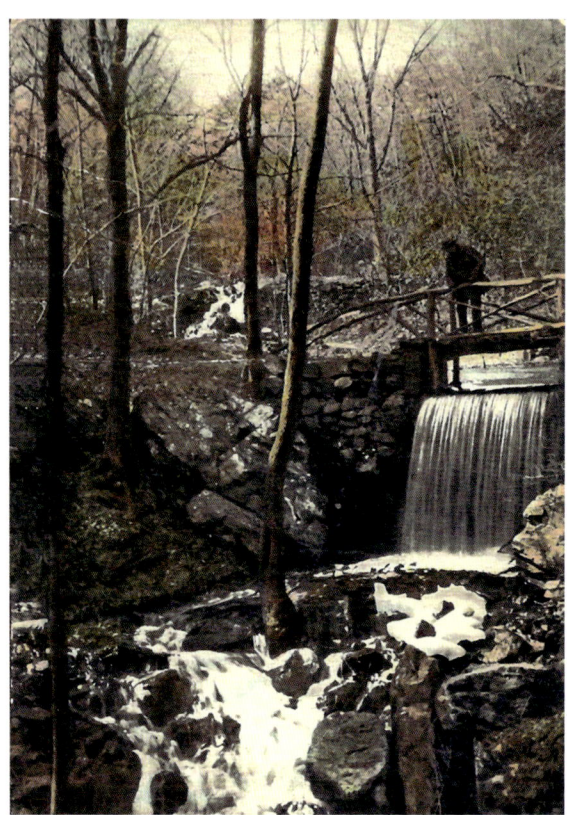

BRIDGE IN THE FELLS: Generations of Medford residents have enjoyed the scenes and trails of the Middlesex Fells. In the nineteenth century, the stone bridge in the Fells was considered to be romantic destination for lovers and was a frequent subject for photographs and postcards.

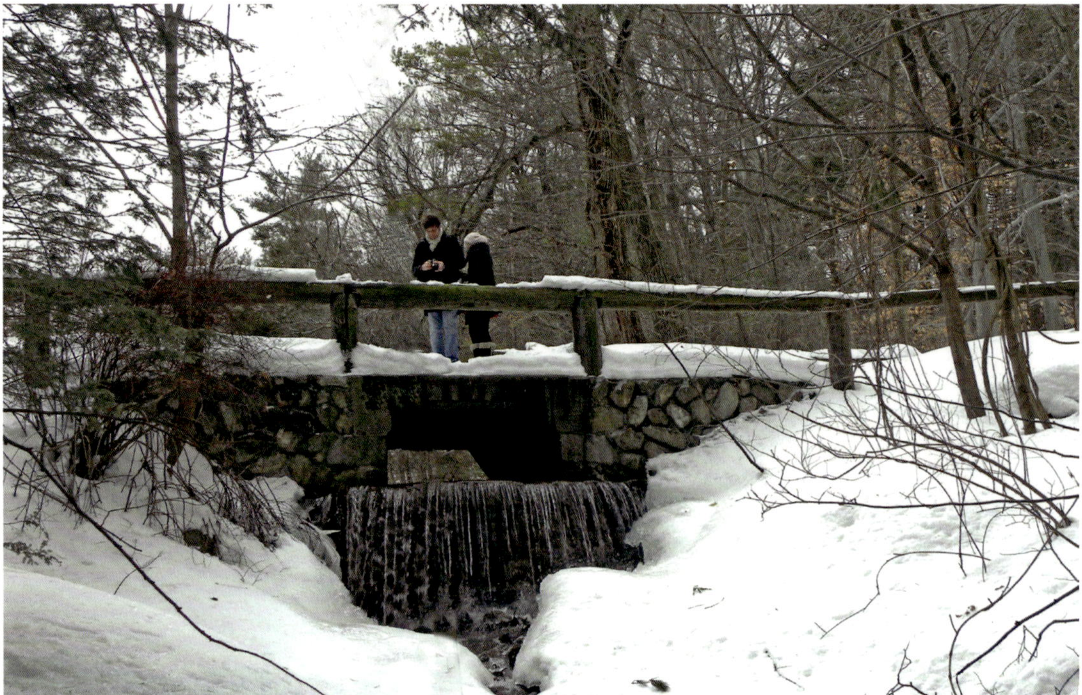

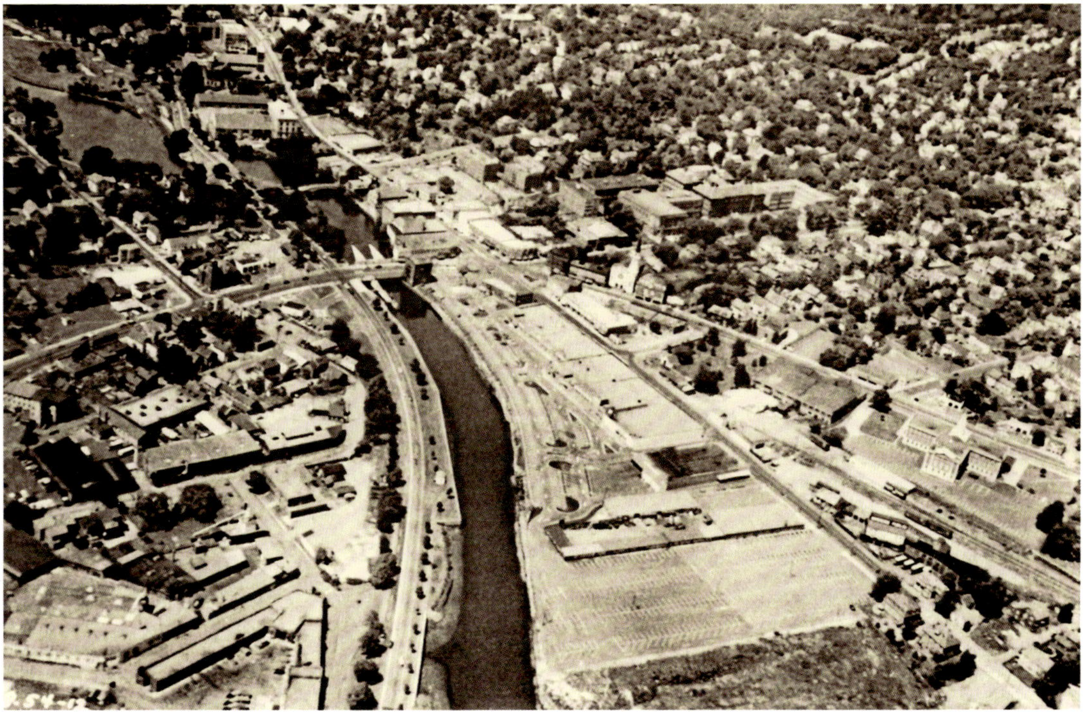

ROUTE 93: In the 1960s Medford's landscape was radically altered during the construction of Route 93. At the same time, the Mystic River was moved and straightened. This 1950s aerial view shows the city before the construction divided the city. Today a similar view from the Fells is dominated by the highway.

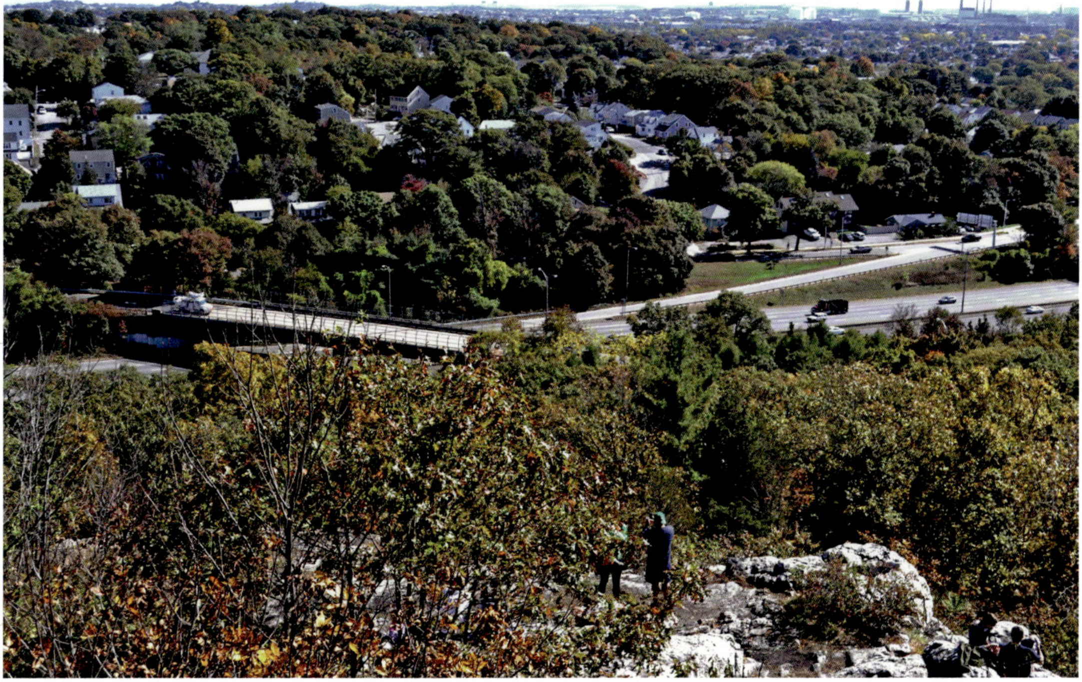

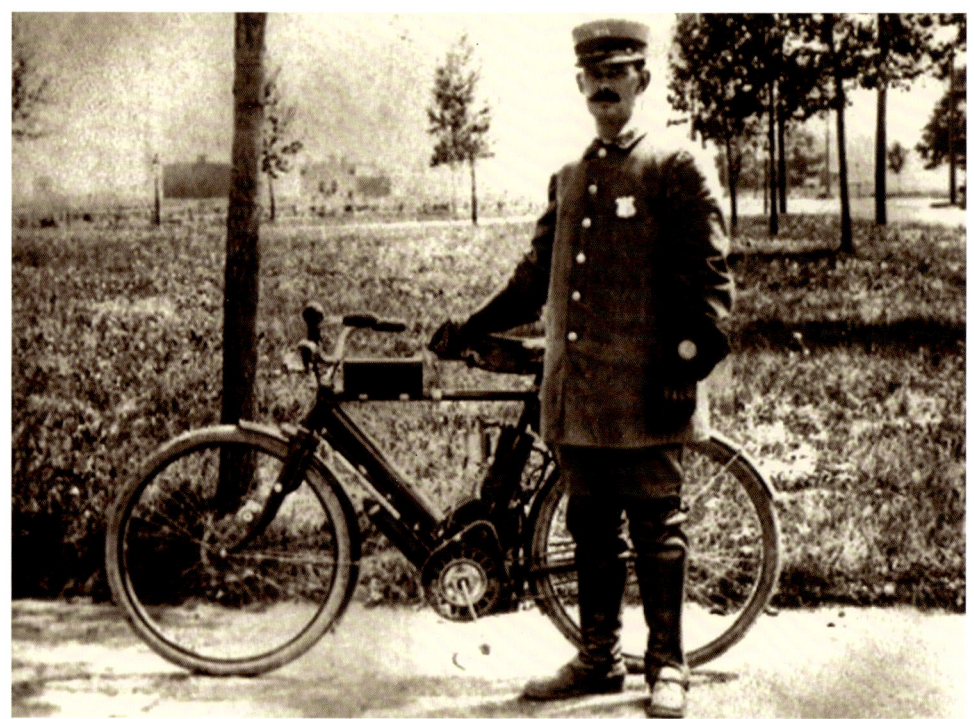

BICYCLES: In the nineteenth century, bicycles became a part of Medford life. Around 1900, the Middlesex Fells were patrolled by bicycle policemen. Pictured here is Metropolitan Park Richard Hanafin, Sr. in full riding uniform. In 2015, members of the Medford Bicycle Advisory commission posed in modern bicycle gear. The Commission was created in 2013 to encourage those who live, work and travel in Medford, Massachusetts, to ride bikes.

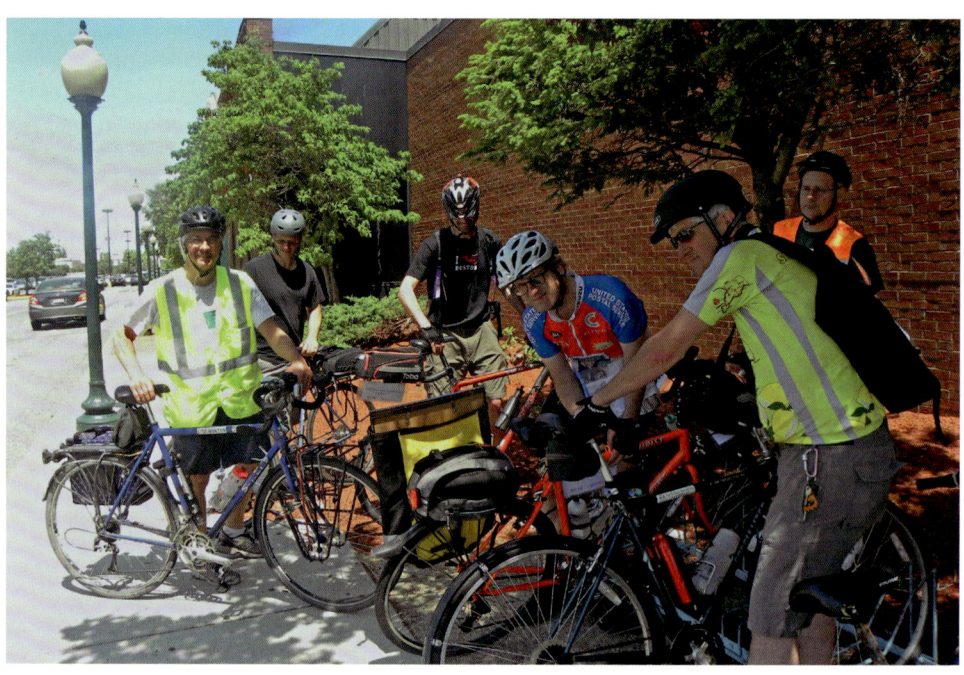

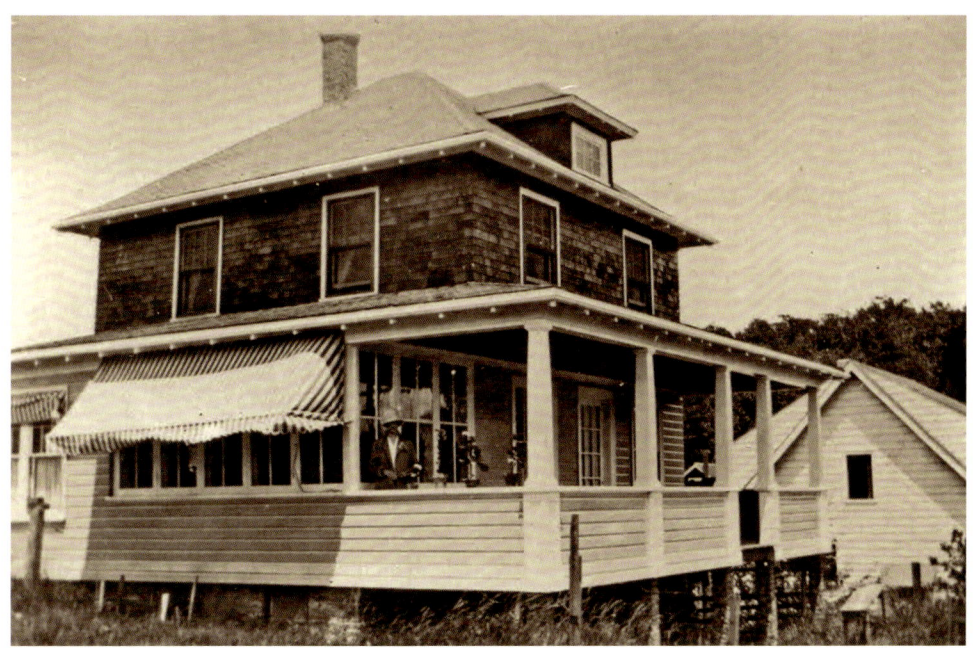

NORTH MEDFORD COTTAGES: It may be hard to believe, but at one time Fulton Heights was a vacation destination. Many of the original houses on the Heights like this one at 115 Wason Street were summer cottages built for vacationers. In the early photo, you can see the exposed foundation of the cottage and the rough landscaping of a seasonal area. North Medford was a desirable getaway because of its proximity to the Middlesex Fells and Wright's Pond. Today many of the former cottages have been turned into attractive year-round houses.

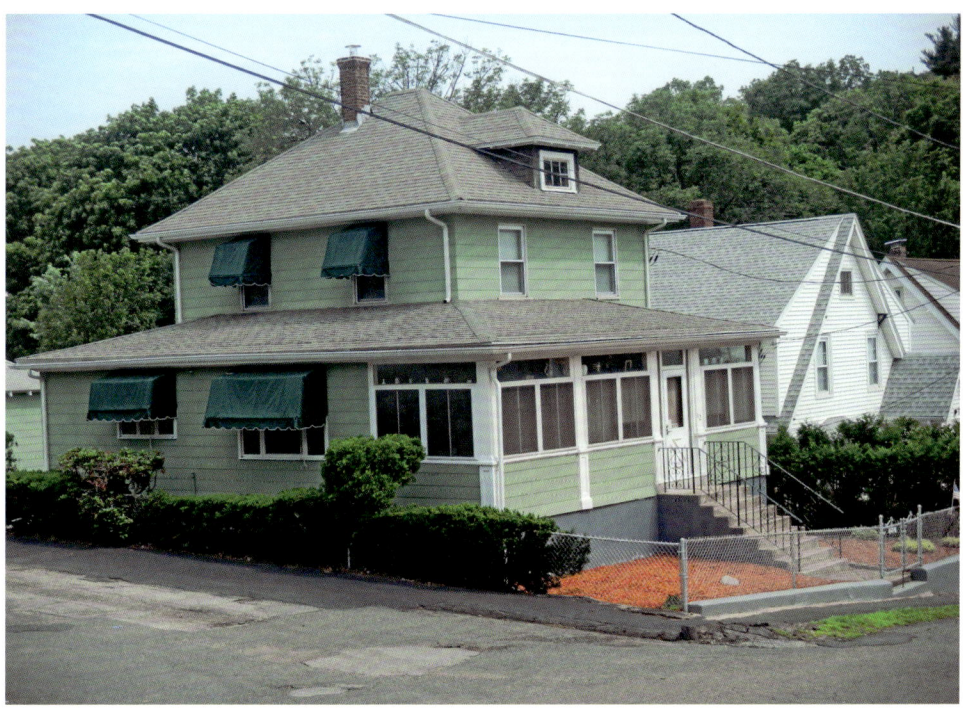

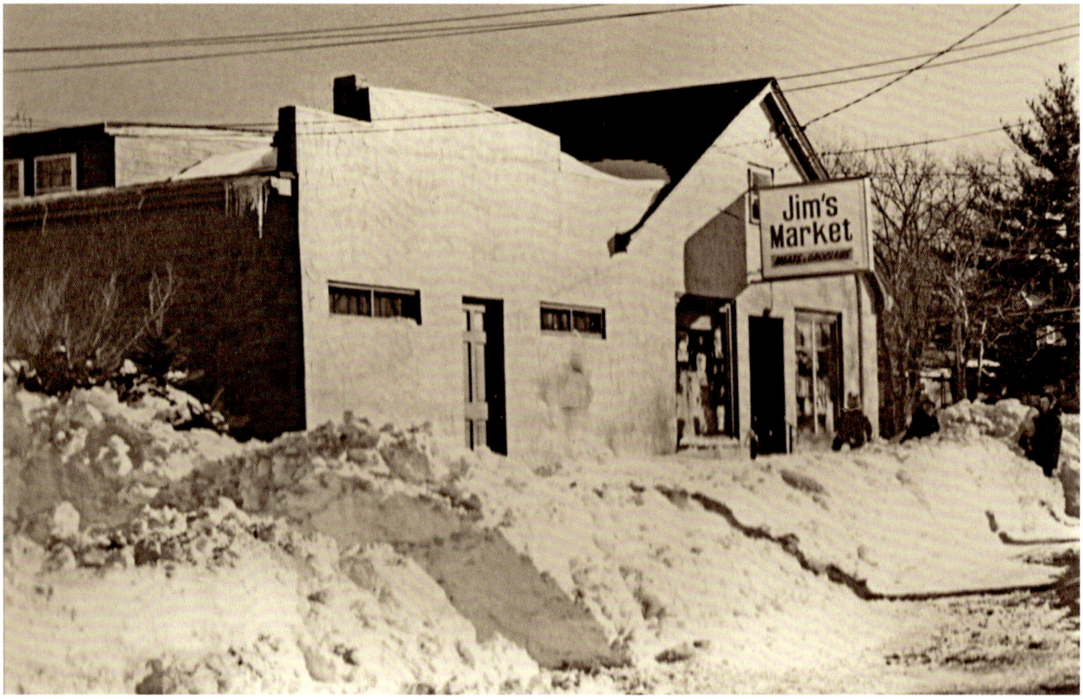

JIM'S MARKET: Like all of Medford's neighborhoods, Fulton Heights has its favorite places. Jim's Market at 463 Fulton Street is a neighborhood institution. The store is seen here during the blizzard of 1978 and in calmer weather in 2015. Jim's B-Boy sandwich of fried egg, ham and two slices of cheese, all grilled in a sub roll, is legendary in the history of Medford cuisine.

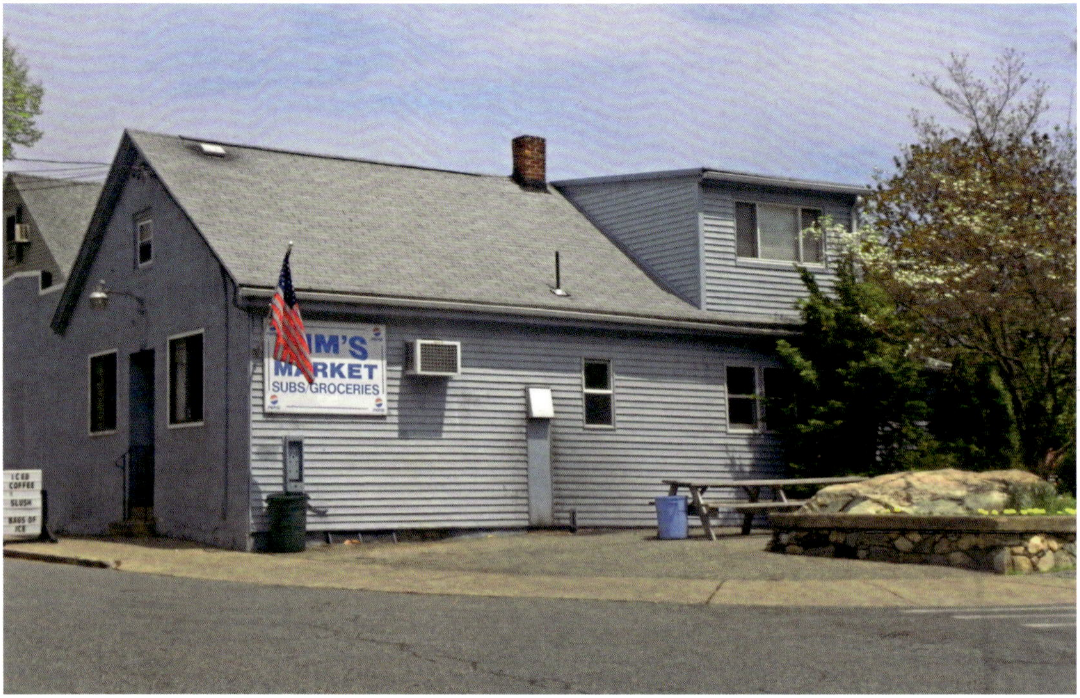

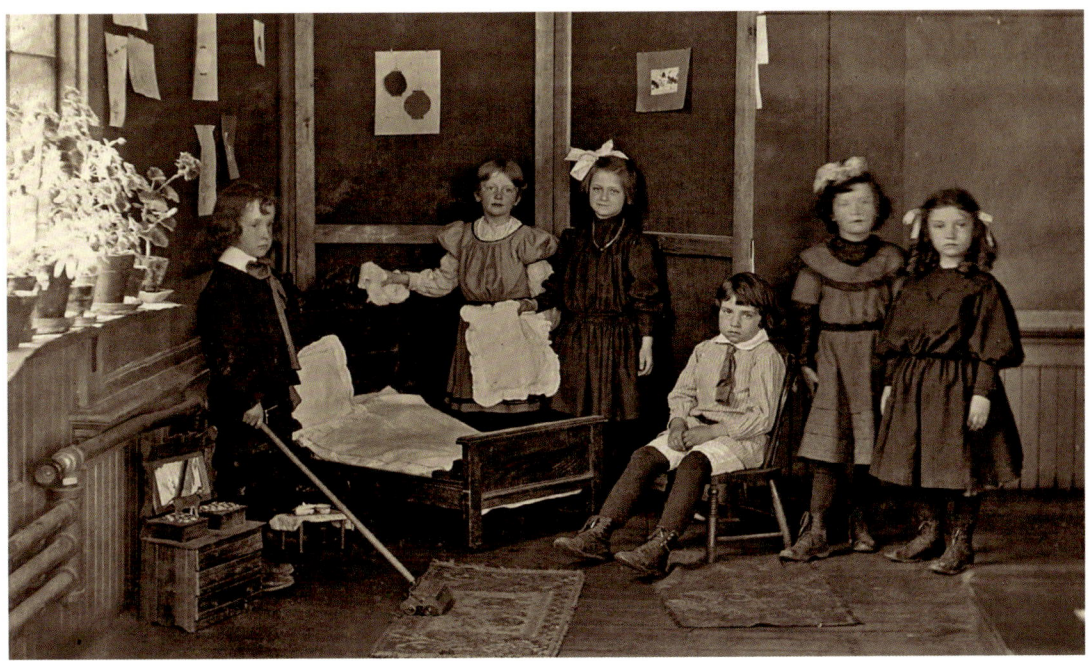

SCHOOL DAYS: Medford schools have educated generations of children. The Tufts School was built in 1868 at the junction of Main and Medford Streets and named after George E. Tufts who donated the land. The brick Davenport School was built in 1926, and named for George A Davenport had been a member of the school committee and was also a photographer. The teacher in the Davenport photo is Anne Theroux, mother of authors Paul and Alexander Theroux.

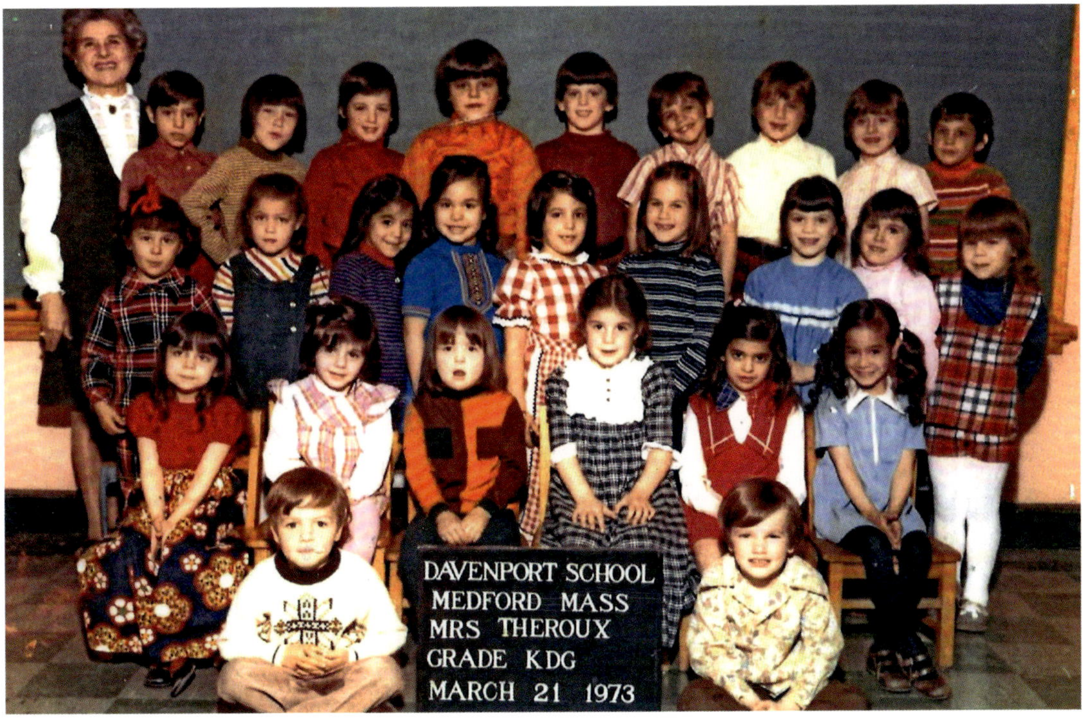

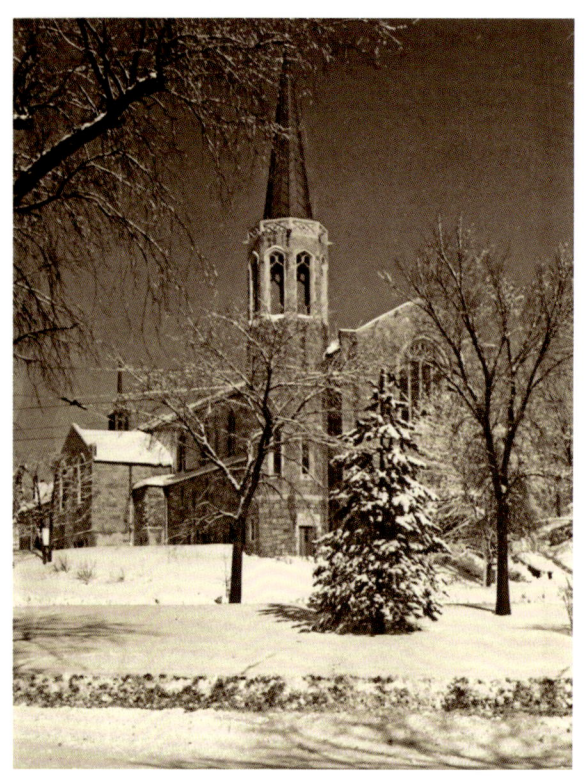

COMBINED PARISHES: St. Francis of Assisi Church began services in 1921 for the people in the North Medford area. St. Joseph's Parish moved into the former First Trinitarian Congregational church building on High Street in 1876. The current church was built a little further up the street in 1912. In the 2000s, the two parishes became a catholic parish collaborative and now share resources and personnel.

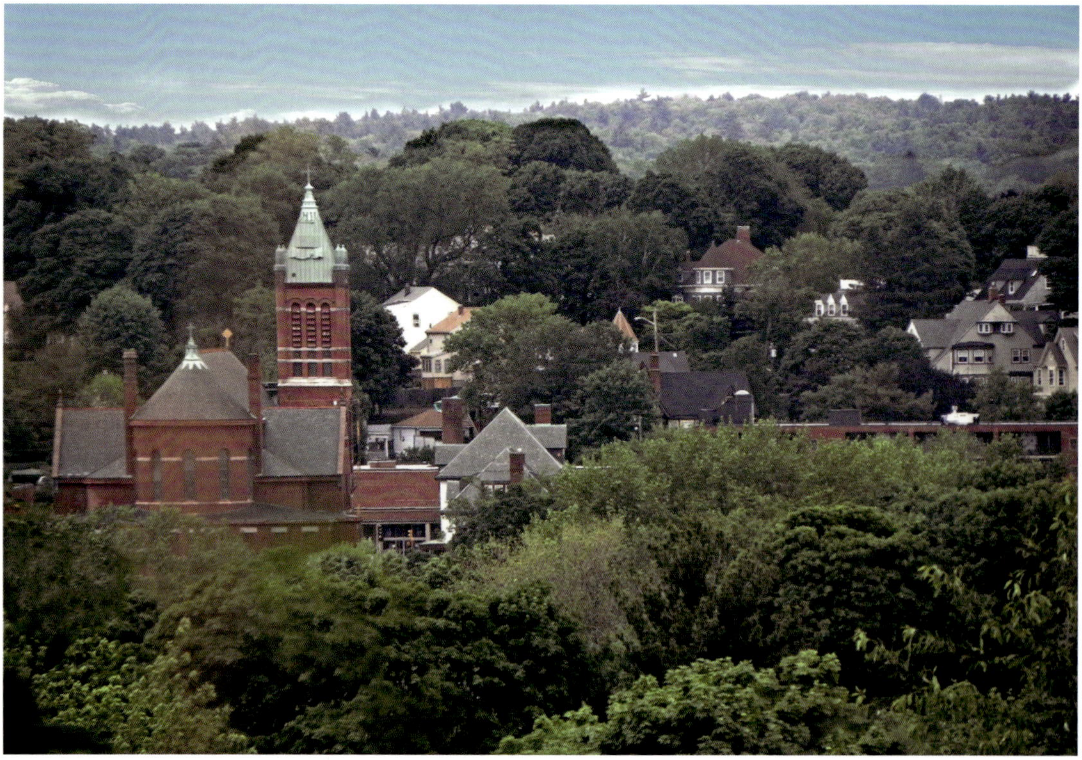

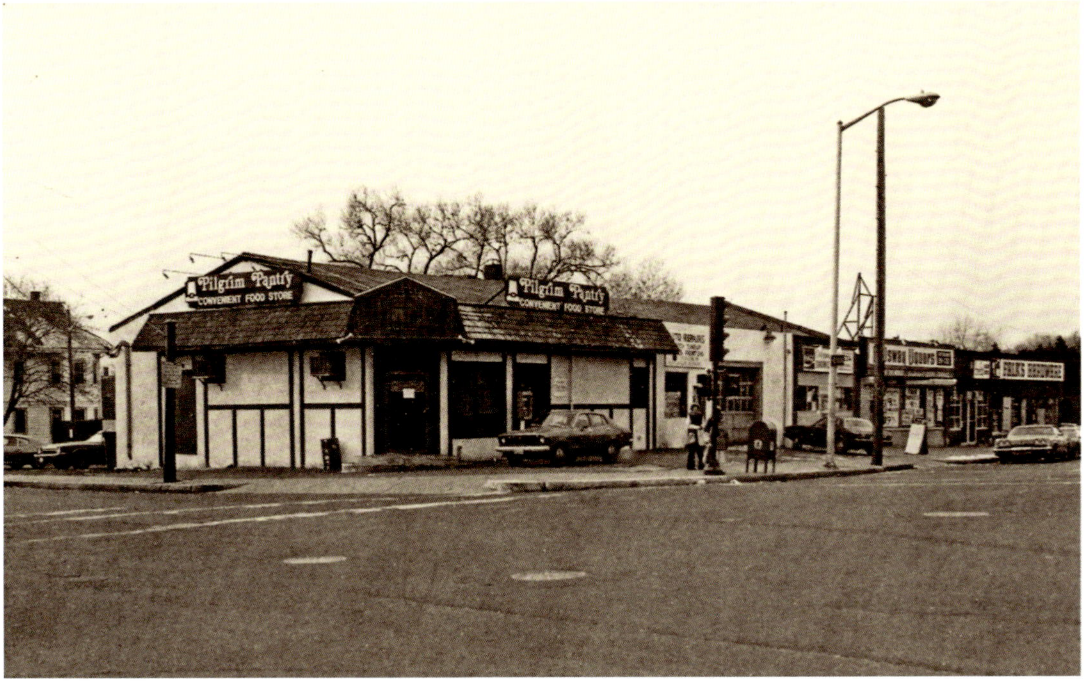

FULTON AND FELLSWAY: The Pilgrim Pantry convenience store was another Fulton Heights institution. Pilgrim Pantry was preceded by Macy's Corner and both corner stores served Town Line donuts. It was tradition for families to cross the street from St. Francis Church after mass on Sundays to snag a dozen donuts and the Sunday paper. The Maple Park Condos were built in 1987 on the site where the Pilgrim Pantry once stood.

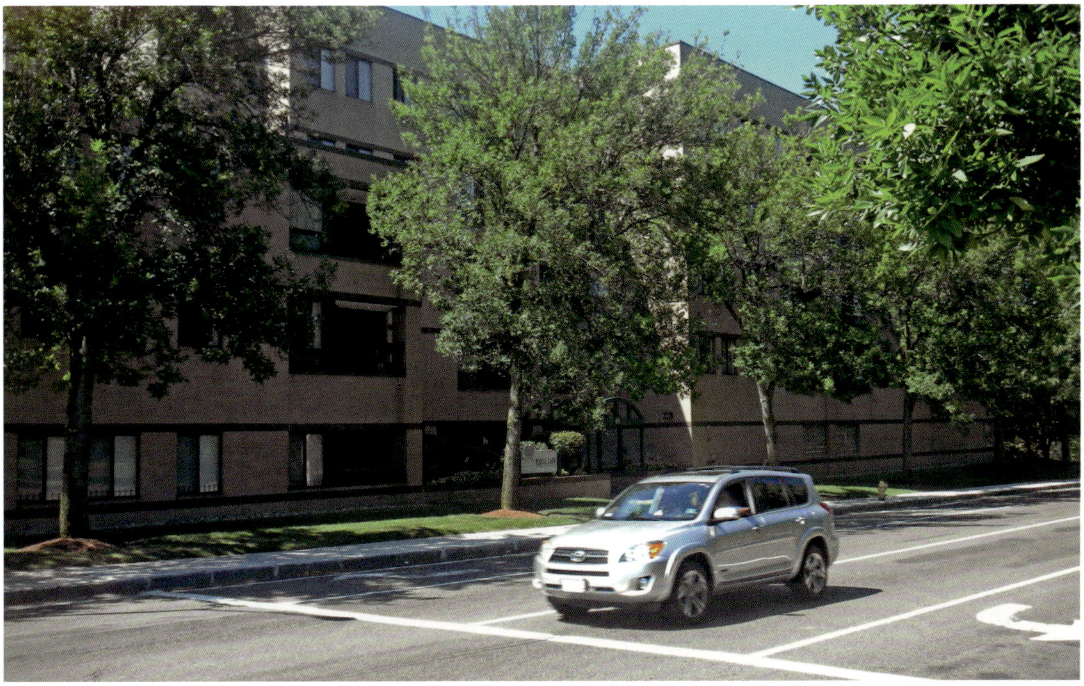

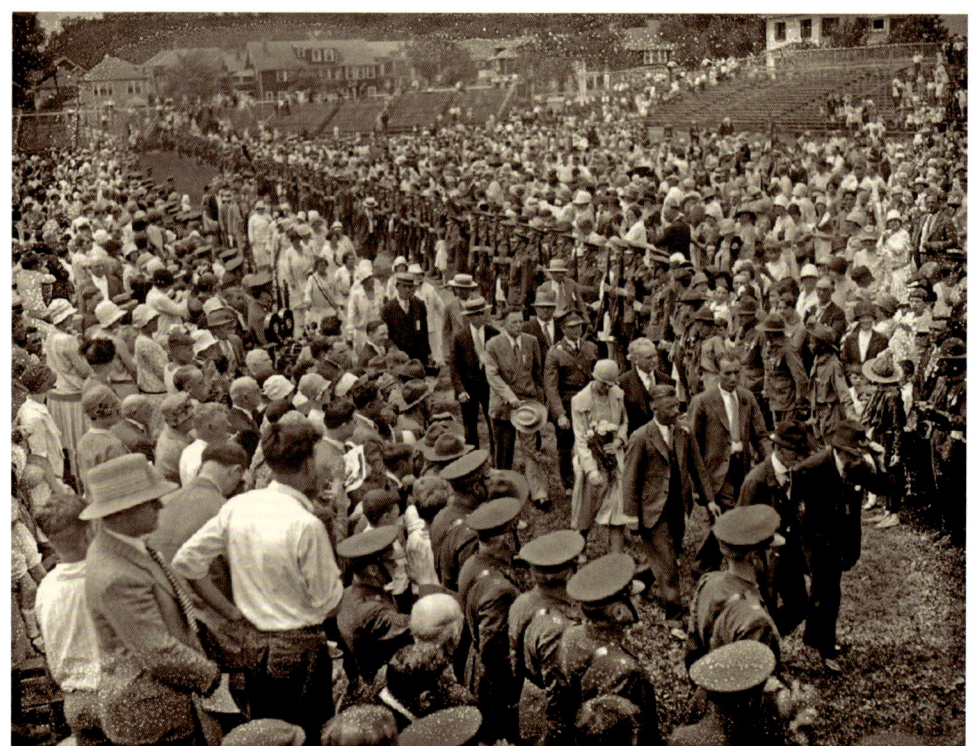

CROWDS: Thousands of people gathered to greet Amelia Earhart during the celebration of her Friendship Flight in 1928. The celebration took place on the Fulton Street Football field which is now known as Gillis Park. In 2013 another great crowd gathered in Medford Square in an attempt to break the Guinness Book of World Records' mark for the most people caroling in Santa hats.

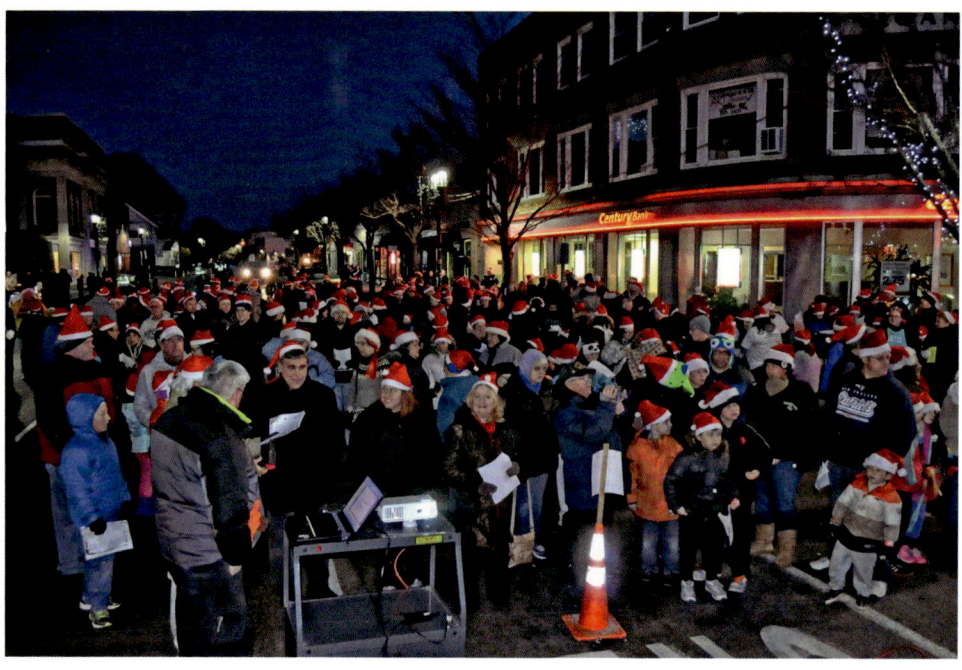

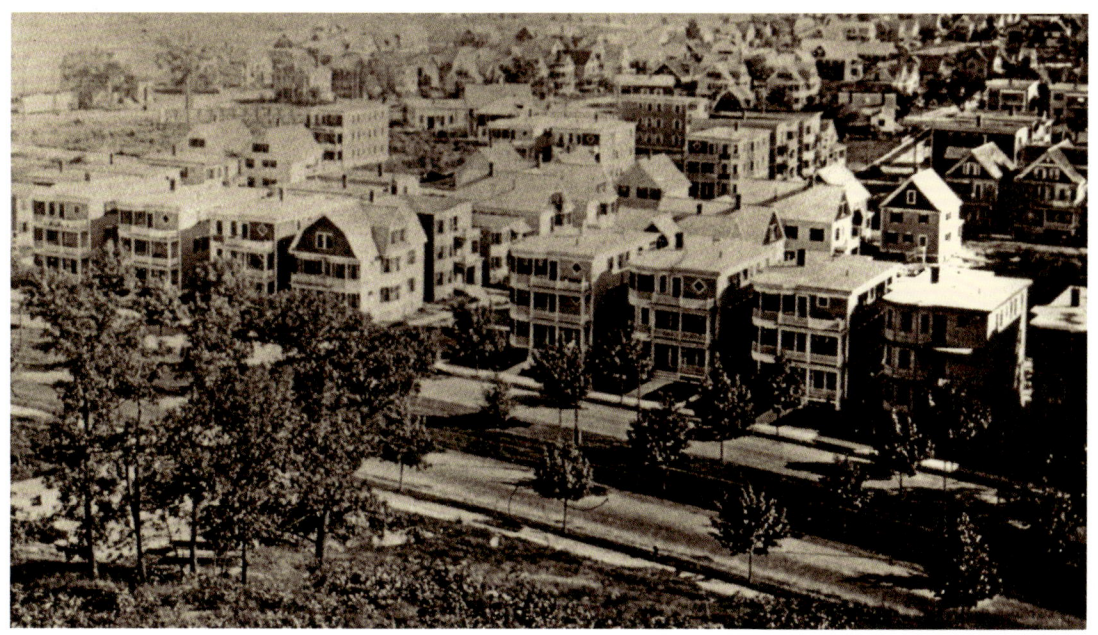

FELLSWAY TRIPLE-DECKERS: During the early twentieth century, tens of thousands of triple-deckers were constructed in New England, as an economical means of housing the thousands of newly arrived immigrant workers. They were regarded as more livable than their brick and stone tenement and row house counterparts, as they allowed for airflow and light on all four sides of each building. Many of the Fellsway triple-deckers seen here were built by John Walker, Jr.

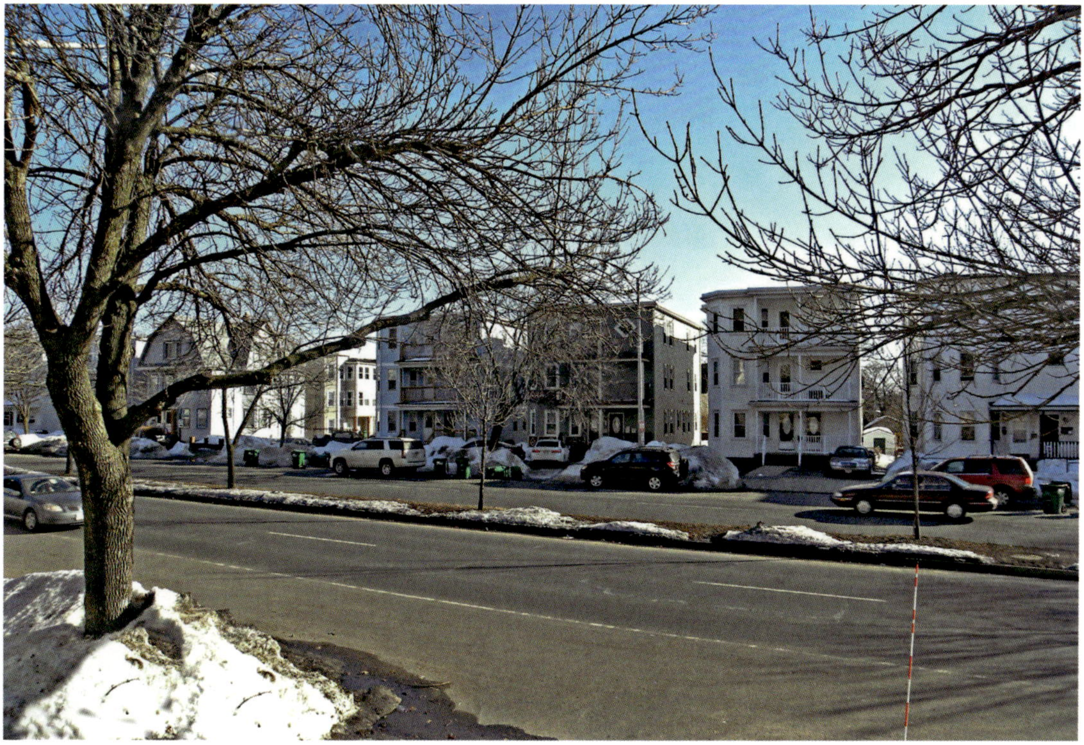

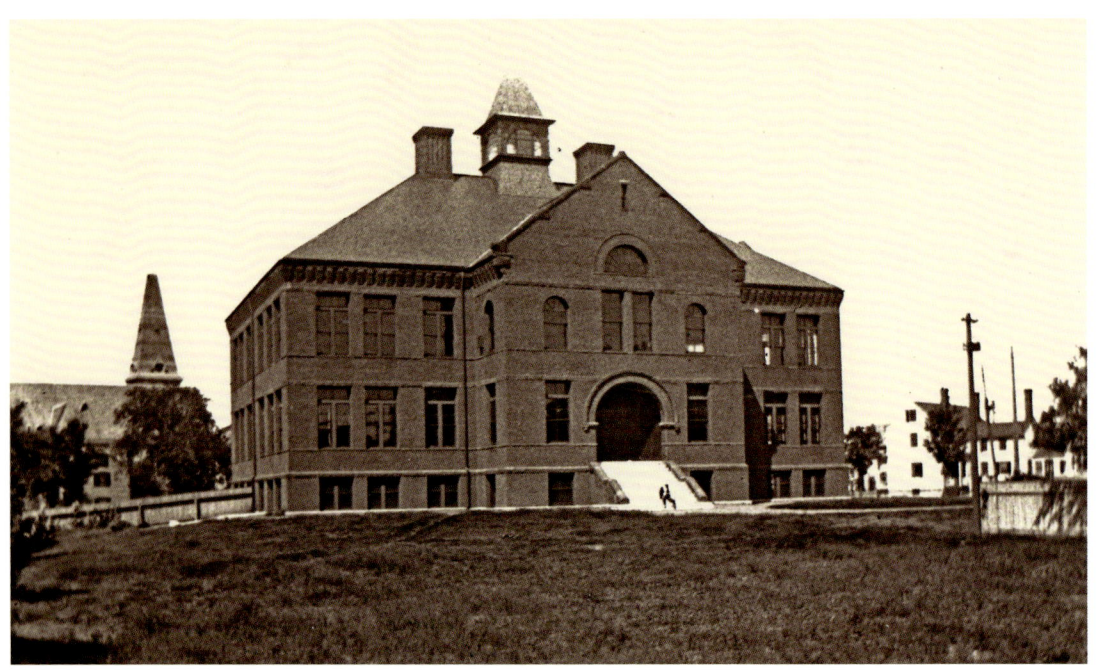

WASHINGTON SCHOOL: Built in 1890, the George Washington School at Cross and Washington was the first Medford school made of brick. The building had six class rooms and an assembly hall. The town loved the new school and considered the brick building a major advancement in school planning. The Medford-Malden Lodge of Elks was constructed near the site in the 1960s after the school was demolished.

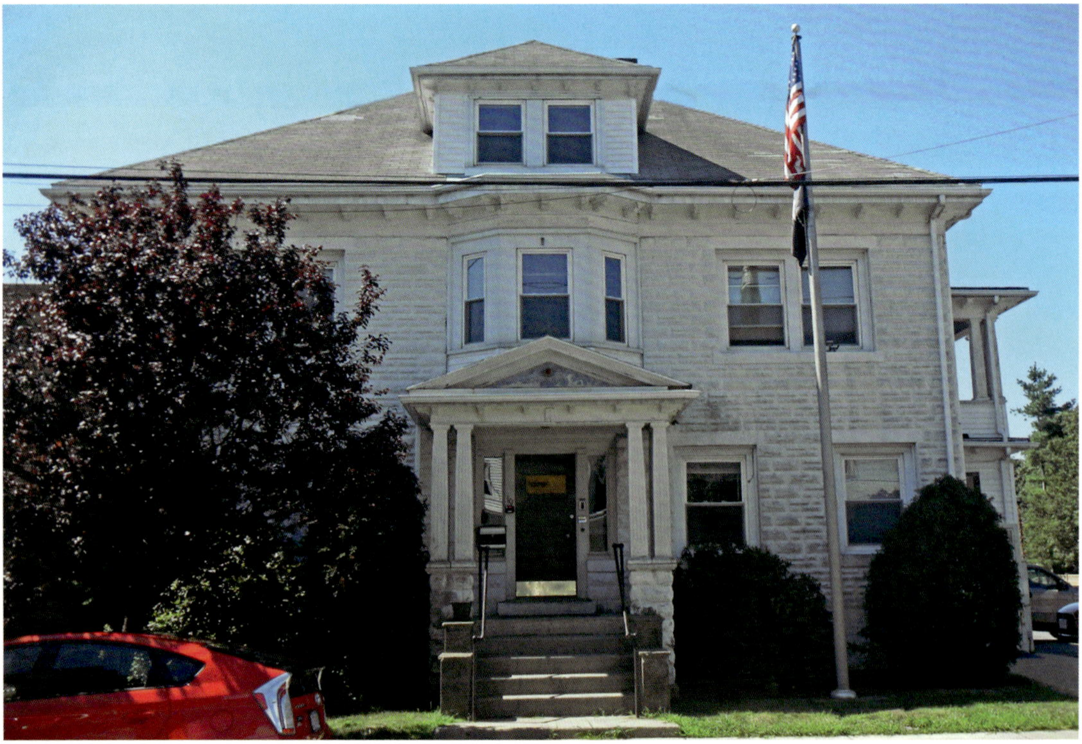

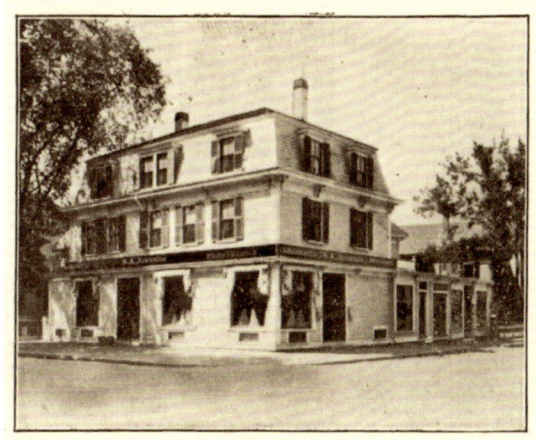

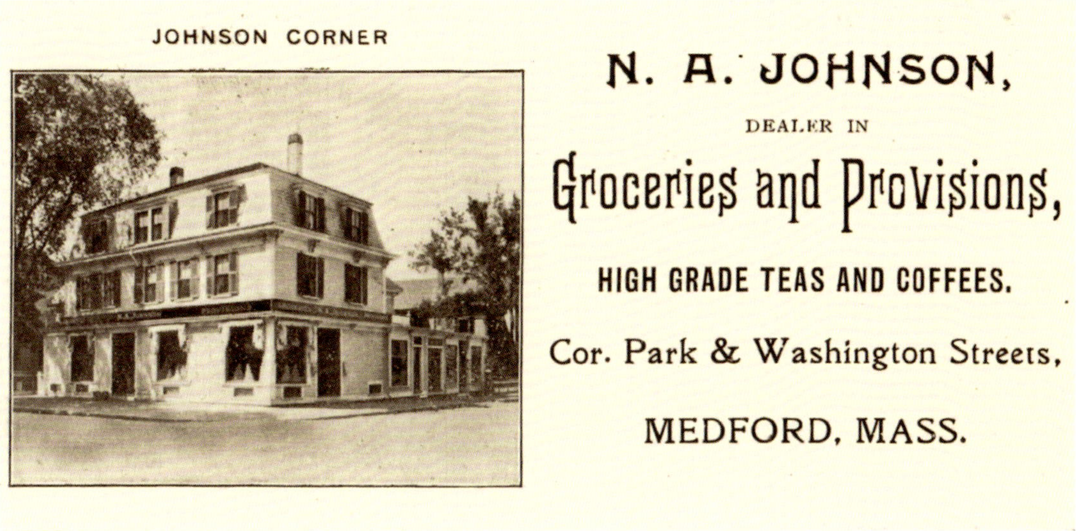

JOHNSON GROCERY: Every Medford neighborhood had its own corner store. N. A. Johnson's grocery supplied the Washington Street area in the 1920s and 1930s. The store was run by Nathan Johnson and his wife Julia who lived upstairs. Today the building look very much as it did when it was constructed in 1901. It is currently a residential property with a number of apartments.

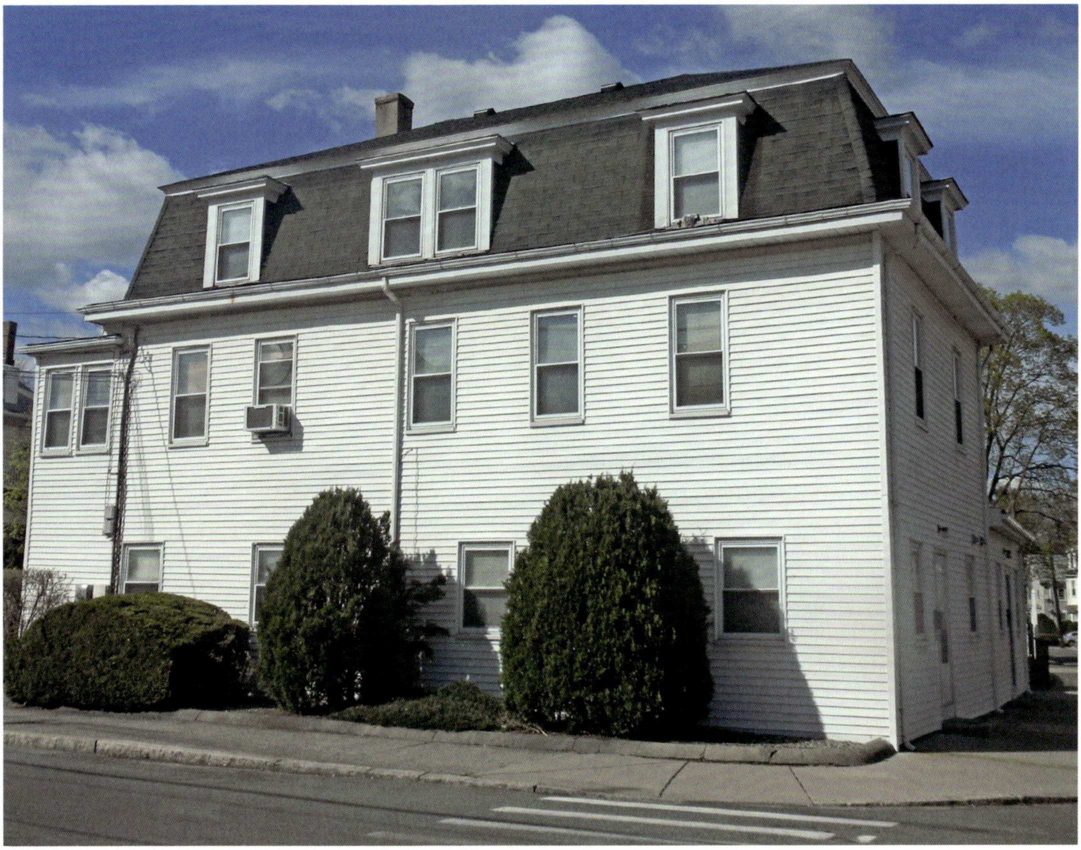

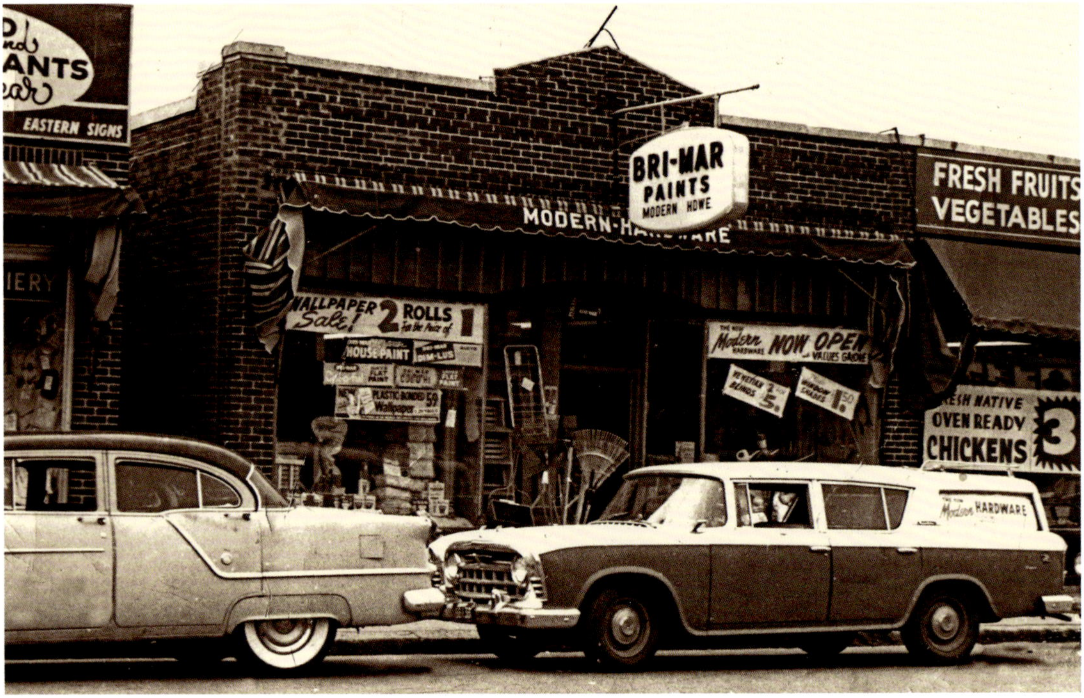

HAINES SQUARE: Each of Medford's neighborhoods had its own business area. Haines Square, at the junction of Salem, Lambert, and Spring Streets offered a mix of local and national businesses. Modern Hardware has made Haines Square its home since 1961. In 1925, the Square was named after Civil War Sergeant Samuel Stevens, but was later renamed in honor of Mayor Benjamin Haines.

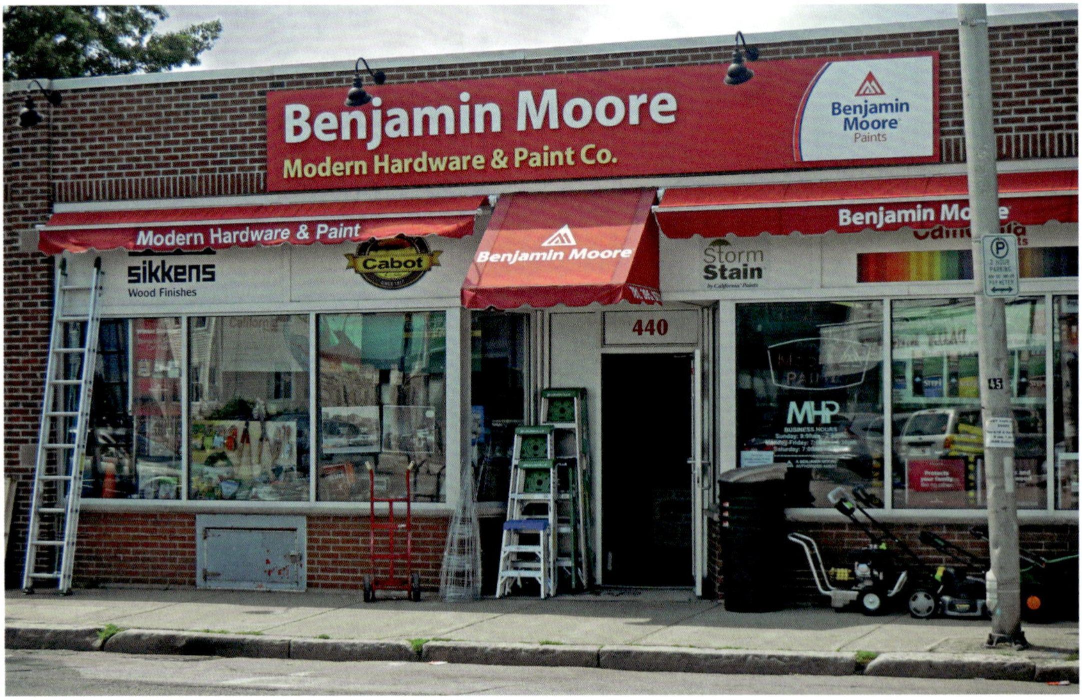

84

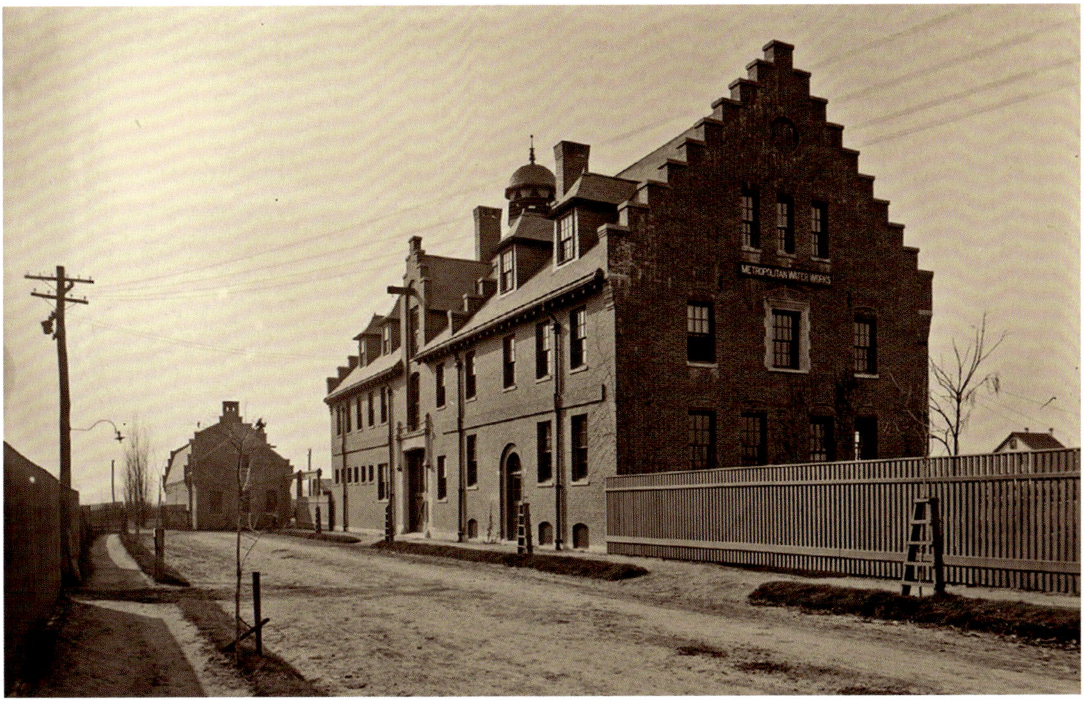

GLENWOOD PUMP HOUSE: Built in 1900, this elegant building was part of the Pipe Distribution Department of the Massachusetts Water Resources Authority. The Glenwood building was headquarters of the northern district of the MWRA. Medford began using Spot Pond for water in the 1870s but became part of the larger MWRA system in the 1890s. Today the pump house is used for living space.

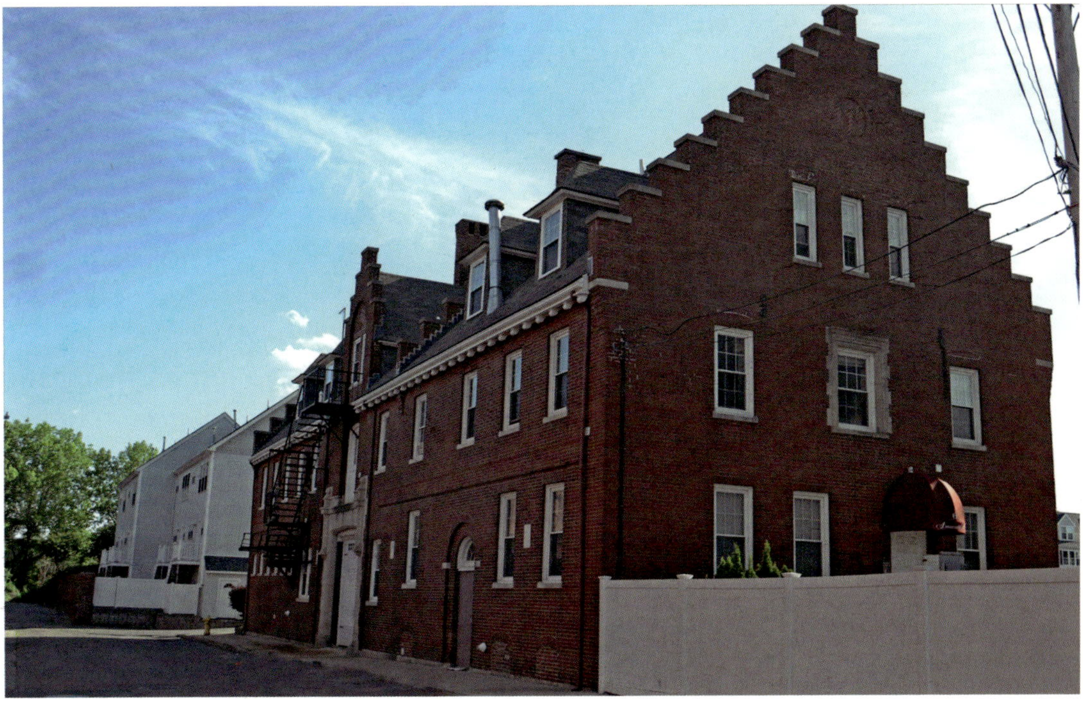

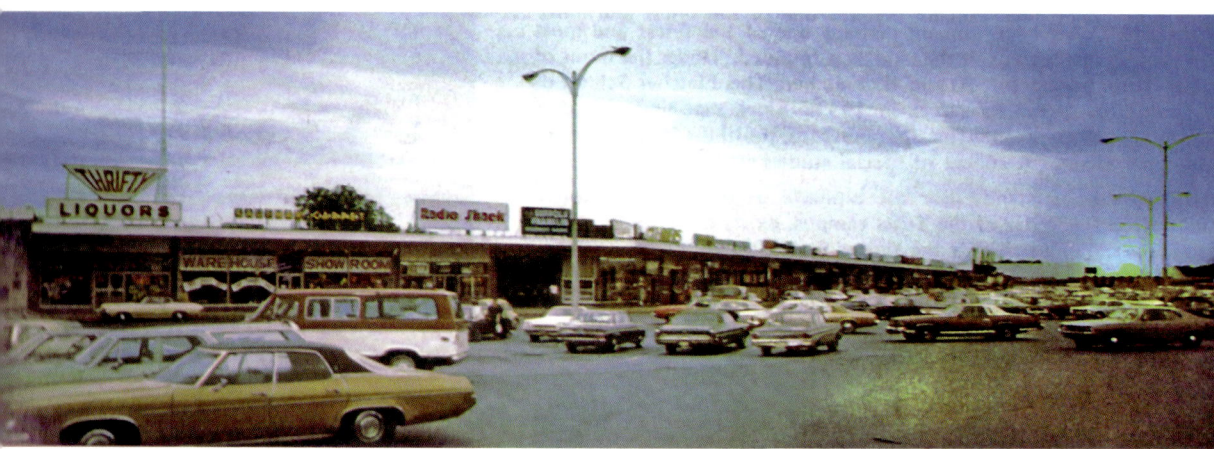

WELLINGTON STORES: Before everyone had a car, Medford's shopping areas were designed for foot traffic. In the mid-twentieth century, however, retail architecture began to be designed with automobiles in mind. Many Medford businesses moved out of the local squares to strip malls like this one in Wellington.

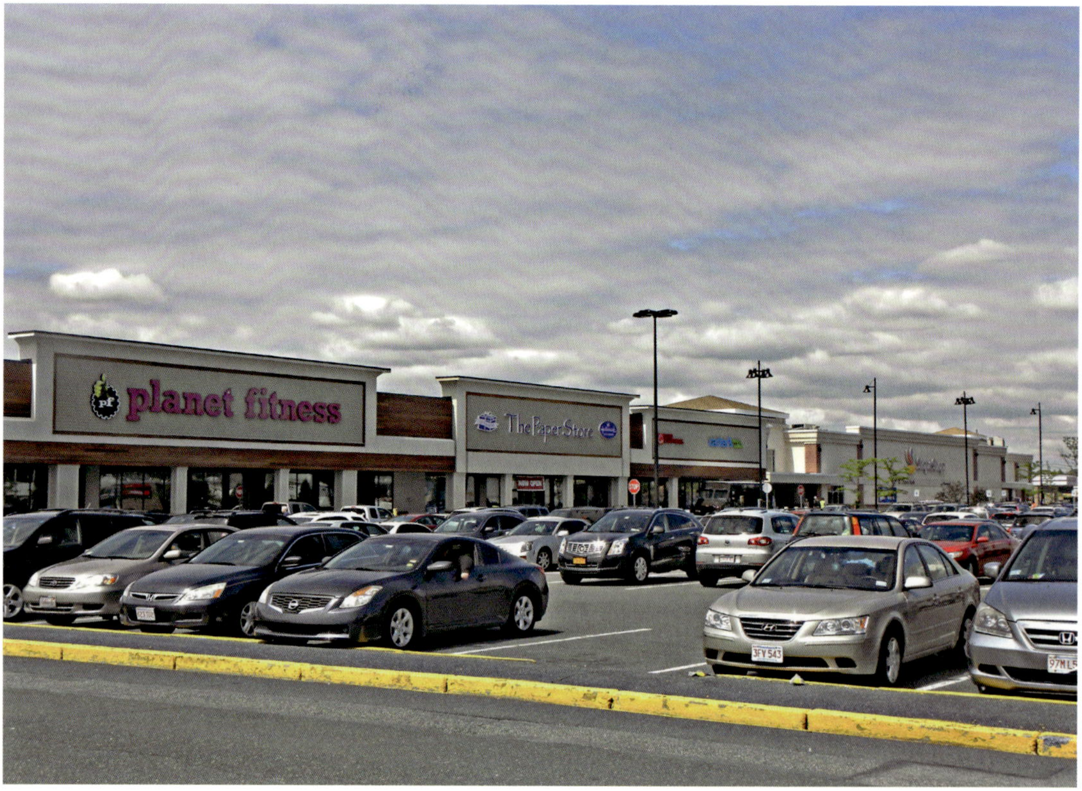

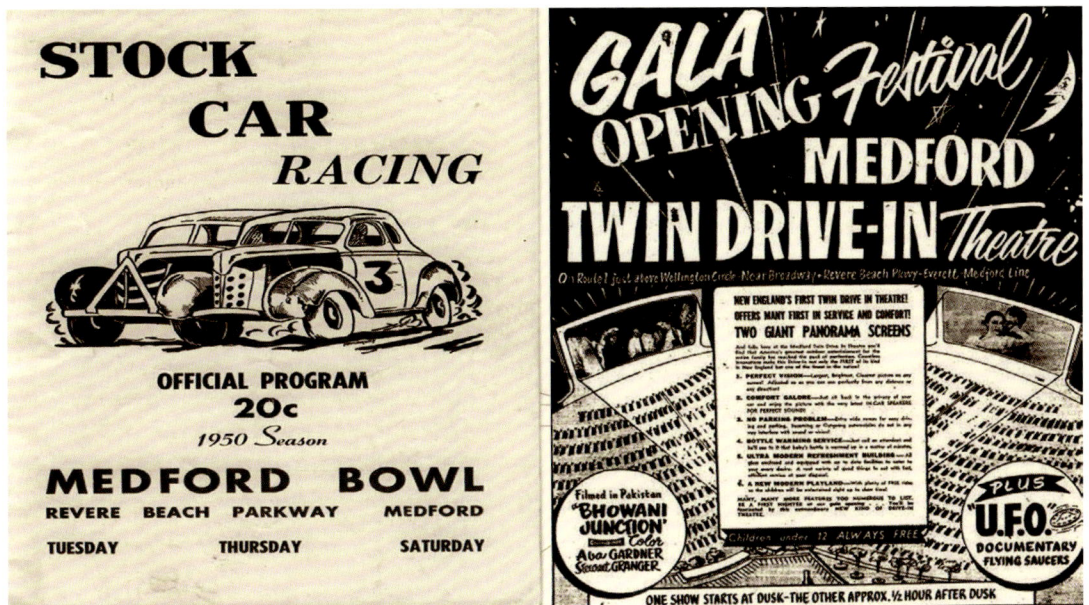

TWIN DRIVE-IN: The Medford Twin Drive In on Revere Beach Boulevard had its grand opening on July 21, 1956 with thousands flocking to see the first twin open-air movie theater in New England. Before the drive-in was constructed the space was a stock car racetrack. Owned by Lloyd Clark, Winthrop Knox, Jr. and George Hackett, the theatre had two separate screens and a car capacity of 900 on each side.

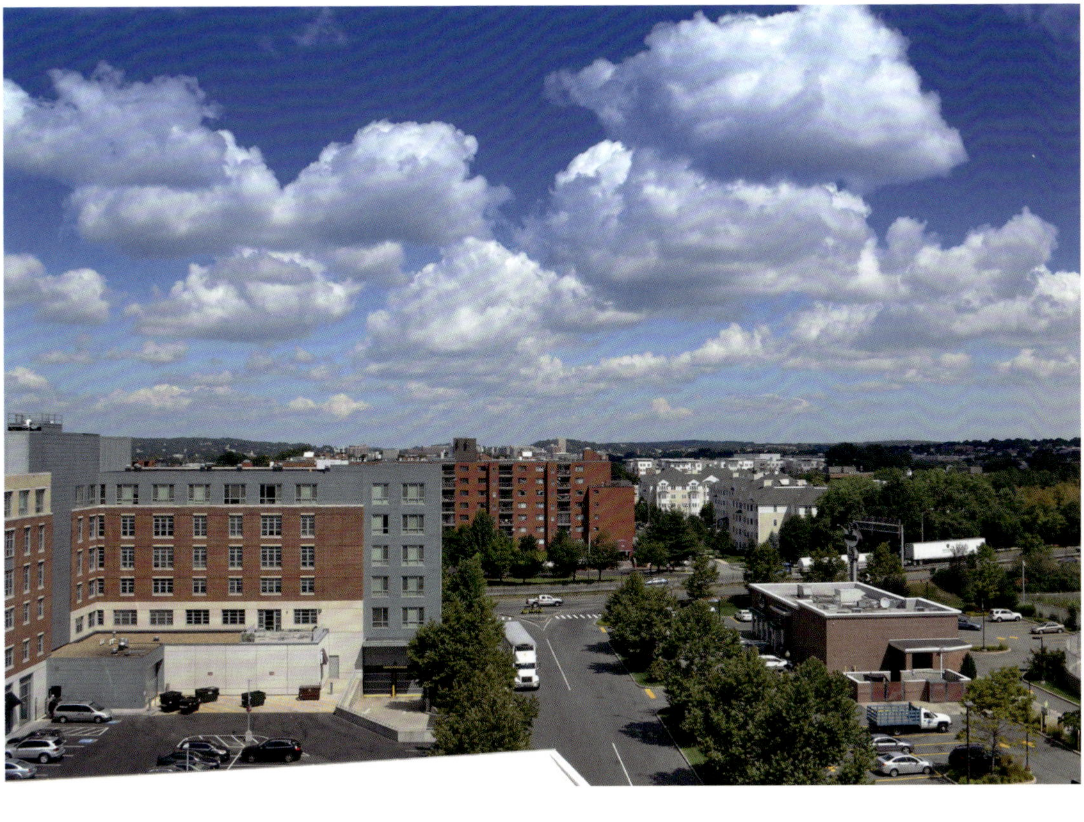

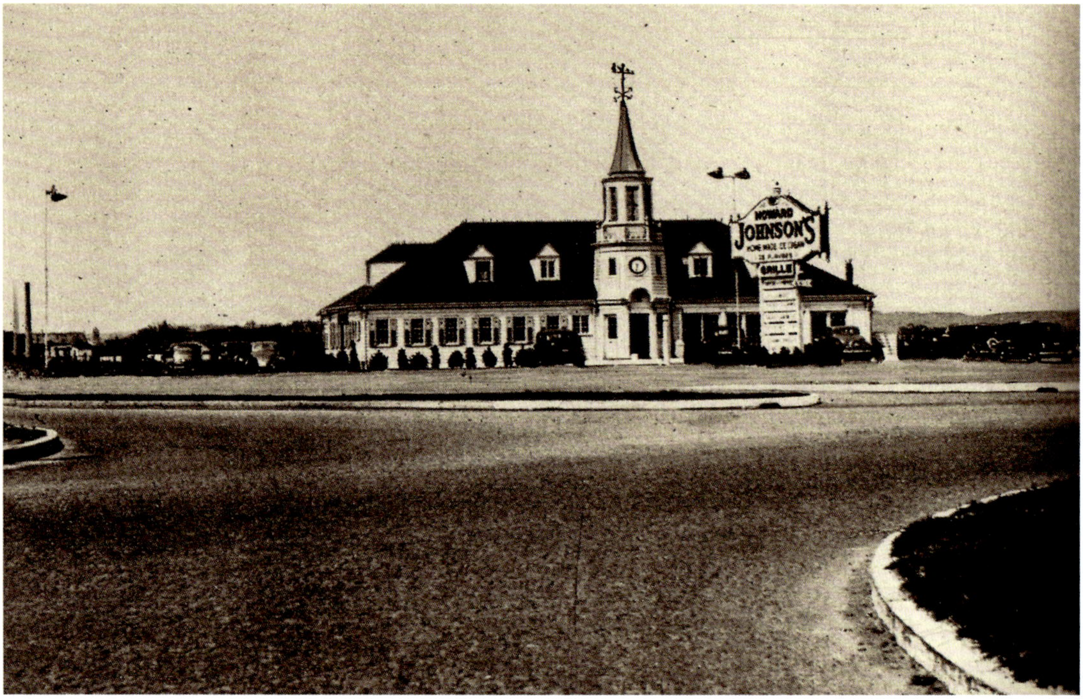

HOWARD JOHNSONS: Medford's Wellington Circle was home to the familiar orange-roofed Howard Johnson's for over sixty years. The original restaurant seen here was built in 1937 and was a popular destination for several Medford generations. The 1937 building was destroyed by fire in the late 1970s but the rebuilt HoJo's served customers until it closed in 1998. CVS now stands on the site in 2015.

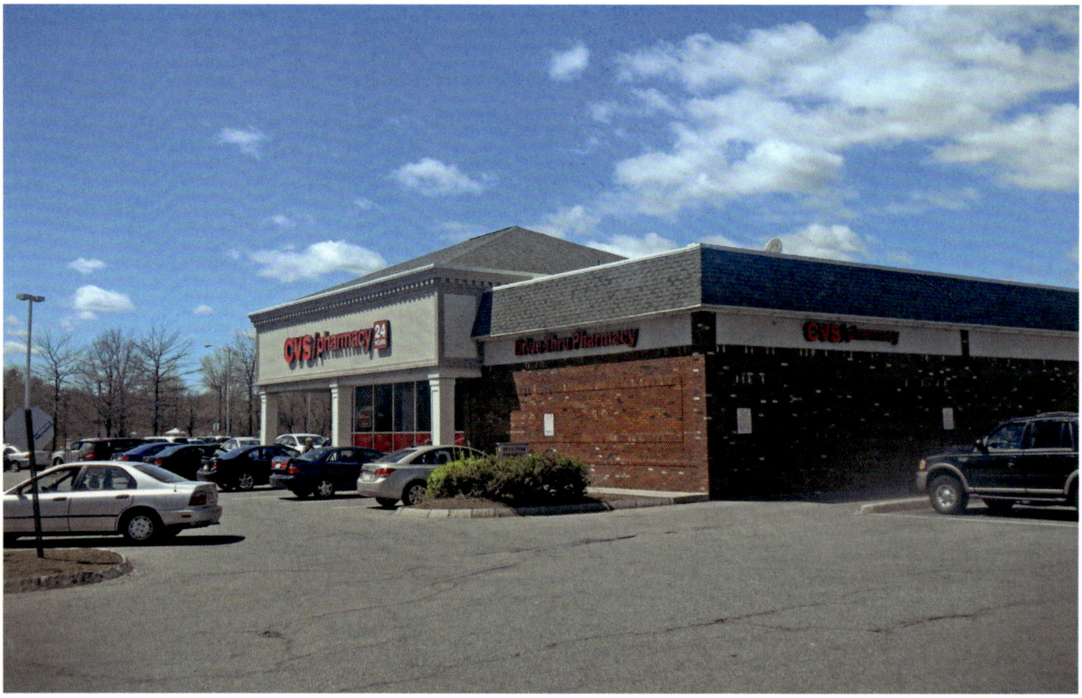

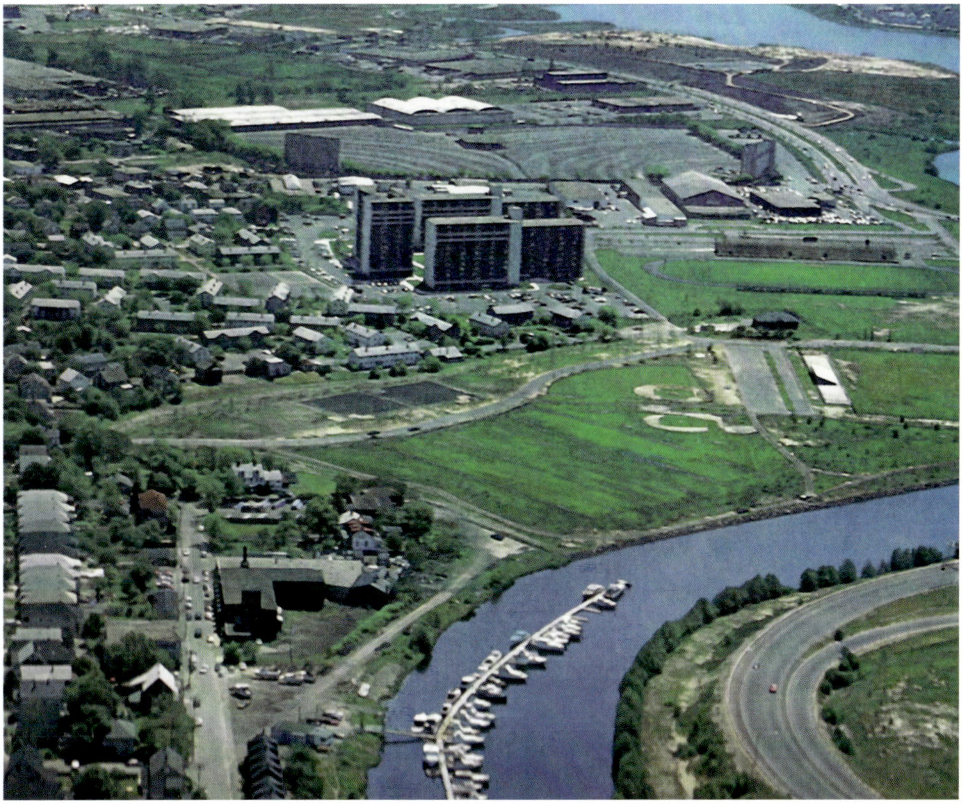

MEADOW GLEN DRIVE-IN: Medford's first drive-in movie theater, The Meadow Glen Drive-in, opened in 1949. The drive-in can be seen at the center left of this aerial view. The drive-in featured two screens, a sixty foot cafeteria bar and a fifty foot snack bar. The drive-in was demolished in the 1970s and the Meadow Glen Mall was constructed on the site.

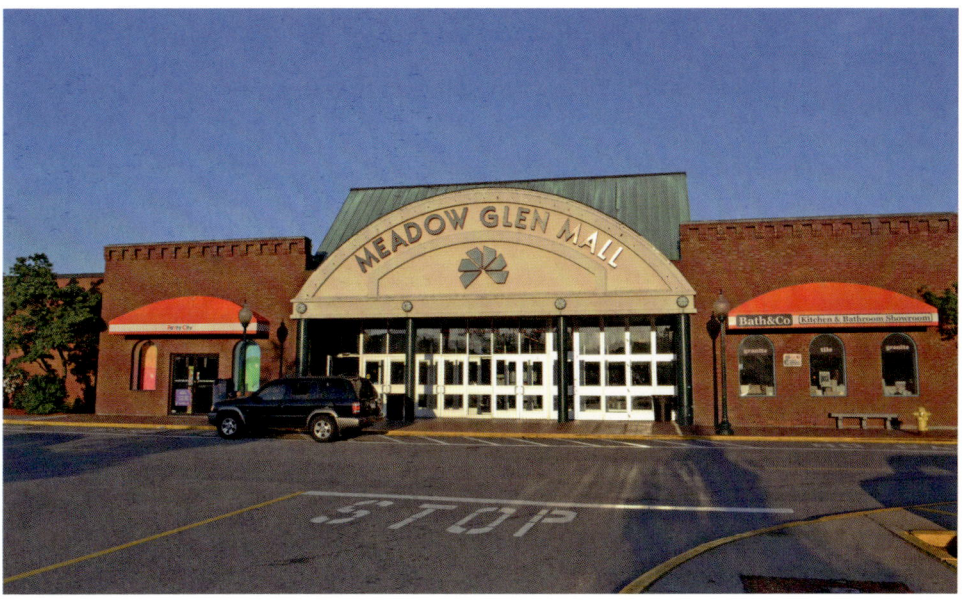

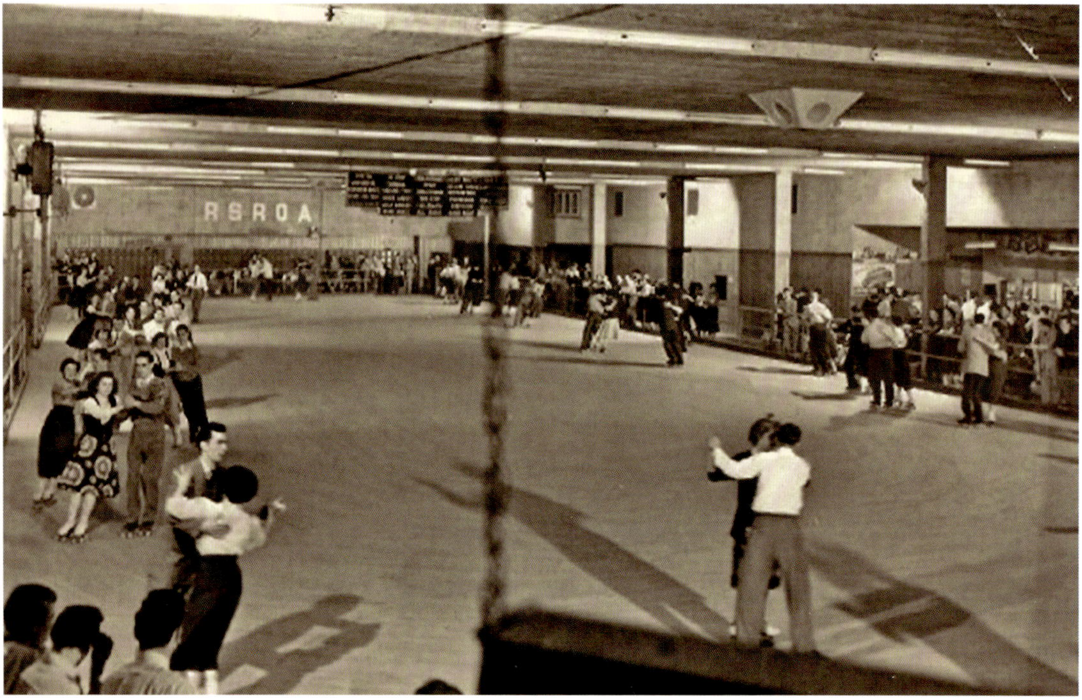

BAL-A-ROUE: Everyone has a memory of the Bal-A-Roue Rollaway. Medford's roller skating rink opened in 1940, just in time for wartime romances. In the decades that followed the rink was the site of countless dates, skating competitions, parties, and long teenage afternoons. The rink closed and was demolished in the 1980s. The Century Bank headquarters now stands on the site.

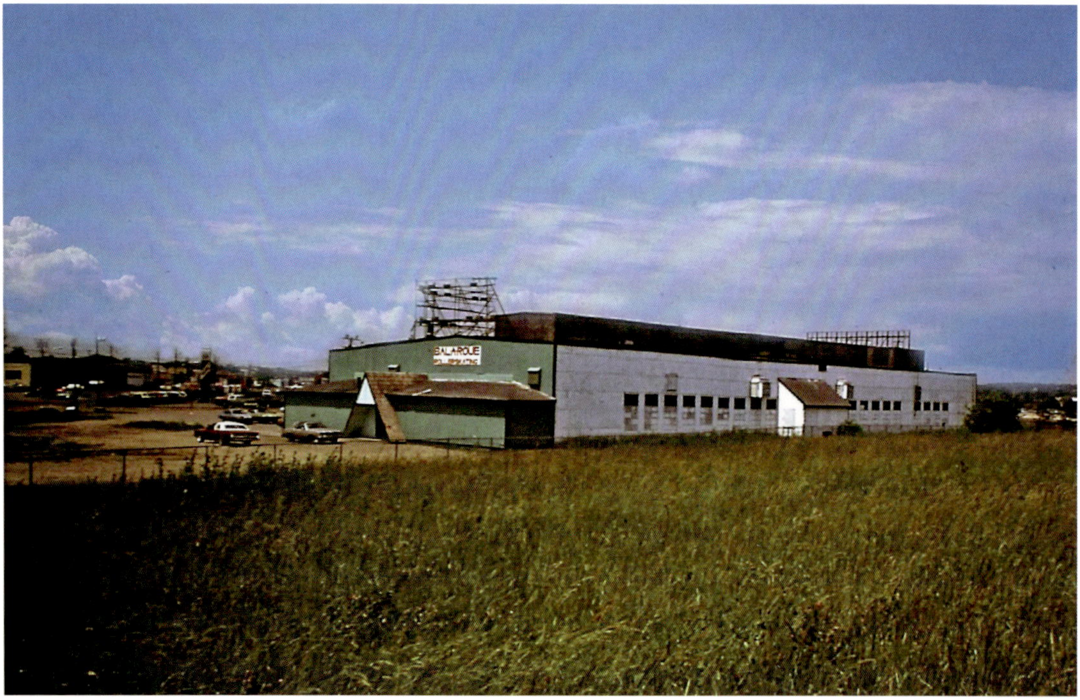

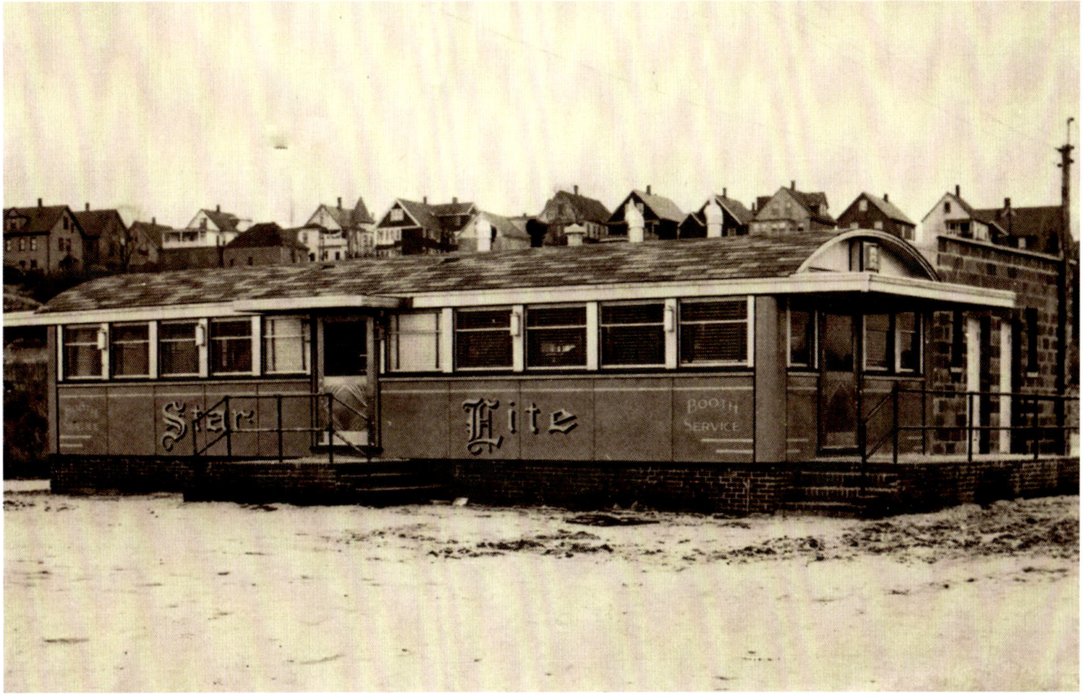

STARLITE DINER: There were several diners in Medford. The Star Lite Diner served customers on Mystic Avenue from the 1940s to the 1960s. The Star Lite was manufactured by the Worcester Lunch Car Company. The decline in popularity of diners is often attributed to the rise of fast food chains. Ironically, the site of the Star Lite is now the location of a Burger King.

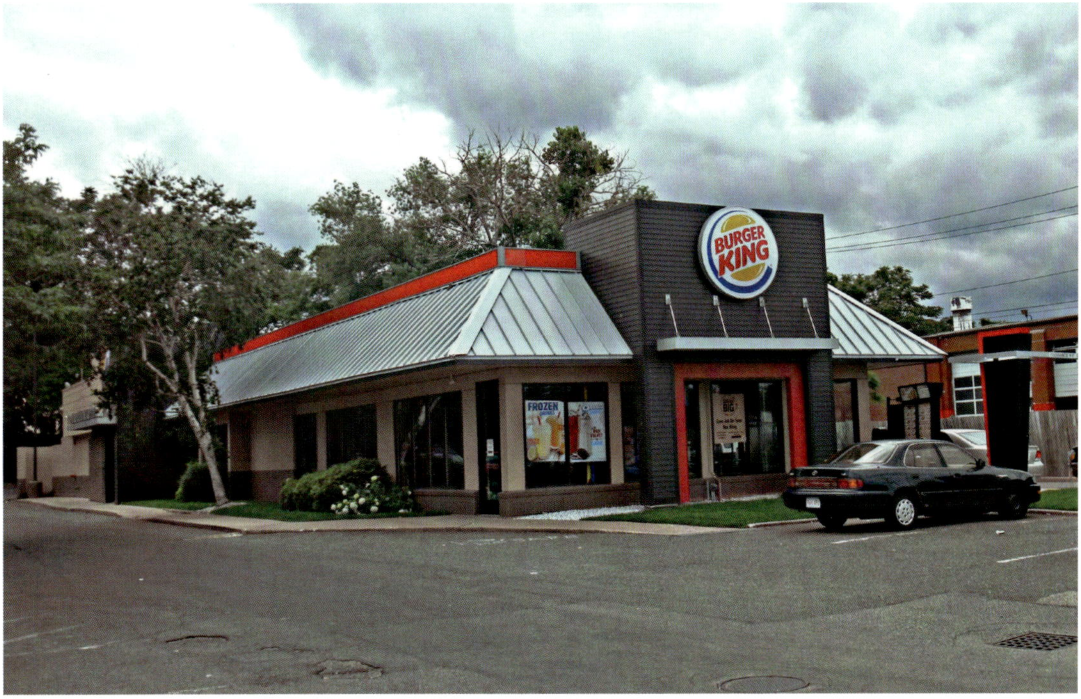

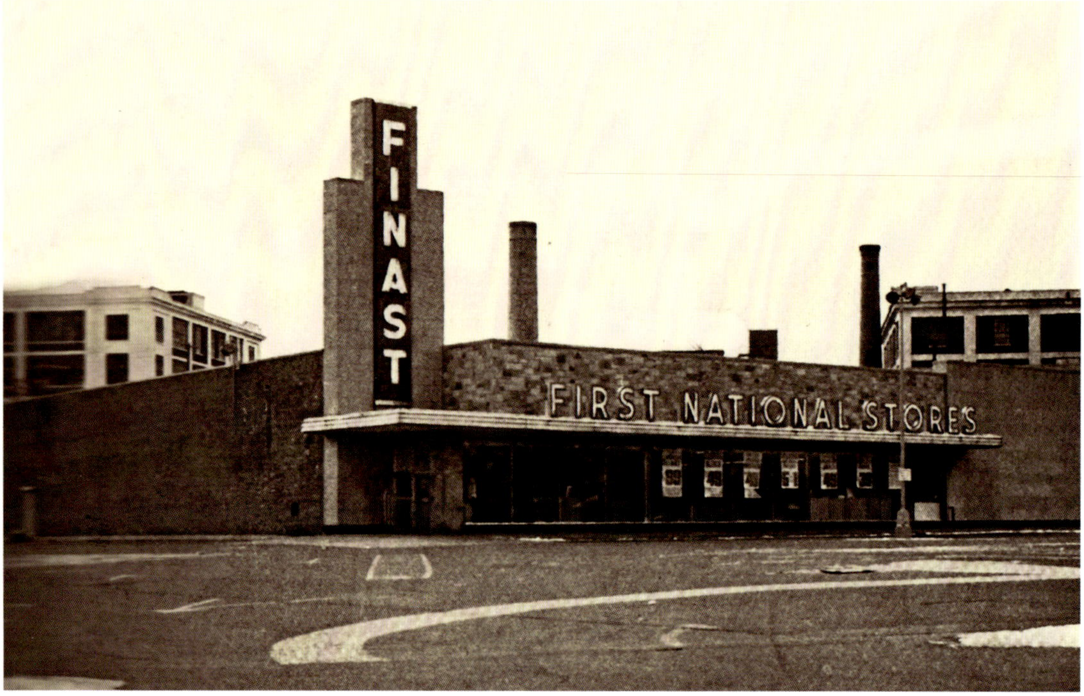

FIRST NATIONAL: It is fitting that Whole Foods now stands on the site of what was the First National Grocery store. First National (or Finast) was a major chain in the Northeast with headquarters in Somerville. There was another First National on High Street in West Medford Square. Today there are no longer any active Finast markets in operation in the US market, with most either being rebranded or closed.

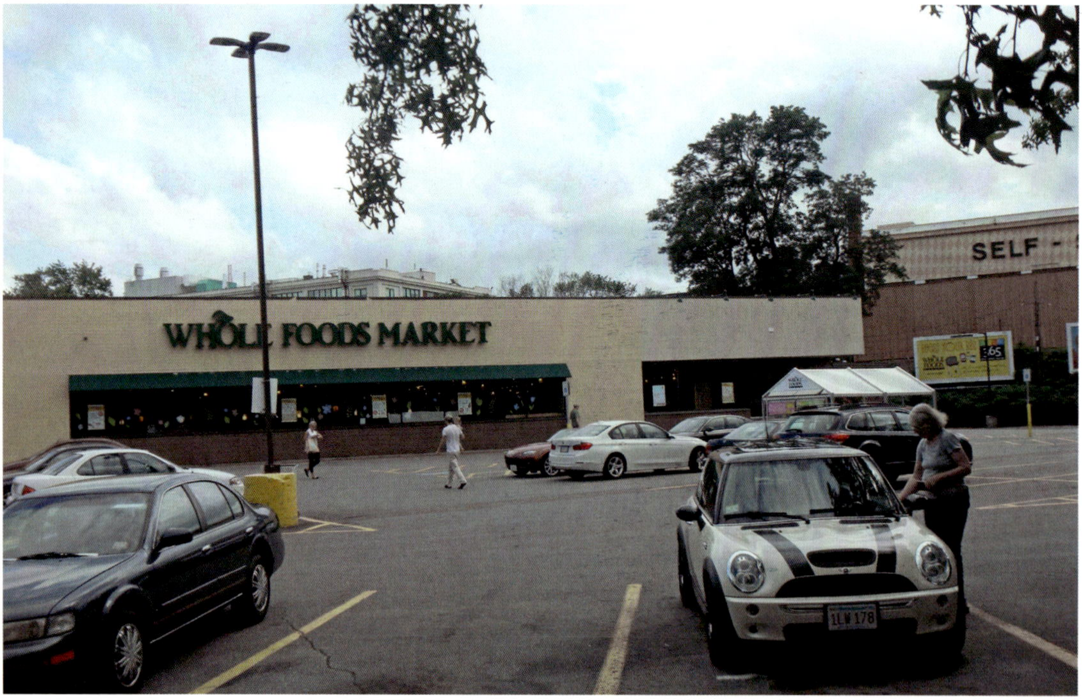

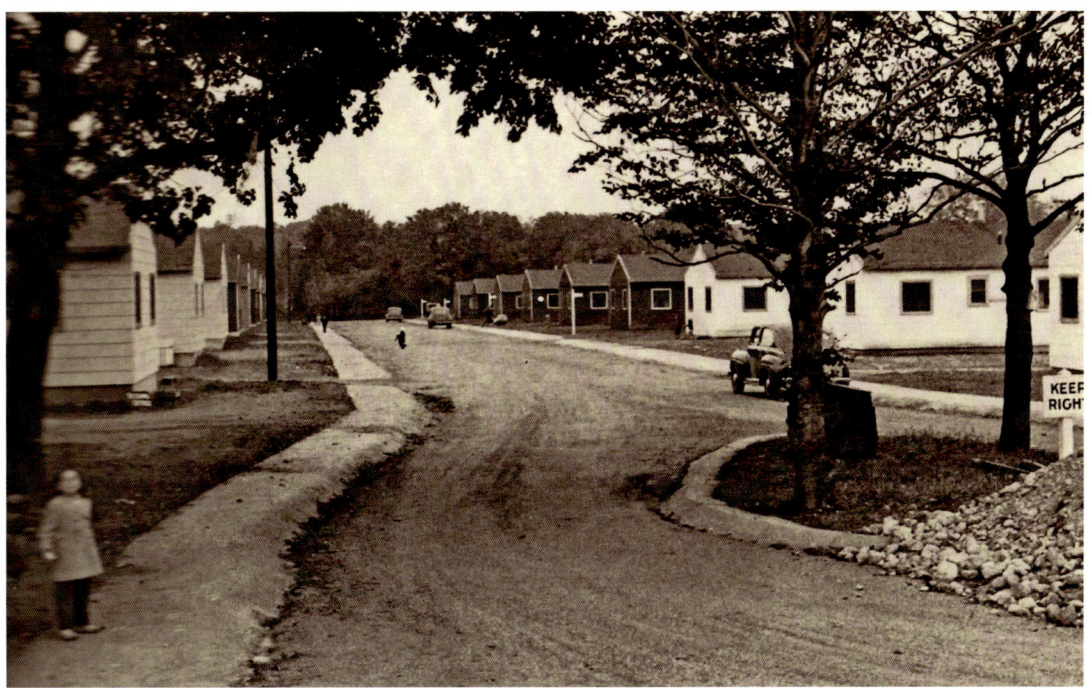

STEARNS VILLAGE: After World War II, a veteran's housing complex was built at Tufts for married students studying on the GI Bill. The "village" on College Avenue, was created out of a dozen prefab buildings that were formerly housing for United Aircraft employees Connecticut. The village was located on the site of the estate which had belonged to abolitionist George Luther Stearns. The site is now the Gantcher Family Sports and Convocation Center, next to Cousens Gym.

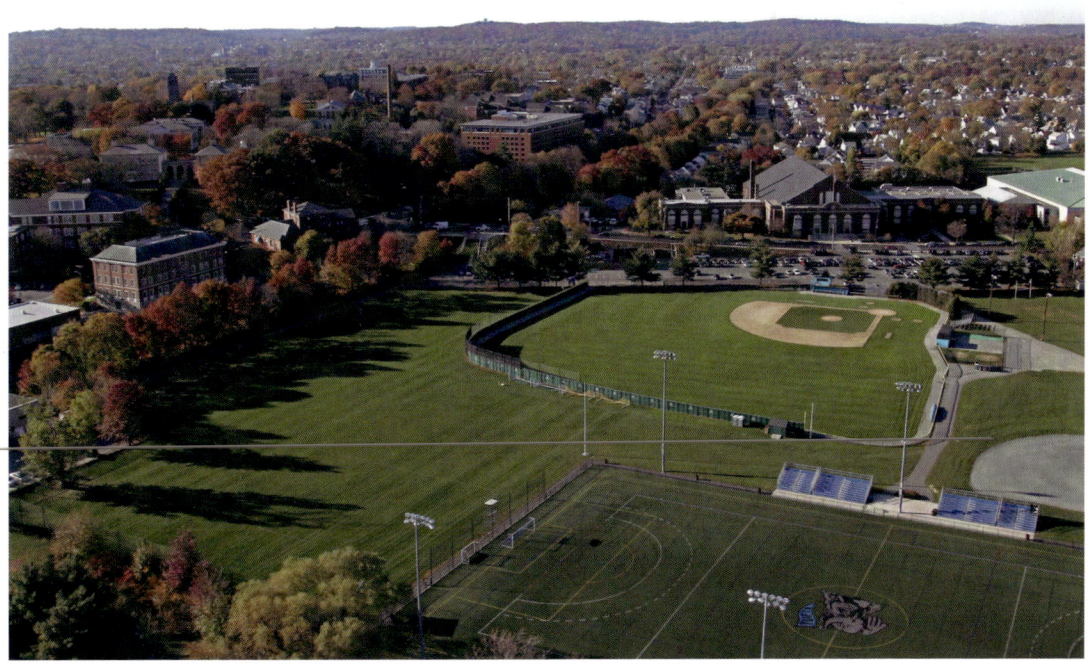

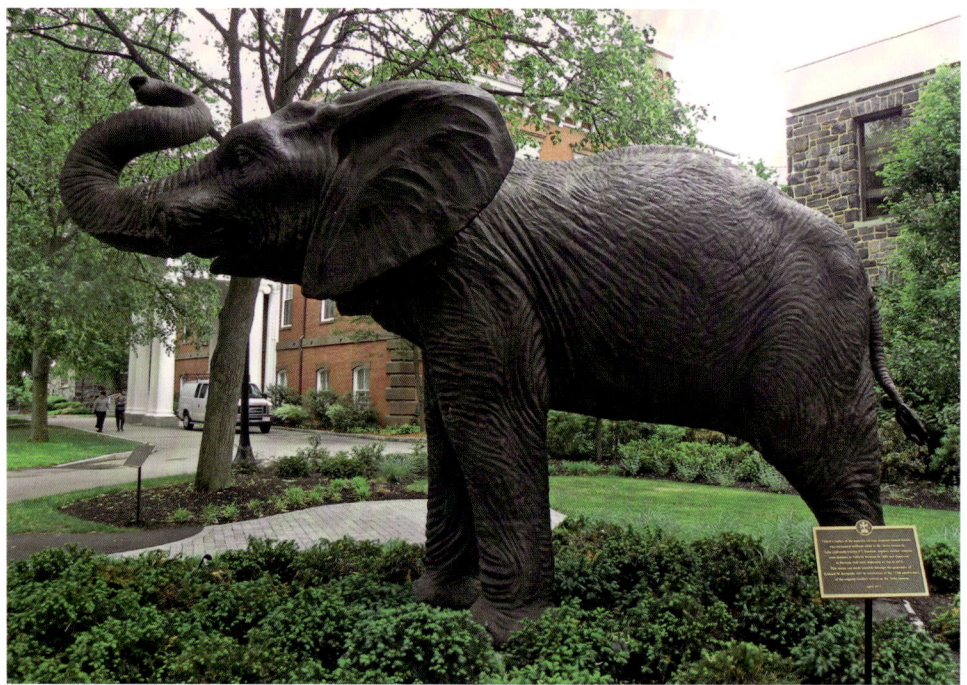

JUMBO: In 1885 the world mourned when Jumbo the elephant, the star of P. T. Barnum's famous circus died in a train accident. Jumbo's preserved hide was donated to the Barnum museum at Tufts University where it became the school mascot. This photo shows the elephant arriving at the Barnum Museum. His hide was destroyed in a fire in 1975. In 2015, Jumbo made a triumphant return to the Tufts campus when this life-sized replica took up residence on the campus.

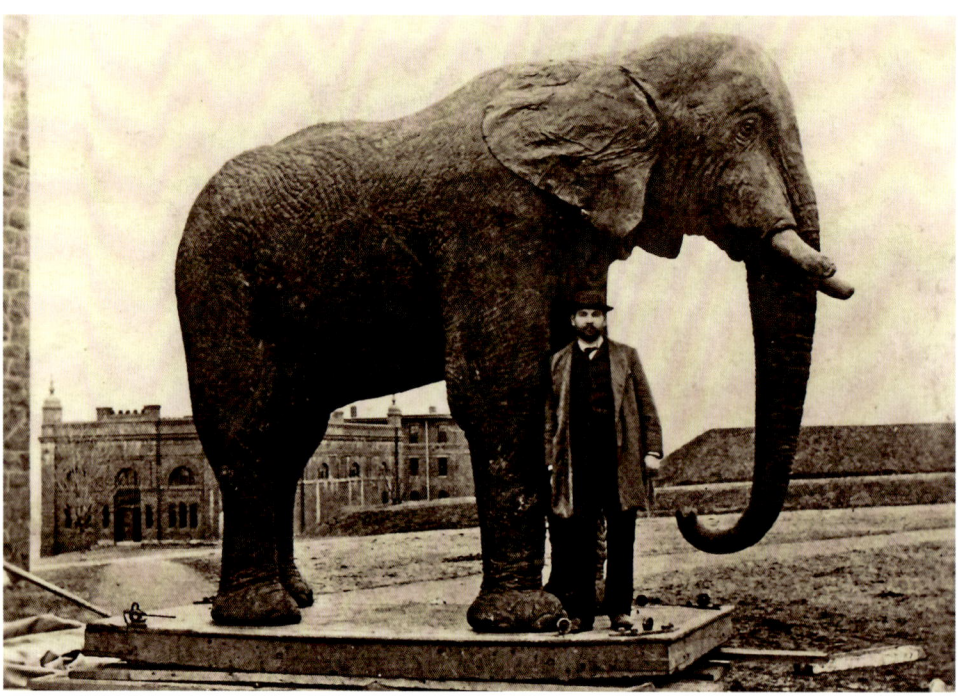

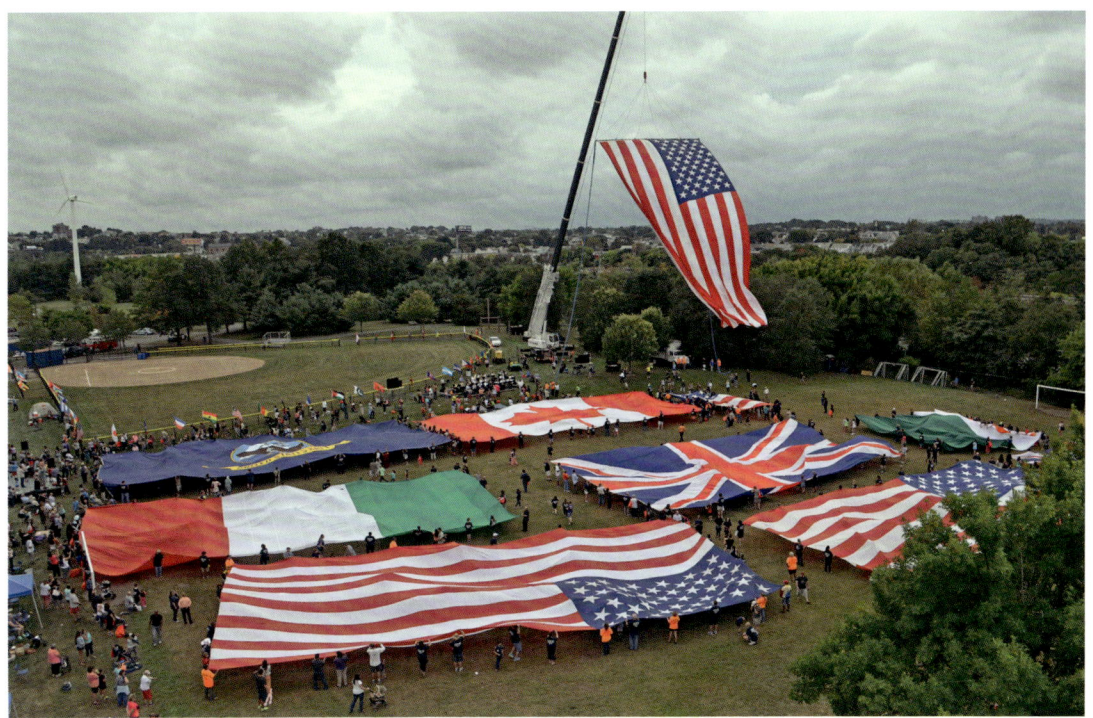

COMMUNITY DAY FLAGS: As you've seen in the pages of this book Medford is all about people and celebration. At Medford Community Day in 2014 hundreds of people turned out to carry giant flags of many nations. Medford never misses a chance to celebrate!

Photo Acknowledgements

Dan Menezes (p.16), David Mussina/MRWA (p.20), Sonan Zoksang (p.26), Michael Bradford (p.30 and p.90), Mayor Michael McGlynn (p.34), Louise Musto-Choate (p.35), Royall House Association (p.50), Margaret Egitto (p.55), Allison Goldsberry (p.64), Joseph F. McCarthy (p.71), Fern Ganley (p.78), George Thurrott (p.84), Anthony Sammarco (p.88).

All other images courtesy of Patricia Saunders, The Medford Public Library, The Medford Historical Society, and Digital Commonwealth. The authors would like to thank Michael Bradford, Ryan Hayward, Koko Kerr, Mayor Michael McGlynn, Dee Morris, and Anthony Sammarco for their generous help with this book.

TUFTS CANNON: This University landmark is painted almost nightly with messages and announcements. The cannon is actually a replica of one from "Old Ironsides." It was given to the city of Medford by the National Park Service and Medford, in turn, gave the cannon to Tufts in 1956, when it was mounted on a small lawn between Goddard Chapel and Ballou Hall. The cannon painting tradition started in the 1970s and is still going strong.

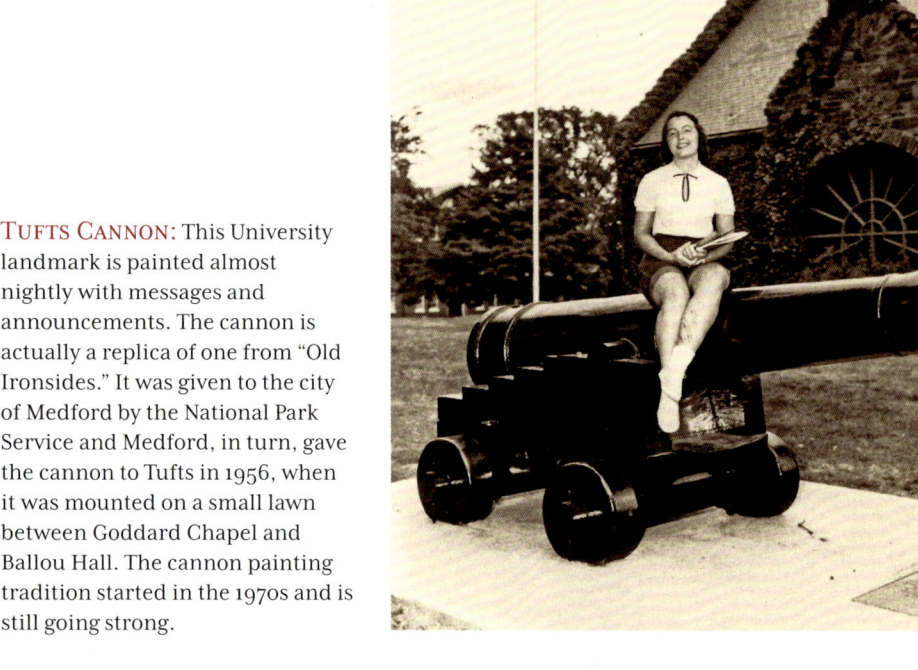

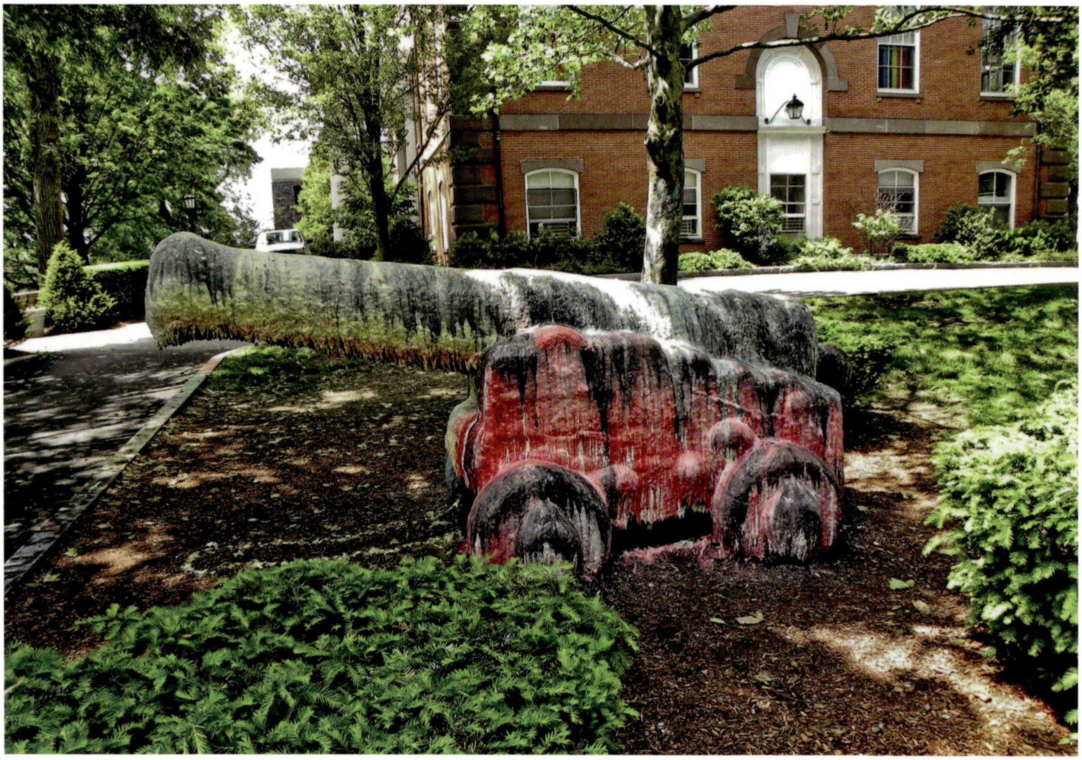